Trend Trading Set-Ups

Founded in 1807, John Wiley & Sons is the oldest independent publishing company in the United States. With offices in North America, Europe, Australia and Asia, Wiley is globally committed to developing and marketing print and electronic products and services for our customers' professional and personal knowledge and understanding.

The Wiley Trading series features books by traders who have survived the market's ever changing temperament and have prospered—some by reinventing systems, others by getting back to basics. Whether a novice trader, professional or somewhere in-between, these books will provide the advice and strategies needed to prosper today and well into the future.

For a list of available titles, visit our Web site at www.WileyFinance.com.

Trend Trading
Set-Ups

Entering and Exiting Trends for Maximum Profit

L.A. LITTLE

WILEY

John Wiley & Sons, Inc.

Published by John Wiley & Sons, Inc., Hoboken, New Jersey.
Published simultaneously in Canada.

For general information on our other products and services or for technical support, please contact our Customer Care Department within the United States at (800) 762-2974, outside the United States at (317) 572-3993 or fax (317) 572-4002.

Wiley also publishes its books in a variety of electronic formats. Some content that appears in print may not be available in electronic books. For more information about Wiley products, visit our web site at www.wiley.com.

Library of Congress Cataloging-in-Publication Data:

Little, L. A. author.
  Trend trading set-ups : entering and exiting trends for maximum profit / L.A. Little.
      pages cm. (Wiley trading series)
  Includes index.
  ISBN 978-1-118-07269-1 (cloth); ISBN 978-1-118-22247-8 (ebk);
  ISBN 978-1-118-23640-6 (ebk); ISBN 978-1-118-26108-8 (ebk)
  1. Portfolio management.   2. Investment analysis.   3. Stock price forecasting.   I. Title.
  HG4637.L582 2013
  332.6—dc23

                                                                          2012020177

Printed in the United States of America

10 9 8 7 6 5 4 3 2 1

Contents

Foreword

Top traders rarely call attention to their many accomplishments, content to execute and perfect their market views, free from self-promotion and outside noise. L.A. Little is that type of rare individual, an experienced trader and educator, with unique insights that are simple, profound and highly actionable. For this reason, I'm pleased to introduce readers to his third book *Trend Trading Set-ups*.

In the real world, most traders enter and exit positions without fully understanding the nature of trend. This omission invariably leads to failure, with participants left scratching their heads and wondering why Mr. Market failed to pay off, as expected. It's a real shame because trends in all time frames can be fully deconstructed through the application of logical observational tools.

Enter top trader and respected market educator, L.A. Little. His first two books, *Trade Like the Little Guy* and *Trend Qualification and Trading*, set into place an original framework for reliable trend analysis and trade management. Little now adds and expands to this impressive curriculum with *Trend Trading Set-ups*, a natural progression to the first two volumes.

His latest book brings his outstanding knowledge base down to earth, with concrete examples and step by step instructions for trade excellence, from position choice to profittaking. This is an important contribution in our 24-hour market environment, allowing at-home gamers and professional money managers to compete on a level playing field with omnipresent computer programs.

I've known L.A. Little for many years as a co-contributor at TheStreet.com. We've also spent quality time discussing the complex issues faced by traders in our fractured market system. Above all else, I view him as a kindred spirit that's as obsessed by the ticker tape as I am. That's no mean feat, given the challenges introduced into the market organism in the last twenty years.

L.A.'s long-time focus on trend qualification has honed a set of symbiotic strategies perfectly in tune with today's fast paced derivative-driven electronic environment. For that reason alone, I expect that readers of *Trend Trading Set-ups* will gain valuable insights that are unavailable through any other market source, online or in print.

Don't be fooled by the apparent simplicity of his systematic approach. Under the hood, he presents a powerful trading system based on classic market principles that work in euphoric bull markets as well as gut-wrenching bear markets. More importantly, these reliable methods are unaffected by the program algorithms we've come to know as high frequency trading (HFT).

This is an amazing accomplishment in a challenging environment that's forced all types of market players to reassess the positive expectancy of their trading systems. Indeed, this resilience offers another advantage in reading this excellent book. Simply stated, it will help your own strategies to overcome the dominance of lighting fast computer trading in the day to day price action.

So, whether you're a new trader just starting out on your journey, or a seasoned veteran looking for fresh insights and a stimulating read to get your performance back on the fast track, I'm proud to recommend *Trend Trading Set-ups*.

Alan Farley

Acknowledgments

As with any endeavor, the twists and turns are what make the journey and for that reason I would like to offer my special thanks to Phillip Campbell and Seth Williams, two avid and knowledgeable traders who took the long and winding road with me serving as sounding boards while spending countless hours proofing and improving the content you hold in your hands.

I would be amiss to overlook the many authors and traders who have offered their contributions over the years, many of which have left indelible footprints in my trading psyche. Names that instantly come to mind are luminaries like Edwards and Magee, Steve Nison, Tom O'Brian, Welles Wilder, Robert Prechter and Alan Farley to name a few. To these and others that have offered their unique insights I offer my sincere gratitude and utmost respect.

Finally to my wife, Nadereh, whose patience over the years has been tested more times than an anchor zone my sincere appreciation for your continued love and thoughtfulness. To my children, Anaheed and Arman, who have had to endure my almost fanatical devotion to research and writing I can only say thank you as well for the love you express each and every day. Without all of you this book, and those that precede it, would never have been realized.

L.A.L.

Trend Trading Set-Ups

Introduction

In life, there are few absolutes while in trading there are none. If you accept that premise, then it follows that the best trades are those trades where the highest opportunity for success is paired with the greatest reward versus risk taken. That is the Holy Grail of trading. The best opportunities are expressed as probabilities, not certainties. Understanding those probabilities across the varied and numerous trading possibilities is what separates this book from all others.

Just like trends, trade set-ups are not created equally. There are good ones and bad ones, great ones and average ones. You should seek the great ones and avoid the rest. This book reduces the complexities surrounding trade set-ups so that you may do just that.

The great trade set-ups are not as hard to find as you might think, but discovering them requires a roadmap—a set of characteristics that, when present, magnetizes the trader to those trade set-ups having high probabilities for success. Once recognized, all that remains is to develop the trading plan and to exploit the opportunity that has presented itself. Sounds simple enough, right?

Much has been written about trading plans, trade execution, and management, and though these concepts are incorporated throughout the book, the real focus is on trade set-ups. What are great trade set-ups? How are they found? What are their characteristics? How can a trader identify and make those trades having the greatest probability for success? That is the crux of the problem after all. It is what separates the average traders from the great ones.

If you back up and ask what makes a trade successful, the answer is reasonably clear—did the trade make money and did it do so without a significant risk of comparatively large drawdowns? If so, it was a success. Anything less is, well, substandard. Notice that it isn't a failure as long as it has a realistic promise of greatness, since trade success or failure is only recognized once the trade has been placed into motion and is dependent on future events. This simple fact reduces every trade, even the trade with the greatest potential, to the possibility of failure. It is an unavoidable fact of trading. What is critical though, is to make certain that each trade taken has the potential to realize greatness, for anything less increases your probability of mediocrity. This trade determination can be visualized as a checklist—a set of key factors that, when present, dramatically increase the probabilities that the trade will result in success and potential greatness. Those key factors are the primary focus of this book but to get to them requires a reasonable amount of preparatory work.

It is not as if this concept of key factors has not been considered already, for it has, whether explicitly or implicitly. For example, fundamental analysts will tell you that the key factors are PE (price-to-earnings) ratios, management, sales and revenue growth rates, and a whole host of other fundamental factors and measurements.

Classical technical analysts will focus on the many technical tools and patterns that have been developed and are abundantly available. Whether it is oscillators, bands, or the numerous trading patterns, the underlying assumption of all these tools and patterns is directed toward the same goal— a marked increase in trade success.

What I am here to tell you is that, yes, the preceding do work—at times—but as a trader and investor, you need the tools that point you to the highest probability trades *all the time*. You cannot have tools that work in just one phase of the market. You need tools that work *in all phases*. You need tools that point out the highest probability trades no matter what the market is doing. You need a checklist that says to either take the trade or to pass on it, and that checklist needs to work in up and down markets. You require the key characteristics that point you toward the best trade set-ups *as a result* of what the market currently offers up as the best trades.

Before creating the checklist, however, it is imperative that trade set-up possibilities be reduced to only those that are fundamental. To do otherwise renders the effort useless since the number of checklists created is most likely unnecessarily large and probably ridden with contradictions and complexities. At the core of all complexity lies simplicity, and that should always be what is sought. Trading and trade set-ups are no different.

In this vein, I offer a simplified view of trading where just two basic trade set-up types exist: retraces and breakouts. From these two basic building blocks flows all else. Chapter 6 reduces the complexities of trade set-up types utilizing these two fundamental building blocks then integrates them with the concept of tests. All price movement in unfettered exchanges is based on the concept of testing, for it is the basis of price discovery. The synthesis of these concepts creates the basis needed to locate trades set-ups possessing the potential for greatness.

Although Chapter 6 is a pivotal chapter, there is a lot of groundwork required to reach that point and it starts with Chapter 1. In my previous book, *Trend Qualification and Trading*,[1] I questioned whether the currently accepted concept of trend was both accurate and sufficient. My findings were that it was not. Trends simply are not created equal. Some are better than others. For this reason I proposed a new definition of trend and a systematic method for determining it. The output of that process provides a distinction between trends; the separation of good from bad, *confirmed* from *suspect*. The distinction is valuable because there is a higher probability that *confirmed* trends will persist longer than *suspect* ones. Chapter 1 presents the data that led to this assertion.

But the real value of a systematic analysis of trend across all stocks, sectors, and the general market is not limited to the realization that a suspect trend has a higher probability of failing as compared to a confirmed one. The real value is that the ability to systematically assess trend across all trading instruments creates an excellent test bed for analysis. How do trends fail? How slowly or quickly does this happen based on the type of trend, its qualification, and the time frame?

Trends are like household appliances. They come into existence and eventually meet their demise. In other words, they have a life cycle and it is predictable. It can be measured. When a microwave oven comes off the assembly line and pops into existence, it has a mean life expectancy of roughly 10 years. When a trend transitions and pops into existence it, too, has a life expectancy. For example, in Chapter 1 you will find that an intermediate term bullish trend exhibits an average life expectancy of roughly 25 bars. For a weekly swing trader, where one bar equates to one week, this would imply that one should expect a failure of the trend, on average, after roughly 25 weeks have passed.

Even though simple trend failure analysis is fascinating and reasonably useful, it only scratches the surface. In fact, there is no reason to limit the analysis of trend failure to stock trends in isolation. It is a widely accepted fact that the general market and even sectors exert an influence on individual stocks. Chapter 3 considers and extends the work of Chapter 1 to include and construct failure probabilities based on the broader context of outside influences.

Although trend failures provide value and play a part in the trade set-up decision process, a study of *trade failure probabilities* rather than *trend failure probabilities* is needed. Chapter 2 defines trade failures and again performs a systematic analysis of the probability curves governing trade

---

[1]L.A. Little, *Trend Qualification and Trading* (Hoboken, NJ: John Wiley & Sons, 2011).

failures. Trade success and failure are highly correlated with entry and exit timing, and Chapter 2 provides the framework and probability analysis that is utilized in later chapters for trade set-up recognition and execution.

Although readers of my previous book, *Trend Qualification and Trading*, will find these first three chapters as somewhat of a review, they should not be skipped. As alluded to earlier, new material is provided and interlaced with the review material. In this way not only are new readers brought up to speed but seasoned eyes are able to find new and interesting insight as well. The end result is that the new is integrated with the old, and all these ideas are illustrated through numerous examples. By the time you reach the end of Part I, you should have a reasonable grasp of the fundamental concepts required for Part II including qualified trends, anchor bars, and support and resistance zones as well as the importance of time frames.

Moving to Part II, it begins with a workable trading plan. Although much has been said by both me and others on trading plans, it is such a fundamental component of trading success that to ignore it completely would represent a greater travesty than its inclusion. For seasoned readers, it may represent the one chapter than can be skimmed but even then it may be found to contain enough uniqueness to interest even their trained eye.

From there the focus shifts to trade set-up identification and execution. Chapter 5 entertains the previously espoused idea that there really are only two basic types of trades: breakouts and retraces. Illustrations are offered to support this simplification, and the concept of tests is integrated into the study, since testing is how a market moves either up or down.

The chapter concludes with the reintroduction of another concept first covered in *Trend Qualification and Trading* which takes on added significance. That concept is the process of retest and regenerate. It turns out that the process can be separated into seven possible outcomes, each of which has varying failure rate probabilities. This analysis thus forms a large and pivotal basis for deciding which trades have the potential for greatness.

Chapters 6 and 7 examine specific trade set-ups in the context of all the material presented. Chapter 6 considers an important facet of trading—range trade set-ups. The market and individual stocks are not always moving directionally (up or down). Sometimes they are stuck in a sideways range. Chapter 6 identifies the key characteristics that set up a range trade and how to exploit them for consistent profits.

Chapter 7 turns to retrace and breakout trades and, again, identifies the key characteristics that separate the great trading opportunities from all others. Numerous examples are drawn upon and extensive integration of prior data is incorporated to clarify and increase the likelihood that you can perform the same identification process going forward.

Breaking with tradition, this book seeks to present the probabilities surrounding trend failures as well as trade failures. It has at its core the desire to understand when a particular trading set-up has the highest probability for success and the potential for greatness. In all cases, the trading set-ups discussed are not based on fancy derivate indicators or complex algorithms. Plenty of work has been offered in those areas. By contrast, this work considers only price, volume, and time across the various time frames and for varying instruments that are known to be related. As with my earlier work, the focus is on measuring supply and demand at critical price points.

When a market participant trades just the bars on a chart, the rules become reasonably simple. Trades are typically made with the qualified trend within the context of a trading plan utilizing the concept of tests to perfect entry and exit timing. The great trades are seen as occurring with sufficient regularity to make them both identifiable and tradable.

The complexities of trading are numerous yet the general concepts need not be. Trading is hard enough without making it more so. Trading in real time is seldom simple yet consistently profitable if the methods are sound. My contribution to this endeavor is a set of methods and principles that further this desirable outcome.

Although this book endeavors to reduce the complexities of trading, it would be a mistake to conceptualize trading as simple and predictable. It is anything but. If a market participant seeks a simple rule that says to always buy this technical indicator or that pattern, then this book will disappoint. What is offered are the data driven trading principals that have driven the conclusions regarding those trades that have the highest probabilities for success. A definition of each trade type is succinctly presented and accompanied by the ideal general market and sector alignment conditions along with the ideal stock trade triggers. It is the trader who takes a potential trade set-up and evaluates its possibilities. With practice, the trades with extraordinary potential can be separated from those with lesser potential. Just as importantly, the weak and worthless opportunities can be avoided. With study and practice, the highest probabilities trades that embody the greatest potential can be recognized and pursued with increased regularity. When accomplished, no longer will success be the result of mere chance but instead the embodiment of predictable probabilities.

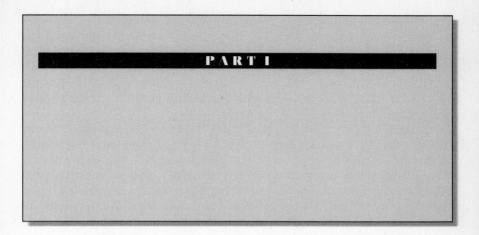

PART I

T rading success is heavily dependent upon being on the right side of the trade and executing the trade at a reasonably optimal time. Neither concept is new. Both are much more difficult to do than they seem.

Take a moment to consider the implications of these two thoughts. What does it mean to be on the *right side* of a trade? For a technical trader, this almost always means that you are trading with the trend, but even that statement is somewhat ambiguous since it implies that the definition of a trend is known and that there is only one trend. Unless you read my first book, *Trend Qualification and Trading*,[1] you are probably unaware that not all trends are created equal and you are unlikely to have a keen appreciation for the fact that there are necessarily multiple trends spread across many time frames that exist simultaneously. What is more, trends across multiple time frames are not necessarily the same. In fact, they differ more often than not. As you can see, once you dig into the concepts a bit, the mental clarity of the high level thoughts quickly becomes murky.

For this reason, before jumping headfirst into a detailed consideration of how to find the highest probability trades, a preliminary discussion of some basic concepts is necessary. Hopefully this will simply be a refresher. Without a common and somewhat precise understanding of the terminology used throughout this book, much of the value will fall upon deaf ears.

---

[1]L.A. Little, *Trend Qualification and Trading* (Hoboken, NJ: John Wiley & Sons, 2011).

For that reason, Part I tackles the thorny question of trend and time frames as well as entry and exit timing. It is necessarily covered with reasonably broad brushstrokes yet with sufficient color to elucidate the general principles of qualified trend and anchored support and resistance. In this way, when I speak of a concept such as *a suspect bullish qualified trend on the short term time frame*, you will understand with exactness both the term and the implications.

Although the material is a review of prior concepts, it is by no means limited to dry definitions regurgitated at a pace that would make a snail appear to be a speed demon. Rather than bore readers of my prior work with three chapters that beg them to skim if not skip, I have instead added significant data to validate the assertion that all trends are not created equal. A distinction is made between trend and trade failures and some simplistic trading rules are implemented to show how timing of entry and exit can yield better trading results through the use of anchored zones.

The third chapter utilizes the Trading Cube to illustrate the broader influences that directly affect trade success and failure. Again empirical data is presented that strongly supports the idea that trading with the trend where that trend is confluent for the stock, the sector, and the general market for the time frame being traded is the most desirable trade set-up. Unfortunately, the market seldom makes it that simple.

The result of the first three chapters is much more than an overview of the basic concepts that comprise the neoclassical concepts of trend trading. Each chapter houses additional and previously unpublished data regarding trend and offers insight into how a trader can benefit from the knowledge. More importantly, these first three chapters lay the groundwork for what follows—finding and executing the best trade set-ups.

The concepts first presented in *Trend Qualification and Trading* are reinforced through real data and presented in a easily understandable manner. There are no fancy formulas, mathematical complexities, or unneeded mental fog. Trading need not be a theoretical formulation of complex and somewhat indecipherable thought. It does not have to depend on models so complex that the originator of the model must muddle through notes when trying to explain it. Elegance is typically hidden in simplicity, and neoclassical trend trading is just that. Like a fine wine it is beautifully simple yet complete and it only improves with time and practice!

CHAPTER 1

Identifying and Qualifying Trend Probabilities

Historically, trend was generally defined as a series of higher highs and higher lows (bullish trend) or a series of lower highs and lower lows (bearish trend). This general definition took hold at the turn of the twentieth century and, for the most part, has held sway ever since.

In *Trend Qualification and Trading*,[1] a more precise and valuable definition of trend was proposed. It suggested the idea that significant price points could be systematically determined on a chart and that these price points would typically end up being at price extremes. These price extremes would have significance because any subsequent test of the price point would provide a comparison. Essentially, the volume on the prior price extreme could be compared to volume on the current price test. This comparison yields insight into the enthusiasm and conviction of the buyers and sellers. If market participants are willing to buy an increasing number of shares at new price extremes, then, for whatever reason, the buyers are expressing their belief that prices will go even higher. The same is true of sellers selling an increasing number of shares at lower and lower price extremes. By measuring this outward expression of conviction, the true equation of the supply and demand of the stock can be made and it is made at the price point where it matters, which typically is at price extremes.

This fundamental approach to a stock's supply and demand characteristics enables observers to gain a far better understanding of the *true trend*

---

[1]L.A. Little, *Trend Qualification and Trading* (Hoboken, NJ: John Wiley & Sons, 2011).

because trend transitions are necessarily determined at price boundaries. It allows one to qualify a trend, and that is important because with trend qualification, all trends are no longer viewed as equals. Some trends are better than others. A quick summary of how to determine trend follows.

TREND DETERMINATION

Figure 1.1 is a short-term annotated chart of Google. The annotations highlight each bar on the chart where a swing point high (SPH) or swing point low (SPL) is observed.

Swing point highs and lows are the result of a simple and methodical calculation. Starting at the leftmost bar on the chart, the high and low of the bar are noted. This high is the potential swing point high while the low is the potential swing point low. Next, the adjacent bar to the right is examined, and if the high is higher than the previous bar's high, this

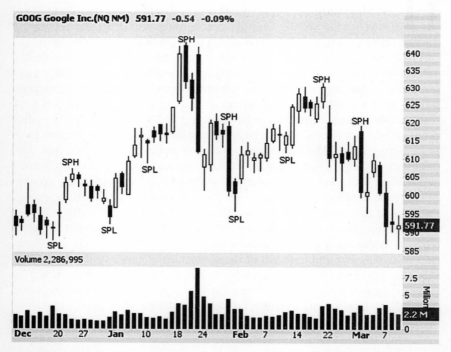

FIGURE 1.1   Swing Point Highs and Lows—Google (December 9, 2010 to March 9, 2011)

higher high becomes the potential swing point high. Likewise, the same operation is completed for the low. When six adjacent bars have been examined without a higher high having been found, then the potential swing point high becomes actualized and the high of the sixth bar is the new potential swing point high going forward. The same is true of lows. In this way, swing point highs and lows are consistently determinable, and the vast majority of these highs and lows end up signifying turning points and/or price extremes on the chart for the time frame under observation. In those cases where they do not, many times value is still produced when it comes to trend determination. In rare cases, they have little value.

With any systematic application of set and sometimes rigid rules, there are times where the price points line up in such a way that a glance at a chart intuitively suggests an up or down trend, yet the rules used to determine swing points fail to make the same determination. While six bars have been found to be optimal, this system is by no means perfect. There are times where a set of human eyes must recognize the deficiency and account for it accordingly in trading. In the vast majority of the cases, the rules outlined work extremely well and the advantages gained from a rigid set of rules when determining trend far outweigh the occasional misreads. In particular, when rigid rules are utilized they can be computer automated. In this way, the systematic and algorithmic trend determination process associated with the *neoclassical trend model* has significant and immeasurable advantages to the *classical trend model* it has replaced.

Once swing point highs and lows are determined, then trend can likewise be ascertained. Historically, trend took the form of three states: bullish, bearish, and sideways. In the neoclassical trend model of trend qualification, there are a total of seven states. *Suspect* and *confirmed* qualifiers are attached to each of the bullish, bearish, and sideways states and one additional *ambivalent* sideways state is introduced. For the six *bullish*, *bearish*, and *sideways* qualified states, trend transitions occur as the result of a swing point test. Only the ambivalent sideways case occurs without a swing point test. Figure 1.2 is the same chart of Google, annotated with qualified trend states.

This short-term chart provides a reasonably good example of trend qualification. Trends transition from one state to another repeatedly over time. Transitions are realized at swing points and are qualified at that time. Take the first trend transition (leftmost). The trend transitioned from an ambivalent sideways trend to a confirmed bullish trend. Why was it bullish, and what causes it to be confirmed?

It is bullish because a higher high is registered on the price bar where the horizontal line is drawn in. Because the close was over the previous swing point, a transition is guaranteed. The qualification comes as a result of a direct volume comparison between the swing point high bar that

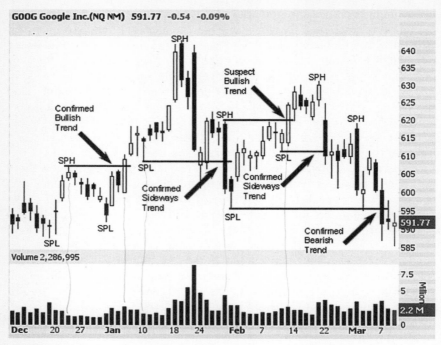

FIGURE 1.2 Trend Qualification Example—Google (December 9, 2010 to March 9, 2011)

was broken and the bar doing the break. The prior swing point high registered approximately 1.2 million shares, while the bar doing the break witnessed about 2.5 million shares or more than twice the amount. When volume expands on a swing point break (high or low) then the trend is qualified as *confirmed*. The adjective *confirmed* is used to signify permanence and determination. The idea behind confirmation is that, for whatever reason, buyers were willing to purchase a greater number of shares at higher prices than had heretofore been paid to obtain a share of this company's future.

Note that just because buyers found it reasonable to increasingly *pay up* to own Google shares at this particular time, doing so was no guarantee that the price would continue higher. They could have simply been wrong. Tomorrow an unforeseen event might have occurred that would have changed their minds. Many things can happen. There is never a guarantee in trading but there are probabilities, and the probabilities tell us that when a trend is confirmed it has a higher probability of continuing higher than if it is suspect. This is worth examining further.

QUALIFIED TREND
FAILURE PROBABILITIES

The increased probability that suspect trends are less likely to continue their trends as compared to confirmed trends is borne out in the data. A trend failure occurs when an existing trend transitions from one qualified state to another. Trend failures, although not used in isolation as a reason to enter or exit a trade, are nevertheless useful to examine. The data set is rich with ideas and, with further refinement, offers excellent and significant insight for all market participants.

To test the increased probability of confirmed trends having longer staying power than suspect trends, data was gathered and applications written to determine each trend transition from the period of January 2002 through July of 2011 across all time frames. Time frames are discussed in more detail later but essentially there are three: the short, intermediate, and long term as observed through their corresponding daily, weekly, and monthly charts.

The data examined included all liquid stocks exclusive of exchange traded notes and funds for this period of time listed on the New York Stock Exchange (NYSE), the NASDAQ, and Amex stock exchanges. The determining characteristic used for trend termination was a trend transition. For example, if a trend transitioned from bearish (suspect or confirmed) to any form of bullish or sideways trend, then the trend was construed as having ended. If, however, a bearish trend (suspect or confirmed) transitioned to a differing bearish state (suspect or confirmed), then the trend was not considered as having ended. The reasoning behind this distinction with respect to trend termination is that this sort of action denotes a case where trend was reaffirmed either in a weaker or stronger form yet it had not ended.

After compiling this data for bullish, bearish, and sideways trends on all three time frames, there was a definite difference noted in the durability of confirmed trends as compared to suspect ones. In some cases the difference is not overly pronounced but is distinguishable nevertheless. In other situations, there are obvious and significant differences. The following series of charts display and extrapolate the findings for the three types of trends and their trend termination characteristics.

Trend Failures (Suspect and Confirmed)

Ask any market participant whether bullish or bearish trends are more prevalent, and the overwhelming response is that bullish trends are much more common. Although the data does bear out those assumptions, for

TABLE 1.1 Occurrence Ratios for Trend Types for Differing Time Frames

Time Frame	Prevalence of Bullish Trends versus Bearish Trends
Short Term	11.03%
Intermediate Term	11.15%
Long Term	10.59%

Note that the data in Table 1.1 recognizes a trend *when it ends*, not when it begins. This implies that all trends that were in effect at the data sampling cutoff date (July 2011) are not represented in these data samples.

the most part, bullish trends are not in fact all that much more common than bearish ones. Depending on the time frame, bullish trends are approximately 10.5 percent to 11 percent more prevalent than their bearish counterparts as shown in Table 1.1.

Table 1.1 considers all trends irrespective of their qualification. In other words, it cares not whether a trend was suspect or confirmed just that it was bullish or bearish. From that perspective, the data confirms the notion that bullish trends are more likely to occur than bearish ones but again, the data is not nearly as lopsided as one would likely have guessed. A closer look also indicates that there is not much variation in the degree to which bullish trends outnumber bearish trends based on time frames either.

WHAT IS THE TRADING SIGNIFICANCE?

The market tends to be bullish more than bearish, and that bullishness is reasonably equal across all time frames. Unfortunately, this snippet of knowledge does not offer the market participant a discernible trading advantage other than the fact that short selling an instrument must necessarily occur on a shorter time frame as compared to buying.

Table 1.2 takes this high level view of the data and begins to examine it in differing ways. Again, the metrics measure the occurrence of a given trend, but in this table the trends are qualified. Rather than just bullish trends compared to bearish trends, it is interesting to know whether the qualified trend of confirmed bullish or bearish is more prevalent than the suspect trend, and indeed it is.

TABLE 1.2 Prevalence of Confirmed versus Suspect Trends

Occurrence Ratios for Confirmed Trends versus Suspect Trends

Time Frame	Bullish Trends—Confirmed versus Suspect
Short Term	9.04%
Intermediate Term	4.95%
Long Term	40.87%

Time Frame	Bearish Trends—Confirmed versus Suspect
Short Term	9.42%
Intermediate Term	17.42%
Long Term	111.06%

This cross-sectional view reveals that *confirmed* bullish trends as compared to *suspect* bullish trends show a great deal of variation between time frames, particularly with respect to the long-term time frame. Long-term time frames are almost 41 percent more likely to be confirmed bullish rather than suspect. The same metric for confirmed bearish trends as compared to suspect ones shows a similar story but is even more pronounced for the long-term time frame. In this case, when bearish trends occur on the long-term time frame, they are 111 percent more likely to be confirmed rather than suspect. When you stop to think about it, this does make sense, since volume tends to expand when prices begin to fall over time.

Table 1.3 provides another view of this same data, but for the first time the concept of persistence is introduced. When a trend comes into existence, how long does it persist? Persistence is critical to a market participant because it is a measure of the expected duration. For the trend trader, this provides a predictive indicator for the increased probability of trend failure, providing value to both those betting for and against the prevailing trend.

The persistence aspect of the data in Table 1.3 is presented as a function of the number of bars for which the trend existed. For any time frame there exists a bar. On a daily chart, each day would be represented by a bar. Likewise, on a weekly chart, one bar would equal one week. Finally, on a long-term chart, one bar would represent one month's worth of data. Thus, when observing the data presented in Table 1.3, the leftmost column shows the number of bars that the trend persisted. All other rows in the table display the percentage of trends that persisted for the relationship depicted in the header for each column.

Starting with the first column entitled "Ratio of All Sideways to All Bullish and Bearish Trends," this set of data is probably the most

TABLE 1.3 Comparative Analysis of the Ratio of Differing Trend Types with Respect to Time

Column 1	Column 2	Column 3	Column 4	Column 5	Column 6	Column 7
Number of Bars	Ratio of All Sideways to All Bullish and Bearish Trends	Ratio of All Bullish to Bearish Trends	Ratio of All Confirmed Bullish to Confirmed Bearish Trends	Ratio of All Suspect Bullish to Suspect Bearish Trends	Ratio of All Confirmed Bullish to Suspect Bullish Trends	Ratio of All Confirmed Bearish to Suspect Bearish Trends
0 to 1	2,762.35%	117.94%	134.97%	102.53%	119.14%	90.51%
1 to 5	194.03%	94.10%	94.99%	93.34%	87.64%	86.11%
6 to 10	64.14%	94.79%	94.46%	95.12%	96.72%	97.41%
11 to 15	40.73%	94.55%	94.35%	94.78%	106.78%	107.27%
16 to 20	26.98%	99.98%	95.75%	104.91%	106.09%	116.24%
21 to 25	17.87%	102.31%	97.60%	108.15%	112.13%	124.25%
26 to 30	10.72%	97.77%	91.05%	106.60%	112.27%	131.45%
31 to 35	6.89%	111.38%	109.66%	113.44%	115.95%	119.95%
36 to 40	4.41%	121.18%	117.00%	126.37%	115.06%	124.26%
41 to 45	2.48%	121.91%	119.03%	125.46%	117.17%	123.50%
46 to 50	1.40%	138.15%	135.88%	140.90%	116.96%	121.28%
51 to 55	1.10%	148.20%	146.14%	150.64%	115.13%	118.68%
56 to 60	0.64%	137.85%	134.72%	141.80%	119.77%	126.06%
61 to 65	0.41%	151.02%	148.58%	154.06%	119.82%	124.25%
66 to 70	0.25%	168.11%	173.01%	162.73%	116.89%	109.95%
71 to 75	0.18%	172.45%	166.07%	179.81%	106.43%	115.23%
76 to 80	0.36%	173.67%	163.40%	186.10%	106.22%	120.98%
81 to 85	0.08%	200.57%	202.84%	198.17%	107.99%	105.50%
86 to 90	0.09%	200.28%	182.58%	222.81%	104.31%	127.29%
91 to 95	0.04%	210.61%	208.74%	212.61%	105.61%	107.57%
96 to 100	0.18%	250.00%	238.91%	262.37%	101.55%	111.53%

revealing. The story this column tells unequivocally is that the persistence of all sideways trends is fleeting. Indeed, the number of occurrences of sideways trends that last for only a single bar when compared to both bullish and bearish trends is off the scale, clocking in at more than 2,700 percent. Unlike bullish and bearish trends, the persistence of sideways trends is virtually nonexistent. This data strongly suggests that the markets are mostly trending either in a bullish or in a bearish fashion with short periods of sideways activity in between.

WHAT IS THE TRADING SIGNIFICANCE?

Sideways trends typically come into and go out of existence very quickly when compared to bullish and bearish trends. Their persistence is fleeting on a relative basis. Market participants typical trade sideways trends by selling the top of the sideways trading range and buying the bottom. With knowledge of this relative absence of trend persistence for sideways trends and with further data analysis still to come, profitable trading of sideways trends has strict parameters associated with the trade set-up.

Moving to the third column, note that between 1 and 20 bars, the occurrence of bearish trends slightly outnumbers bullish ones, but bullish trends tend to increasingly outnumber bearish trends from 31 bars on, irrespective of the quality of the trend. Recognize that the data in this table represents a rather broad brushstroke view of the varying relationships between differing types of trends across all time frames. From this perspective though, this column strongly suggests that the when trend persistence becomes reasonably extreme (80 bars or more), bullish trends have a much greater likelihood of being the trend observed.

Again, 80 bars is abstracted because the data in this table is derived for all samples across all time frames; thus, 80 bars on the short-term time frame implies approximately 4 months of trading, whereas for the intermediate-term time frames the equivalent timing would be 16 months or a little over a year's worth of time. For the long term, this would represent roughly a six-and-a-half-year trend.

WHAT IS THE TRADING SIGNIFICANCE?

Bullish trends typically last longer than bearish trends. This needs to be engrained into the trading consciousness of all market participants—bearish trends will necessarily disappear more quickly than bullish ones.

Columns 4 and 5 further dissect Column 3 into two component parts: confirmed bullish trends as compared to confirmed bearish trends (Column 4) and those where the quality of the trend was suspect (Column 5). In doing this you can see that for bearish trends, it is much more important that they be confirmed if they are to last.

WHAT IS THE TRADING SIGNIFICANCE?

Bearish trends are more likely to fail after 15 bars than bullish trends if they are suspect. The implication is that if a market participant is short selling a stock because it is bearish, unless it is confirmed bearish, a trader must be quicker to pull the trade if it begins to falter once 15 bars is approached.

The final two columns consider the number of confirmed versus suspect trend occurrences for bullish (Column 6) and bearish (Column 7) trends. The numbers are reasonably well contained yet supportive of the notion that there are more confirmed trends than suspect ones for both bullish and bearish trends. This data complements the data presented in Table 1.2. Another noticeable characteristic of the data that span Columns 3 through 7 is that suspect trends generally outnumber confirmed trends at the short end of the time spectrum.

In summary, using the data from Columns 3 and 4, if a trend fails within the first 30 bars, it is more likely to have been a bearish trend. This data once again emphasizes that, in general, all bullish trends tend to last longer than bearish trends and that this is true for both qualified and unqualified trends. Generally speaking, if a trend lasts longer than 10 bars, it is more likely to be a confirmed trend (bullish or bearish). Persistence of trend is dependent on the quality of that trend.

WHAT IS THE TRADING SIGNIFICANCE?

In general, the quality of a trend has a direct impact on the longevity of the trend. Since there is typically a greater probability of realizing profits with a longer lasting trend, Table 1.3 suggests that, generally speaking, confirmed trends offer a greater probability of a profitable outcome.

Bullish and Bearish Trend Persistence   In general, for a market participant, there is great significance to the concept of persistence when trading. Generally, the longer a trend continues the better because it typically takes a while for a market participant to recognize a trend and begin to trade it. If trend persistence is tooshort, then by the time a market participant jumps aboard it may simply be too late to profit by it and worse, the participant may lose.

Trend persistence can be examined in a number of ways, and Table 1.3 was one such method. The basic question is whether confirmed trends show a greater tendency to persist longer than suspect ones, and if so, are there particular trend types that have higher persistence probabilities than others? Do the data exhibit such characteristics? Is there a measurable probability that could be generically used to guide a market participant's approach to more consistent probability in their trading endeavors?

Before examining the data though, the definition of a trend failure is reemphasized. For a trend to fail, a trend transition must occur. A trend transition starts a trend and also ends it. For a trend transition to occur, price must exceed either a swing point high or a swing point low and close above or below it.

For several years I have postulated that there is a difference in persistence rates and that it is discernible. Using data from the January 2002 to July 2011 time period, Figure 1.3 is a comparison of suspect and confirmed trends on the short-term time frame, which, for the purposes of this study, is understood to mean a period consisting of three months of daily bars.

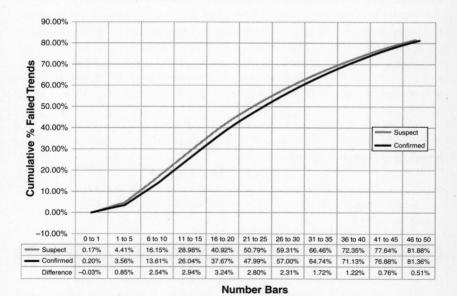

	0 to 1	1 to 5	6 to 10	11 to 15	16 to 20	21 to 25	26 to 30	31 to 35	36 to 40	41 to 45	46 to 50
Suspect	0.17%	4.41%	16.15%	28.98%	40.92%	50.79%	59.31%	66.46%	72.35%	77.64%	81.88%
Confirmed	0.20%	3.56%	13.61%	26.04%	37.67%	47.99%	57.00%	64.74%	71.13%	76.88%	81.36%
Difference	−0.03%	0.85%	2.54%	2.94%	3.24%	2.80%	2.31%	1.72%	1.22%	0.76%	0.51%

Number Bars

FIGURE 1.3 Trend Failure Rate for Confirmed versus Suspect Bullish Trends on the Short-Term Time Frame (2002 to 2011)

Figure 1.3 displays the cumulative failure rate for qualified trends on the short-term time frame over the various bar intervals starting from 1 bar and proceeding through 50 bars in 5-bar intervals. The simplest way to read this graph (and others to follow) is to look to the sequence of numbers at the bottom of the graph. The first row is labeled "Suspect," and each cell of the row contains the cumulative percentage of trend failures (a transition to a different trend) that occurred for a given number of bars since the trend began. The last row is the difference between suspect and confirmed persistence (suspect minus confirmed). If the number is negative, then the suspect trend lasted longer than confirmed trend, and if the difference is positive, then just the opposite was the case.

To illustrate, take a look at the fourth cell, which contains the value of 28.98 percent in the "Suspect" row. The cell just above denotes that somewhere between 11 to 15 bars, an existing trend failed and that the cumulative number of trend failures having occurred starting with 1 bar up until 15 bars is 28.98 percent.

Juxtaposed to this are confirmed trends, which show a lesser number of cumulative failures (26.04 percent) for the same number of bars. The difference between these two failure rates is 2.94 percent and is the increased cumulative probability that a suspect trend is more likely than a confirmed trend to fail within 15 bars of the trend having begun on this time frame, which is the short term.

Is 2.94 percent significant? After all, it is not that large of a difference. Consider that in trading, a small advantage, when wrapped within a trading plan, can create large profits over time. There is a lot more to be said about trading plans and trade set-ups, but for now, suffice it to say that this measurable difference over a longer period of time in which the data is believed to be representative of the population being extrapolated to is indeed significant.

Figure 1.4 is the same comparison but for the intermediate-term time frame, which, for the purposes of this study, is defined as one year of data where each bar represents one week.

On this time frame, the variance between the two cumulative failure rates is slightly less pronounced as compared to the short-term time frame, but again it shows an increased probability of failure for suspect versus confirmed trends.

WHAT IS THE TRADING SIGNIFICANCE?

For both short and intermediate-term time frames, after the first five bars, bullish trends offer a greater probability of trading success when compared to suspect trends. The increased probability is generally around 2 to 2.5 percent.

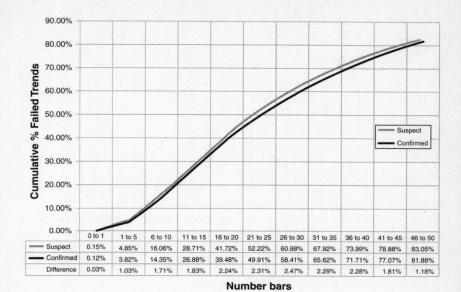

	0 to 1	1 to 5	6 to 10	11 to 15	16 to 20	21 to 25	26 to 30	31 to 35	36 to 40	41 to 45	46 to 50
Suspect	0.15%	4.85%	16.06%	28.71%	41.72%	52.22%	60.88%	67.92%	73.99%	78.88%	83.05%
Confirmed	0.12%	3.82%	14.35%	26.88%	39.48%	49.91%	58.41%	65.62%	71.71%	77.07%	81.88%
Difference	0.03%	1.03%	1.71%	1.83%	2.24%	2.31%	2.47%	2.29%	2.28%	1.81%	1.18%

Number bars

FIGURE 1.4   Trend Failure Rate for Confirmed versus Suspect Bullish Trends on the Intermediate-Term Time Frame (2002 to 2011)

Moving to the long-term time frame, Figure 1.5 shows the cumulative failure rate for bullish trends where each bar is one month in duration.

As can be seen in this figure, unlike the other time frames, for the long-term time frame suspect trends are more durable than confirmed ones. This stands in stark contrast to the expected results. Does it mean that on this time frame trend qualification has little value or, worse, that the assumptions made about qualified trends are just plain wrong?

Fortunately the answer appears to be neither. The reason for the aberration is found within the data itself and is a testament to just how devastating the 2008–2009 bear market really was. You have no doubt heard that the declines experienced in the economy as well as the stock markets were the worst since the Great Depression, and the data bears that out. Due to the algorithmic nature of swing point determination, the volume expansion experienced during the late 2008 and early 2009 declines left an abundance of swing point highs where volume was tremendous on the monthly bars. The result was that when prices finally began to rise in 2009 and on through 2011, these high volume swing points, once surpassed, resulted in trend transitions that were overwhelmingly suspect yet they persisted. A confluence of factors, not the least of which included unprecedented

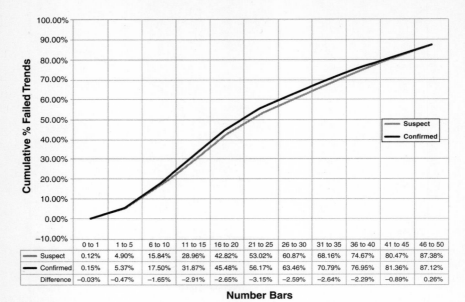

	0 to 1	1 to 5	6 to 10	11 to 15	16 to 20	21 to 25	26 to 30	31 to 35	36 to 40	41 to 45	46 to 50
Suspect	0.12%	4.90%	15.84%	28.96%	42.82%	53.02%	60.87%	68.16%	74.67%	80.47%	87.38%
Confirmed	0.15%	5.37%	17.50%	31.87%	45.48%	56.17%	63.46%	70.79%	76.95%	81.36%	87.12%
Difference	−0.03%	−0.47%	−1.65%	−2.91%	−2.65%	−3.15%	−2.59%	−2.64%	−2.29%	−0.89%	0.26%

Number Bars

FIGURE 1.5 Trend Failure Rate for Confirmed versus Suspect Bullish Trends on the Long-Term Time Frame (2002 to 2011)

actions taken by the Federal Reserve that served to prop up equity prices, has resulted in this aberration.

To illustrate this, consider Figure 1.6, which represents the same data points but only from 2002 to 2007. Once again, the familiar pattern of suspect trends failing prior to confirmed trends is restored.

Although this explanation does nothing to change the fact that there are situations where, for some period of time, the probabilities that favor the termination of suspect trends at a faster rate than confirmed trends do not hold true, the fact is that this period of history was indeed historic.

It also underscores the fact that even though a trend is suspect, that in itself does not necessarily mean that the trend will fail. A suspect trend, on all time frames, has a higher probability of failure prior to a confirmed trend—nothing more. How much more probable is contained in the prior figures. Although it differs on each time frame and is dependent upon how far the trend has already extended in terms of the number of bars that have transpired, the increased probability varies from about 2 to 4 percent. This may not seem like much, but in trading it is huge to have that kind of an edge in your favor.

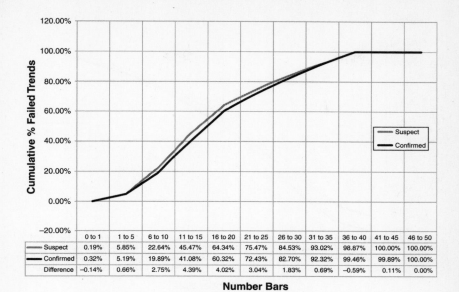

	0 to 1	1 to 5	6 to 10	11 to 15	16 to 20	21 to 25	26 to 30	31 to 35	36 to 40	41 to 45	46 to 50
Suspect	0.19%	5.85%	22.64%	45.47%	64.34%	75.47%	84.53%	93.02%	98.87%	100.00%	100.00%
Confirmed	0.32%	5.19%	19.89%	41.08%	60.32%	72.43%	82.70%	92.32%	99.46%	99.89%	100.00%
Difference	−0.14%	0.66%	2.75%	4.39%	4.02%	3.04%	1.83%	0.69%	−0.59%	0.11%	0.00%

Number Bars

FIGURE 1.6 Trend Failure Rate for Confirmed versus Suspect Bullish Trends on the Long-Term Time Frame (2002 to 2007)

WHAT IS THE TRADING SIGNIFICANCE?

Suspect trends will not necessarily fail because they are suspect; they just have a higher probability of failure when compared to confirmed trends. A market participant should resist the attempt to short sell a suspect bullish trend because it is suspect. In fact, a market participant should generally not trade against an established trend regardless of its qualification unless attempting to time a turn, and in those cases, there need to be other technical factors that support such a stance.

So, what about bearish trends? Do they exhibit the same sort of failure characteristics when comparing suspect to confirmed trends? Indeed they do. Figure 1.7 exhibits the short-term time frame trend failure probabilities for a bearish trend termination.

Another comparison that can be made is to compare Figure 1.3 to 1.7, which reveals a steeper slope for the failure rate in Figure 1.7 as compared to Figure 1.3. The unavoidable implication is that bearish suspect trends are more apt to fail faster than its suspect bullish trend brethren.

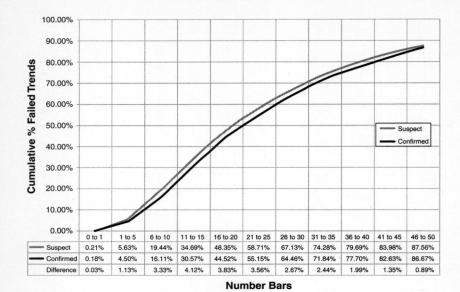

	0 to 1	1 to 5	6 to 10	11 to 15	16 to 20	21 to 25	26 to 30	31 to 35	36 to 40	41 to 45	46 to 50
Suspect	0.21%	5.63%	19.44%	34.69%	48.35%	58.71%	67.13%	74.28%	79.69%	83.98%	87.56%
Confirmed	0.18%	4.50%	16.11%	30.57%	44.52%	55.15%	64.46%	71.84%	77.70%	82.63%	86.67%
Difference	0.03%	1.13%	3.33%	4.12%	3.83%	3.56%	2.67%	2.44%	1.99%	1.35%	0.89%

Number Bars

FIGURE 1.7 Trend Failure Rate for Confirmed versus Suspect Bearish Trends on the Short-Term Time Frame (2002 to 2011)

What's true of short-term bearish trends is even truer on the intermediate term as shown here in Figure 1.8.

Not only is a bearish suspect trend more apt to exhibit a trend failure on this time frame, but the increased probabilities top 5 percent from 11 to 20 bars. Is this an aberration again as a result of the historical turmoil witnessed during the 2008 debacle?

Logically, it makes sense that when selling does begin, if volume swells as price depreciates (confirmed bearish trend), then the intensity of the selling is not as likely to reverse (fail) quickly. Add to this fact the knowledge that the vast majority of the stocks follow the general market (see Chapter 3 for the data behind this assumption) and that all general market indexes experienced confirmed bearish trends during this time, then one would expect to find that the difference between the failure rates of suspect versus confirmed trends would be less during the late 2008 to early 2009 period.

Indeed the data bears these facts and assumptions out. The next two figures take the same data displayed Figure 1.8 and once more divide the data into two groups—from 2002 to 2007 (Figure 1.9) and from 2007 to 2011 (Figure 1.10).

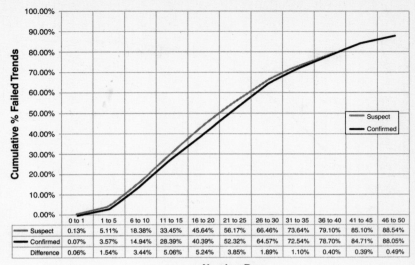

FIGURE 1.8   Trend Failure Rate for Confirmed versus Suspect Bearish Trends on the Intermediate-Term Time Frame (2002 to 2011)

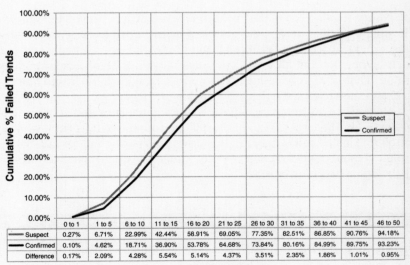

FIGURE 1.9   Trend Failure Rate for Confirmed versus Suspect Bearish Trends on the Intermediate-Term Time Frame (2002 to 2007)

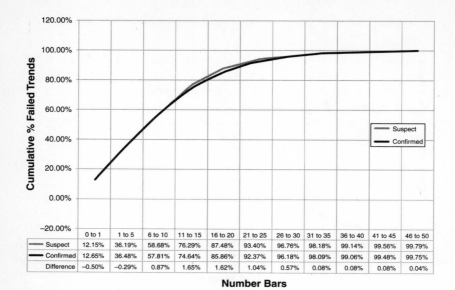

	0 to 1	1 to 5	6 to 10	11 to 15	16 to 20	21 to 25	26 to 30	31 to 35	36 to 40	41 to 45	46 to 50
Suspect	12.15%	36.19%	58.68%	76.29%	87.48%	93.40%	96.76%	98.18%	99.14%	99.56%	99.79%
Confirmed	12.65%	36.48%	57.81%	74.64%	85.86%	92.37%	96.18%	98.09%	99.06%	99.48%	99.75%
Difference	−0.50%	−0.29%	0.87%	1.65%	1.62%	1.04%	0.57%	0.08%	0.08%	0.08%	0.04%

Number Bars

FIGURE 1.10 Trend Failure Rate for Confirmed versus Suspect Bearish Trends on the Intermediate-Term Time Frame (2007 to 2011)

Notice the flatness of the curve in Figure 1.10 as opposed to Figure 1.9. The shape of the curve is indicative of a fast move lower (which turned most stocks bearish on this time frame) followed by an equally fast move back higher, forcing an end to the bearish trend. Think back about this period. That is what happened. The market cascaded lower into March of 2009 and then reversed quickly off the lows.

Once more, as before, given the historical declines and volume swells witnessed in the late 2008 to early 2009 period, the data is somewhat distorted for this period of time. In this case, the historic failure rates of confirmed versus suspect trends is likely *understated* and that the rates will likely top 5 percent over time.

WHAT IS THE TRADING SIGNIFICANCE?

Bearish trends differ from bullish trends in two important ways.

1. Confirmed bearish trends tend to have a much higher probability of persistence when compared to suspect bearish trends. This is true of both short and intermediate-term time frames with increased probabilities for persistence approaching 5 percent.

2. Overall, bearish trends fail sooner than bullish trends (compare Figures 1.3 and 1.4 versus 1.7 and 1.8).

The implication to a trader is that bearish trends, when confirmed, offer greater opportunity versus risk, and they do so in a more compacted time period. If the trend can be joined quickly, the opportunity exists for faster profits and with a greater probability of success.

The risk for those holding long positions is just the opposite when a confirmed bearish trend comes into existence, for the losses can mount very quickly.

Finally, when previously viewing the long-term time frame for bullish trends we noted the uncharacteristically higher occurrence of confirmed versus suspect trend failures. Unlike bullish long term trends, this is not the case for confirmed bearish trends. If the data is sliced up again between pre-2007 and post-2007, it suggests that the tendency for suspect trends to fail sooner than confirmed trends is understated in Figure 1.11. Note that this is consistent with what was seen in Figures 1.9 and 1.10.

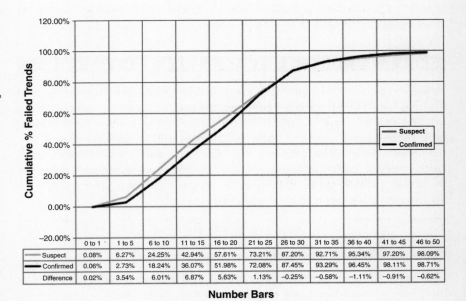

	0 to 1	1 to 5	6 to 10	11 to 15	16 to 20	21 to 25	26 to 30	31 to 35	36 to 40	41 to 45	46 to 50
Suspect	0.08%	6.27%	24.25%	42.94%	57.61%	73.21%	87.20%	92.71%	95.34%	97.20%	98.09%
Confirmed	0.06%	2.73%	18.24%	36.07%	51.98%	72.08%	87.45%	93.29%	96.45%	98.11%	98.71%
Difference	0.02%	3.54%	6.01%	6.87%	5.63%	1.13%	−0.25%	−0.58%	−1.11%	−0.91%	−0.62%

Number Bars

FIGURE 1.11 Trend Failure Rate for Confirmed versus Suspect Bearish Trends on the Long-Term Time Frame (2002 to 2011)

Both long- and intermediate-term bearish trends have excellent failure probability distinctions between confirmed and suspect trends—probabilities that range from 4 to 7 percent between 6 and 20 bars. There are a number of ways that a market participant could exploit this probability distribution, such as a spread trade not only across trading instruments (short selling the confirmed bearish trend and buying the suspect bullish trend) but, better yet, doing this when the stock being shorted is at the beginning of its trend (between 1 and 10 bars, for example) while the stock being purchased in an equal dollar amount is nearing the end of the its likely lifespan (20 bars or more, for example).

Figures 1.3 to 1.11 considered qualified trend persistence for both bullish and bearish trends. The data offers a glimpse into the probabilities for trend continuance based on how long the trend has already persisted. Generally speaking, qualified trends offer a market participant an increased insight into the likelihood of trend failure in general and more specifically for suspect and confirmed trends. Since the vast majority of trading systems are grounded in trend in one form or another, having increased insight into failure probabilities has value. With this kind of data in front of you, it does not take a lot of imagination to consider numerous ways to utilize the data to one's advantage.

WHAT IS THE TRADING SIGNIFICANCE?

As another example, in Figure 1.11 the probability matrix is screaming out that if a long-term bearish trend is confirmed, the probability that it will fail during the first five bars is a minimal 2.73 percent. If this is Bar 1 or 2 of a long-term bearish trend, then you know that there is a 97.27 percent chance that the bearish trend will persist for at least four more bars (months in this case). Furthermore, it is a fact that when a suspect trend has witnessed persistence for more than 11 bars, the probability of seeing trend failure is almost 7 percent greater than if you are trading a confirmed trend.

Sideways Trend Persistence

In the preceding paragraphs, both bullish and bearish trend failure probabilities were considered, but what about sideways trends? They are trends, too. Do they share the same characteristics?

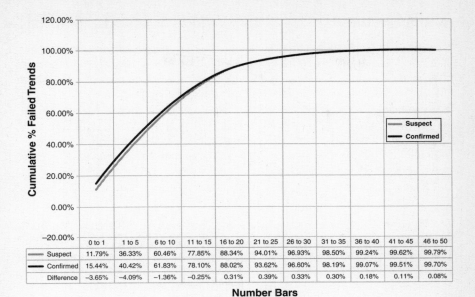

	0 to 1	1 to 5	6 to 10	11 to 15	16 to 20	21 to 25	26 to 30	31 to 35	36 to 40	41 to 45	46 to 50
Suspect	11.79%	36.33%	60.46%	77.85%	88.34%	94.01%	96.93%	98.50%	99.24%	99.62%	99.79%
Confirmed	15.44%	40.42%	61.83%	78.10%	88.02%	93.62%	96.60%	98.19%	99.07%	99.51%	99.70%
Difference	−3.65%	−4.09%	−1.36%	−0.25%	0.31%	0.39%	0.33%	0.30%	0.18%	0.11%	0.08%

Number Bars

FIGURE 1.12 Trend Failure Rate for Confirmed versus Suspect Sideways Trends on the Short-Term Time Frame (2002 to 2011)

In my previous book, *Trend Qualification and Trading*, I considered sideways trends as akin to a way station between bullish and bearish trends. My trading experience led me to believe that they shared the same qualified trend characteristic—that is, that suspect trends would show less likelihood to persist as compared to confirmed trends—but the data have proved that assumption to be somewhat misguided. The next three figures (1.12 through 1.14) are for sideways trends that fail. Note that, unlike bullish or bearish trends, sideways trends can fail in one of two ways. They can either transition to a bullish or to a bearish trend. Bullish trends only have one way to go—down. Similarly, bearish trends can only fail by reversing and heading higher. Not true of sideways trends because they are in the middle of bullish and bearish.

In the following figures, sideways trend termination is shown as one data point independent of whether the replacement trend (the one transitioned to) was bearish or bullish. The characteristic difference between the two transition directions appears reasonably insignificant, so there is not really a reason to examine them exhaustively.

Upon observation, there are three noteworthy facts displayed across all three time frames for sideways trend termination. The first is that the

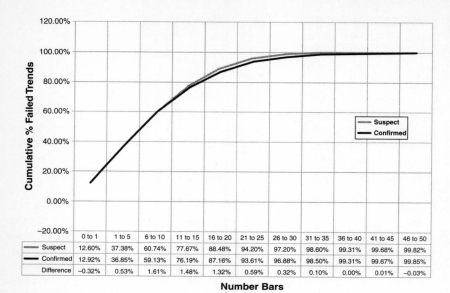

FIGURE 1.13 Trend Failure Rate for Confirmed versus Suspect Sideways Trends on the Intermediate-Term Time Frame (2002 to 2011)

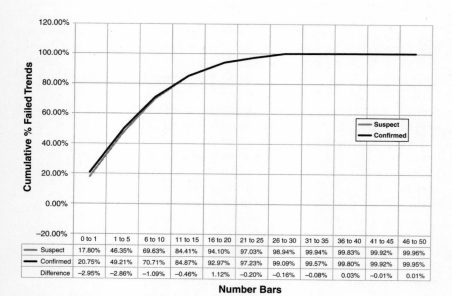

FIGURE 1.14 Trend Failure Rate for Confirmed versus Suspect Sideways Trends on the Long-Term Time Frame (2002 to 2011)

difference between trend failure rates for suspect versus confirmed trends is not all that significant. The intermediate-term time frame is the only one of the three time frames that sees a consistently higher rate of failure for suspect trends as compared to confirmed trends, but even then, it is reasonably minor.

A second and somewhat consistent observation (true of two of the three time frames) is that confirmed trends are more likely to fail than suspect sideways trends during the first 10 bars. Although there is probably a reasonable rationalization for this fact, it is not clear as to what it is. Again, other than one particular data point, the increased failure rates are not all that much greater.

Finally, the most valuable takeaway is that sideways trends have a very high probability of failing within 10 to 15 bars across all three time frames. In fact, some 70 to 80 percent of all sideways trends fail regardless of their qualification (suspect or confirmed) within 15 bars. They simply do not last very long comparatively and are little more than way stations between bullish and bearish trends.

QUALIFIED TRADE FAILURE PROBABILITIES

In the prior section, the focus was centered on trend failures where a failure was measured as a trend transition. Returning to Figure 1.2, there were five trend transitions in the chart resulting in four different trend failure categorizations. The first qualified trend was confirmed bullish and it persisted for 15 bars before it met its fate. At that point, a confirmed sideways trend replaced it and lasted for 9 bars before failing, and so forth and so on. The rate of failure (trend failure) between suspect and confirmed trends is the entire premise behind the statement that *unlike men, not all trends are created equal*. Though extremely valuable and somewhat profound, the trend failure data previously presented simply validate the fact that trends have qualitative differences and a market participant can both recognize and trade off of those differences. But there are other ways to look at failures. One such way is to draw a distinction between failures as they apply to trends as opposed to trades. Allow me to digress.

When trading, the objective is to locate and utilize some criterion to enter into a trade. The success or failure of the trade is predicated on whether money is made or lost. The parameters for trade exit in the failure case can be based upon many factors—subjective or objective. For example, some market participants always use a particular percentage loss as a stop out.

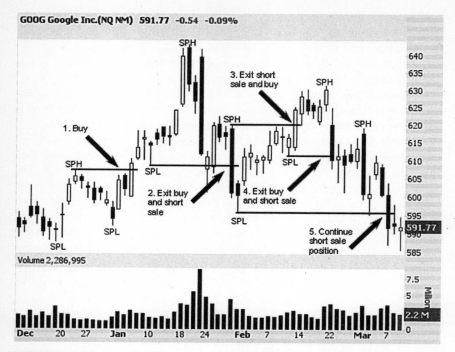

FIGURE 1.15 Example Where Trend and Trade Failure Are Identical—Google (December 9, 2010 to March 9, 2011)

If, for example, the losses mount to the point that they are more than 7 percent, then the trade is closed at a loss. There are countless strategies for trade exit that trigger a trade failure.

Now, if the trading parameters for trade failure exit are aligned identically to trend failure, then trend and trade failure will necessarily be exactly the same. To illustrate, Figure 1.15 is the same chart of Google once more (Figure 1.2) but this time annotated to identify the entry and exit price points based entirely upon trend failure. No attempt is made to exit with a profit—just to identify where the trade would fail if the exit criterion for trade failure was exactly the same as trend failure.

In this illustration, each time trend transitions to a differing trend state, the trade fails right along with the trend failure. They are the same. Although this could be the case, trade failure exit criteria are highly unlikely to be identical to trend transition. Most market participants do not enter a trade based on a trend transition and exit based on a failure of that trend. Market participants typically utilize trend as one factor as part of a larger set of factors to trigger trade entry and exit. It may be a factor but typically it is not the only factor. For this reason, trend and trade failures are generally not the same.

Qualified trends are primarily concerned with direction and the strength of the directional price movement. Trend, per se, is not necessarily meant to be the trigger for trade execution. Said another way, trend really is not meant for timing trade entry and exit. Trend tells a market participant which way to point—not when to start pointing. To know when to point requires additional timing tools that complement trend transition.

Thus far, all the data presented have centered on *trend failure*, which is quite different from *trade failure*. Trade failure accounts for the needs of a market participant to time entry and exit within the context of trading a qualified trend. Trade success and failure is all about optimizing both trade entry and exit for both the success and failure possibilities.

Trade Failures (Suspect and Confirmed)

In the preceding analysis, a trend was assumed to have failed when the trend transitions to a differing trend type. Assuming that the real objective of trading is trade success and knowing that there is an apparent value in trading qualified trends, the question arises as to whether the data presented previously differ if *failure* is defined differently. For example, what if the definition of a *trade failure* is revised from a trend transition to a trade below the breakout bar that begins a bullish trend? Similarly, a *failure* for a bearish trade would be a trade above the breakout bar that begins a bearish trend. Would the results prove to be better or worse than what were observed previously? Realize that this is only one of a myriad of trade entries and exit timings, but it is a simple one that can be utilized to illustrate the concept of marrying qualified trend to entry and exit timing.

To illustrate this revised *failure criteria*, Figure 1.16 once more takes the same Google chart and illustrates how a trade failure would appear based on the preceding stop out criteria in the two bullish buy set-ups. The bearish short set-ups could have been illustrated as well but essentially are the same idea—just the opposite direction. Rather than clutter the chart too much, just the bullish set-ups and resultant stops are identified.

When comparing Figure 1.15 to 1.16, it is quite apparent that there is a distinct difference between trade and trend failures. In this particular example, use of the trade failure criteria did not really change the outcome much, but in many cases it significantly reduces the trend's persistence and avoids what would otherwise be significant drawdowns in an investor's capital.

To examine the effects when using trade failure criteria rather than trend failure criteria on the question of suspect versus confirmed trend

FIGURE 1.16 Google Bullish Trade Failure Example

transitions, the same raw data used in the prior examination was again utilized and simulations were run with a change to the single variable—the notion of when a failure occurs. So rather than a failure occurring upon a trend transition, a failure is instead defined as a trade below the opposite extreme of the bar that resulted in a trend transition. For a bullish trend transition, this implies a trade and close below the low of the breakout bar. For a bearish trend transition, then, it implies a trade and close over the high of the breakout bar.

The results are remarkably different, as seen in Figure 1.17. For a direct comparison, use Figure 1.3 as the equivalent time period and trend direction.

The significance of the difference is unmistakable. In Figure 1.3, the cumulative trend failure rate from zero through five bars was less than 5 percent for both confirmed and suspect trends. In the case where a trade back below the low of the breakout bar is used as the failure criteria for the trade, more than 60 percent of the trades fail before five bars (note the granularity of the bar observations is greater in this graph than previous graphs).

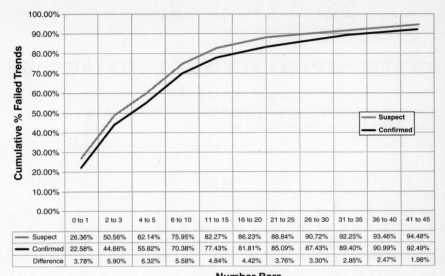

	0 to 1	2 to 3	4 to 5	6 to 10	11 to 15	16 to 20	21 to 25	26 to 30	31 to 35	36 to 40	41 to 45
Suspect	26.36%	50.56%	62.14%	75.95%	82.27%	86.23%	88.84%	90.72%	92.25%	93.46%	94.48%
Confirmed	22.58%	44.66%	55.82%	70.38%	77.43%	81.81%	85.09%	87.43%	89.40%	90.99%	92.49%
Difference	3.78%	5.90%	6.32%	5.58%	4.84%	4.42%	3.76%	3.30%	2.85%	2.47%	1.98%

Number Bars

FIGURE 1.17 Cumulative Trade Failure Rate for Confirmed versus Suspect Trades on the Short-Term Time Frame for Bullish Trends (2002 to 2011) (Failure Based on a Violation of Breakout Bar's Opposite Price Extreme)

If you stop to think about it, this makes a lot of sense. To fail early when a failure has to be a trend failure (such as it was in Figure 1.3), price must collapse precipitously or a prior swing point low must be located in close proximity to the swing point high that was just broken. Neither of these conditions is common and thus, the odds of an immediate trend failure are unlikely.

In Figure 1.17, though, the use of a trade failure stop out results in more than 76 percent of all suspect trend breakouts failing within 10 bars of the trend transition. Even confirmed trades witness a failure rate of just over 70 percent using this stop out criterion.

From a trading perspective, it is unlikely that this particular stop out criterion is worth pursuing but it does shed additional light on another data point that does have critical significance. That data element is the pronounced difference observed between suspect and confirmed trend failure rates when using differing stop out criteria.

In Figure 1.3, the largest observed difference between suspect and confirmed trend never registered more than 3.24 percent. Recall that Figure 1.3 measures *trend failures*. Here in Figure 1.17, the difference escalates to over 6 percent for three to four bars' duration and in general is much higher across all sample rates. Note that the only difference is that now the failure is based on a different criterion—it is now a *trade failure*.

WHAT IS THE TRADING SIGNIFICANCE?

These data overwhelming suggest that, with the proper stop out criterion, the difference in confirmed versus suspect failure rates is significant and emphasizes that confirmed trends should be a trader's preferred trend.

     For completeness, the following figures illustrate that the results observed in Figure 1.17 are consistently true across the intermediate- and long-term time frames for bullish trends. Likewise, the results are evident in bearish trends as well. Since sideways trends have been shown to be a way station between bullish and bearish trends, they are no longer analyzed during the remainder of the book.

     Figures 1.18 and 1.19 display the results for the intermediate and long-term trends, respectively, based on the same trade failure criterion reflected in Figure 1.17.

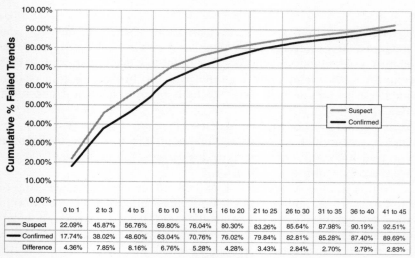

	0 to 1	2 to 3	4 to 5	6 to 10	11 to 15	16 to 20	21 to 25	26 to 30	31 to 35	36 to 40	41 to 45
Suspect	22.09%	45.87%	56.76%	69.80%	76.04%	80.30%	83.26%	85.64%	87.98%	90.19%	92.51%
Confirmed	17.74%	38.02%	48.60%	63.04%	70.76%	76.02%	79.84%	82.81%	85.28%	87.40%	89.69%
Difference	4.36%	7.85%	8.16%	6.76%	5.28%	4.28%	3.43%	2.84%	2.70%	2.79%	2.83%

Number Bars

FIGURE 1.18 Cumulative Trade Failure Rate for Confirmed versus Suspect Trades on the Intermediate-Term Time Frame for Bullish Trends (2002 to 2011) (Failure Based on a Violation of Breakout Bar's Opposite Price Extreme)

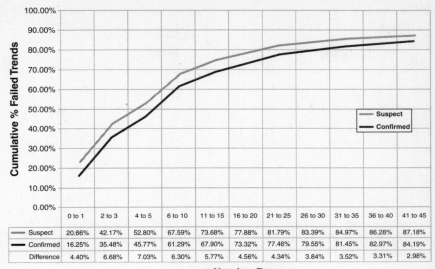

	0 to 1	2 to 3	4 to 5	6 to 10	11 to 15	16 to 20	21 to 25	26 to 30	31 to 35	36 to 40	41 to 45
Suspect	20.66%	42.17%	52.80%	67.59%	73.68%	77.88%	81.79%	83.39%	84.97%	86.28%	87.18%
Confirmed	16.25%	35.48%	45.77%	61.29%	67.90%	73.32%	77.46%	79.55%	81.45%	82.97%	84.19%
Difference	4.40%	6.68%	7.03%	6.30%	5.77%	4.56%	4.34%	3.84%	3.52%	3.31%	2.98%

Number Bars

FIGURE 1.19 Cumulative Trade Failure Rate for Confirmed versus Suspect Trades on the Long-Term Time Frame for Bullish Trends (2002 to 2011) (Failure Based on a Violation of Breakout Bar's Opposite Price Extreme)

In each of these graphs, the pronounced difference between suspect and confirmed trade failures remains as such. Although bearish trend trade failures continue to show a demarcation between suspect and confirmed trends, it is not nearly as well defined as what was observed for bullish trends. An attempted rationalization of this is that bullish accumulation and market tops have differing characteristics when compared to price mark downs and market bottoms. Selling tends to be climatic and swift whereas buying tends to be more systematic and slow.

For completeness, Figures 1.20 through 1.22 display the results of the same trade failure criterion for short, intermediate, and long-term bearish trade failures, respectively.

SUMMARY

All serious market participants understand that trading is primarily based on probabilities. If they do not, they should not be trading. There is no guaranteed trade. Most anything can happen and, if you trade long enough, it probably will.

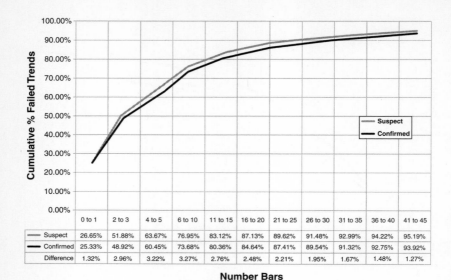

Number Bars

	0 to 1	2 to 3	4 to 5	6 to 10	11 to 15	16 to 20	21 to 25	26 to 30	31 to 35	36 to 40	41 to 45
Suspect	26.65%	51.88%	63.67%	76.95%	83.12%	87.13%	89.62%	91.48%	92.99%	94.22%	95.19%
Confirmed	25.33%	48.92%	60.45%	73.68%	80.36%	84.64%	87.41%	89.54%	91.32%	92.75%	93.92%
Difference	1.32%	2.96%	3.22%	3.27%	2.76%	2.48%	2.21%	1.95%	1.67%	1.48%	1.27%

FIGURE 1.20   Cumulative Trade Failure Rate for Confirmed versus Suspect Trades on the Short-Term Time Frame for Bearish Trends (2002 to 2011) (Failure Based on a Violation of Breakout Bar's Opposite Price Extreme)

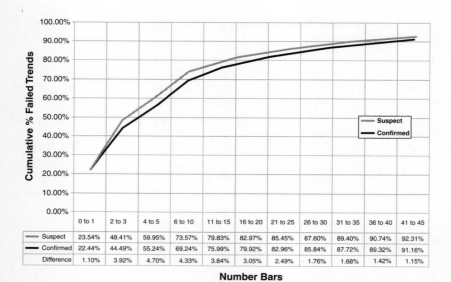

Number Bars

	0 to 1	2 to 3	4 to 5	6 to 10	11 to 15	16 to 20	21 to 25	26 to 30	31 to 35	36 to 40	41 to 45
Suspect	23.54%	48.41%	59.95%	73.57%	79.83%	82.97%	85.45%	87.60%	89.40%	90.74%	92.31%
Confirmed	22.44%	44.49%	55.24%	69.24%	75.99%	79.92%	82.96%	85.84%	87.72%	89.32%	91.16%
Difference	1.10%	3.92%	4.70%	4.33%	3.84%	3.05%	2.49%	1.76%	1.68%	1.42%	1.15%

FIGURE 1.21   Cumulative Trade Failure Rate for Confirmed versus Suspect Trades on the Intermediate-Term Time Frame for Bearish Trends (2002 to 2011) (Failure Based on a Violation of Breakout Bar's Opposite Price Extreme)

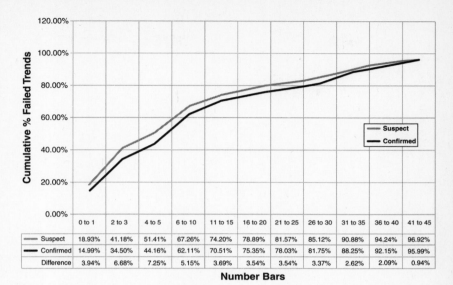

FIGURE 1.22 Cumulative Trade Failure Rate for Confirmed versus Suspect Trades on the Long-Term Time Frame for Bearish Trends (2002 to 2011) (Failure Based on a Violation of Breakout Bar's Opposite Price Extreme)

In the preceding figures (Figures 1.3 through 1.14), it was observed that, in almost all situations, confirmed trends have a higher probability of continuing than suspect trends when utilizing trend transition as the criterion for trend failure.

By broadening the definition of a failure to *trade failure* and defining that as the case where price trades below the opposite extreme price of the bar where the breakout occurs, a significant distinction between suspect and confirmed trends is evidenced. The differing trade failure rates begin to uncover the possibilities that trend qualification provides to a market participant. If a suspect trend breakout has a trade failure probability rate that is 6 percent higher than a confirmed trend over the first five bars of a trend transition breakout, that sort of knowledge can be very valuable indeed.

What remains, however, is to expand the baby steps taken thus far to include additional entry and exit criteria that can greatly enhance a market participant's success rates as well as profit potential. To do that requires the expansion of this somewhat simplistic start to include additional timing criteria. In *Trend Qualification and Trading*, it was noted that trend provides direction while anchor zones provide timing, so what better place to move but to anchor zones. With anchor zones, further refinements to trade failure can be made and a more valuable trading system pursued.

CHAPTER 2

Anchor Zones: The Key to Timing Trades

I n the preceding chapter, a methodological approach to qualifying trends was reviewed and some of the data that lie behind the methodology were revealed. A distinction was made between *trend failure* and *trade failure* because a change in trend typically is not the most optimal time to make a trade. Despite that, the previous chapter showed how the application of a simplistic stop out rule could dramatically alter the probability of failure when comparing confirmed trends to suspect ones. This chapter takes that idea a bit further.

In *Trend Qualification and Trading*,[1] there was a reasonably significant amount of time spent examining price and volume with the idea of identifying areas on the chart where supply and demand were apparent. That was true of swing points as well as of anchor bars and anchor zones. It stands to reason that if price zones can be identified that have a reasonably good record of supporting or resisting a further decline or advance in price, then that would be the ideal place to use as entry and exit point when trading. This chapter reintroduces anchor bars and zones, briefly reviewing what they are and then expanding the trade analysis presented in Chapter 1 to include anchor zones for trade entry and exit.

---

[1]L.A. Little, *Trend Qualification and Trading* (Hoboken, NJ: John Wiley & Sons, 2011).

41

ANCHOR BARS AND ZONES

An anchor bar is a place on the chart where buyers and sellers meet with a result that is anything but ordinary. Ordinary is where the volume of trading is somewhat subdued, the price range is relatively small, swing point highs and lows are not being created or tested, and no price gaps are apparent. When anchor bars appear, they exhibit at least one or more of these characteristics.

Think of anchor bars as a price bar where the appearance of conviction is unmistakable. Either the buyers are totally convinced that they are correct in their view or the sellers are, or in some situations, both parties to the transaction have certainty with respect to their correctness in belief. When buyers or sellers become convinced that they are correct, then that belief is displayed in one or more of three possible ways on the charts. Either volume begins to expand relative to any volume witnessed previously at the same price area on the chart, or the length of the bar becomes elongated (the spread between the high and low on the bar), or prices may gap higher or lower. Any and all of these occurrences may also involve swing point highs and lows.

Heavy volume bars are easy to spot on a chart because they usually tower above all other bars. They represent situations where volume swells hugely on a comparative basis for the time frame under examination.

A wide price spread bar is any bar where the width of the bar is relatively wide as compared to all other bars on the same time frame. Wide price spread bars can happen when one side of the trade takes control and relentlessly pushes price throughout the bar. Another common occurrence is a reversal during the bar where one side initially takes control, but somewhere during the bar is reluctantly forced to retrace. The result many times leads to violent and fast price reversals that leave telltale markings on the charts. Many times wide price spread bars double as high volume bars.

Gaps occur whenever some event transpires that results in the odd situation where no trades take place for a given price range. Many times the event occurs outside of trading hours, but it can happen during trading hours. In the latter case, one would usually only see this gap on an intraday trading chart. Gaps can, in a way, be viewed as a subset of wide price spread bars, and many times they double as wide price spread bars. When measuring a wide price spread bar where a gap is evident on that trading day, the width of the gap is added to the spread of the *gap bar*. The result is the true width of the bar (the width of the gap plus the width of the gap bar).

Anchor Bars

If you examine most any chart, you will find anchor bars.

Anchors—An anchor is a price bar that contains one or more of the following patterns: a gap formation; significantly noticeable volume escalation; significantly noticeable price spread

Anchor Top—The high price of an anchor bar; a swing point high or low

Anchor Bottom—The low price of an anchor bar

The importance of anchor bars is that they are one of the few places on a chart where supply and demand can be both identified and measured. The identification is that the anchor bar consists of one or more of the characteristics described earlier. The measure is the number of transactions that occurred while forming the anchor bar. That measure is volume.

In general, charts should be viewed in the context of about 60 bars per chart, not because 60 is some sort of magical number, but because it embodies some characteristics that are important. For one, a chart constructed of roughly 60 bars is an ample number of bars but not too many for trend analysis. You want a chart that is not too cluttered, otherwise it becomes unusable. Too much information is just as bad as too little.

When viewing a daily chart, for example, three months of data creates a readable chart with about 60 bars. A weekly chart of one year's worth of data is about 60 bars as well. When viewed in this manner, there is unlikely to be a proliferation of anchor bars and that is good a good thing.

Figure 2.1 is a chart of the Technology Select Sector SPDR Fund ETF (XLK), an exchange traded fund that is representative of the broad technology sector in the Standard and Poor's 500 (S&P 500). It just so happens that this chart displays several examples of each of the three anchor bar formations.

The leftmost annotations are four separate wide price spread bars. All of these bars also happened to be high volume bars. Many times wide price spread bars double as high volume bars. Additionally, high volume and wide price spread bars many times are located adjacent to each other. When located adjacently, they are referred to as *clustered anchor bars*. Clustered anchor bars such as those witnessed on this chart tend to anchor prices for some time to come. In this particular chart, price highs and lows were more or less contained within the highs and lows of the wide price spread, high volume bars for a good eight weeks before breaking free.

FIGURE 2.1 Anchor Bar Examples—Technology Select Sector SPDR ETF (XLK) (Jul 13, 2011 to Oct 13, 2011)

Many times such price action creates a range trade set-up as discussed in Chapter 6.

There are a number of gap sequences on this chart. One example of this is highlighted in the leftmost oval. That price bar doubles as another wide price spread and high volume bar when the gap is added to the width of the bar. The final annotation is another example of a gap sequence that ends up as both wide price spread and high volume.

In *Trend Qualification and Trading*, an entire chapter was devoted to proper identification of anchor bars and zones. Their significance is paramount to a market participant because timing is a critical part of success. When the tops and bottoms of anchor bars are combined, anchor zones take form. Anchor zones are useful constructs because they have much greater significance when attempting to identify areas on the charts where prices should trade to, yet not beyond.

Anchor Zones

Anchor zones are a significant improvement to old-school support and resistance lines and channels. They have increased value because they are

FIGURE 2.2 Anchor Zones Example—Technology Select Sector SPDR ETF (XLK) (Jul 13, 2011 to Oct 13, 2011)

anchored to chart events that have greater significance, and what better significance than that of strength or weakness exhibited through increased supply or demand for the stock?

Figure 2.2 is the same chart as presented in Figure 2.1 but annotated with two anchor zones constructed from a subset of the anchor bars highlighted in the prior figure. Note that anchor zones can also consist of swing points as well since they too tell a story about supply and demand in most cases.

Anchor bars, when interlaced, form anchor zones that represent price areas on the chart where significance has been demonstrated through price and volume. Anchor zones are identified as those areas on the chart where anchor bar highs and lows overlap or form a congruent price zone on the chart.

Reflecting back on the previous chapter, the failure rate for confirmed versus suspect trends improved once a set of simplistic entry and exit rules were imposed. Those rules resulted in confirmed trends becoming even more persistent as compared to suspect trends. The rule, as you recall, was that a trade failure occurred if the stock traded under or over the opposite extreme price bar once the trend transitioned.

With the introduction of anchor bars and zones, what happens if the rule is extended to examine the trade failure rate if the nearest anchor zone is utilized as the stop out criterion? In fact, anchor zones could be viewed as the target profit object as well as the stop loss failsafe.

RECONSIDERING TRADE FAILURES

Given that anchor zones provide a far better methodology to gauge stock entry and exit, it seems quite reasonable to utilize anchor zones for trade failure determination rather than the opposite extreme price on the bar where trend transition occurred.

To that end, Figure 2.3 displays the results of such a stop out policy. There are two significant differences to this chart with respect to those presented in Chapter 1. First, a trade can now terminate for one of two reasons—it meets either the profit target objective or the stop loss protection. Both are realized when price overruns an anchor zone. Specifically, for every trade examined over the decade of data, when a trend transitions,

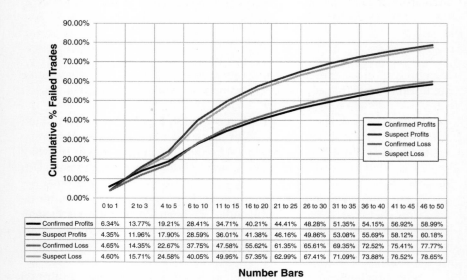

	0 to 1	2 to 3	4 to 5	6 to 10	11 to 15	16 to 20	21 to 25	26 to 30	31 to 35	36 to 40	41 to 45	46 to 50
Confirmed Profits	6.34%	13.77%	19.21%	28.41%	34.71%	40.21%	44.41%	48.28%	51.35%	54.15%	56.92%	58.99%
Suspect Profits	4.35%	11.96%	17.90%	28.59%	36.01%	41.38%	46.16%	49.86%	53.08%	55.69%	58.12%	60.18%
Confirmed Loss	4.65%	14.35%	22.67%	37.75%	47.58%	55.62%	61.35%	65.61%	69.35%	72.52%	75.41%	77.77%
Suspect Loss	4.60%	15.71%	24.58%	40.05%	49.95%	57.35%	62.99%	67.41%	71.09%	73.88%	76.52%	78.65%

Number Bars

FIGURE 2.3 Bullish Short-Term Trade Terminations Using Anchor Zones for Target and Stop Criteria (2002 to 2011)

the nearest support and resistance zones are located. For bullish trades, if the top of the resistance zone is penetrated, then the trade is terminated and recorded as a trade that reached its profit objective. The opposite case is where the bottom of the support is penetrated, in which case a stop loss occurs and terminates the trade. For bearish trades the same criteria are utilized but in the opposite direction.

Thus, Figure 2.3 contains four curves. Naturally there is the suspect versus confirmed trends but with each of these there are two possible outcomes—a profit case and a loss case.

In the preceding figure, a number of interesting points are observable with the most prominent being that trade termination for those trades that ended with losses occurred much faster, on average, than those that ended with profits. This was true of both suspect as well as confirmed trends.

WHAT IS THE TRADING SIGNIFICANCE?

Though maybe not intuitive, this data suggests that for bullish trends, the further you get out on the trade duration curve, the greater the likelihood that the trade is a winner rather than a loser. For example, assume a trade that has a duration of 11 to 15 bars so far. At that particular point in the life of all such confirmed bullish trades on the short-term time frame, 47.58 percent or almost half would have terminated with losses already if they were going to fail. Contrast that with only 34.71 percent of trades that have terminated due to resistance zones that have been hit and traded above. When looking at this chart, the old adage of "letting your profits run" comes to mind, driving home the thought that you cannot terminate trades out of boredom because trades that end up as losing trades are much more likely to have occurred already than winning trades.

Looking at the same data in a slightly different way, Figure 2.4 looks strictly at the ratio of trade termination rates for the same criteria. The ratio is between trades that end in profits versus those that end in losses.

To aid in reading the chart, take a look at the first couple of values in the chart. The first is actually a negative 2 percent, which indicates that trade terminations that ended in losses occurred, on average, 2 percent less frequently that those that ended in profits *for trade durations of one bar*. The second number is 1 percent, which indicates that for trade durations of two through three bars, trade terminations that ended in losses occurred, on average, 1 percent *more* frequently than those that ended in profits.

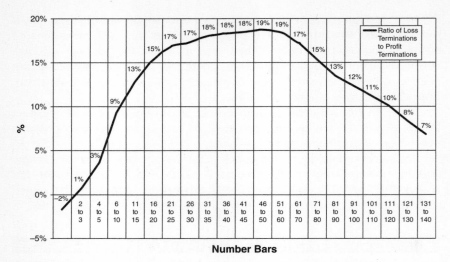

FIGURE 2.4 Ratio of Bullish Profits versus Losses for Trade Failure Rates on the Short-Term Time Frame Using Anchor Zones for Target and Stop Criteria (2002 to 2011)

Echoing Figure 2.3, the data more clearly states the fact that trades that end in losses will, on average, terminate more quickly than those that end in profits.

WHAT IS THE TRADING SIGNIFICANCE?

For a market participant who uses time stops as part of their stop out regimen, stops where losses are taken should be taken within the first 10 or so bars where the curve is the steepest because if the trade does not terminate by then, it has a greater probability of being a winner rather than a loser.

One final note on trade termination ratios: Confirmed trends tend to hit profit targets at a greater rate than suspect trends within the first five bars because they are stronger. After that it is the reverse but the difference is nominal—only about 2 percent in most cases.

Finally, looking back at Figure 1.17 from Chapter 1, another distinct difference is the overall lower trade failure rates that result from a small change in how trades are entered and exited. The differences are dramatic. In Figure 1.17, 70 percent to 75 percent of all trades terminated within

10 bars. In Figure 2.4, that rate was reduced by half, and the change to entry and exit criteria was simple—just stay in the trade unless the nearest anchor zone extreme was violated.

WHAT IS THE TRADING SIGNIFICANCE?

When using anchor zones for trade terminations (both profit and losses), the trade failure rate is reduced substantially. Trade failures when using the extreme opposite breakout bar (Chapter 1) versus the bottom of the anchor support zone (for a bullish trend) heavily favored longer trade durations. In the case of breakout bar stops, 80 percent of confirmed bullish trades between 1 and 15 bars failed. When using the bottom of anchored support as the stop out, less than 35 percent of the trades failed. Anchored zones provide a marked improvement to trade duration.

The other side of the equation to longer trade durations that must be considered is drawdowns. A drawdown is essentially defined as a paper loss. If trade durations are extended at the expense of significantly increased drawdowns, then the benefits are somewhat muted.

For the studies conducted, there was an increase in drawdowns experienced when utilizing anchor zones rather than the opposite extreme of the breakout bar as the stop loss criterion. The paper losses increased to, on average, roughly 5 percent across all time frames. What was not measurable was the added benefit received for those trade terminations that resulted in profits since the initial investigations profit target terminations were not considered.

As for other trade types and time frames, the results displayed in Figures 2.3 and 2.4 are equally observable on the intermediate and long-term time frames.

In Figure 2.5, the same bullish profits versus losses stop out criteria are used to display the long-term time frame. This data suffers from the same inverse relationship explained in Chapter 1, where suspect trends fail at a lesser rate than confirmed ones for the data that encompasses the 2008 stock market crash, but even if corrected for that data, there is an interesting observation. When utilizing this anchor zone stop out strategy, termination rates for long-term time frames do not extend for all qualified trend types. In Figure 1.19, roughly 70 percent of all trends ceased their existence within 15 bars. Here, in Figure 2.5, that number is roughly 85 percent.

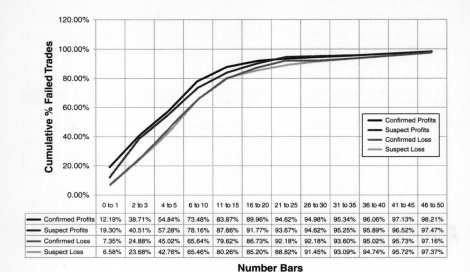

	0 to 1	2 to 3	4 to 5	6 to 10	11 to 15	16 to 20	21 to 25	26 to 30	31 to 35	36 to 40	41 to 45	46 to 50
Confirmed Profits	12.19%	38.71%	54.84%	73.48%	83.87%	89.96%	94.62%	94.98%	95.34%	96.06%	97.13%	98.21%
Suspect Profits	19.30%	40.51%	57.28%	78.16%	87.66%	91.77%	93.67%	94.62%	95.25%	95.89%	96.52%	97.47%
Confirmed Loss	7.35%	24.88%	45.02%	65.64%	79.62%	86.73%	92.18%	92.18%	93.60%	95.02%	95.73%	97.16%
Suspect Loss	6.58%	23.68%	42.76%	65.46%	80.26%	85.20%	88.82%	91.45%	93.09%	94.74%	95.72%	97.37%

Number Bars

FIGURE 2.5   Bullish Profits versus Losses for Trade Failure Rates on the Long-Term Time Frame Using Anchor Zones for Target and Stop Criteria (2002 to 2011)

WHAT IS THE TRADING SIGNIFICANCE?

Long-term trades—bullish and bearish—simply do not last all that many bars once established. There is a reasonably high probability that a long-term trend will stop out (either with a profit or a loss) within a small number of monthly bars (see Figures 1.19 and 2.5). For this reason, buy and hold makes very little sense from an investment perspective without incorporating some sort of hedging strategy or taking partial profits with the passage of time. At 20 to 25 bars, stop outs for both losses and profits approach equality. That equates to one and a half to two years at most.

Although the data previously presented is just a small sampling of trend probabilities, it nevertheless begins to provide a window into the world of trade successes and failures and just how radically different they can appear based on entry and exit criteria, the trend type, the time frames examined, and the direction of the trade.

Considering trade direction, Figures 2.6 and 2.7 highlight a dramatic difference between bullish and bearish trade types. The examples shown are for the short-term time frame. Again, all entry and exit criteria are the same as are the time frames. The data presented is for the aggregate of

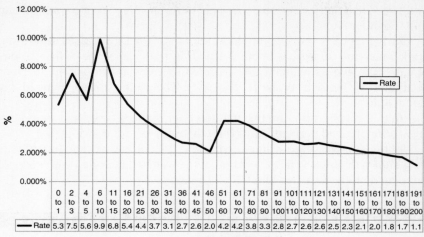

	0 to 1	2 to 3	4 to 5	6 to 10	11 to 15	16 to 20	21 to 25	26 to 30	31 to 35	36 to 40	41 to 45	46 to 50	51 to 60	61 to 70	71 to 80	81 to 90	91 to 100	101 to 110	111 to 120	121 to 130	131 to 140	141 to 150	151 to 160	161 to 170	171 to 180	181 to 190	191 to 200
Rate	5.3	7.5	5.6	9.9	6.8	5.4	4.4	3.7	3.1	2.7	2.6	2.0	4.2	4.2	3.8	3.3	2.8	2.7	2.6	2.6	2.5	2.3	2.1	2.0	1.8	1.7	1.1

Number Bars

FIGURE 2.6 Trade Termination Rates for Bullish Trades Where Profits Are Realized for Short-Term Time Frames Using Anchor Zones for Target and Stop Criteria (2002 to 2011)

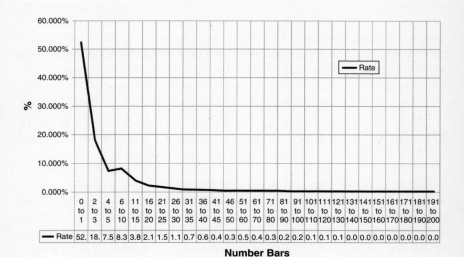

	0 to 1	2 to 3	4 to 5	6 to 10	11 to 15	16 to 20	21 to 25	26 to 30	31 to 35	36 to 40	41 to 45	46 to 50	51 to 60	61 to 70	71 to 80	81 to 90	91 to 100	101 to 110	111 to 120	121 to 130	131 to 140	141 to 150	151 to 160	161 to 170	171 to 180	181 to 190	191 to 200
Rate	52.	18.	7.5	8.3	3.8	2.1	1.5	1.1	0.7	0.6	0.4	0.3	0.5	0.4	0.3	0.2	0.2	0.1	0.1	0.1	0.0	0.0	0.0	0.0	0.0	0.0	0.0

Number Bars

FIGURE 2.7 Trade Termination Rates for Bearish Trades Where Profits Are Realized for Short-Term Time Frames Using Anchor Zones for Target and Stop Criteria (2002 to 2011)

confirmed and suspect trends. The only difference is that one trade is long and the other short.

In Figures 2.6 and 2.7, the data points are for those cases where the trade ends due to a profit being realized. In the case of the bullish trades (Figure 2.6), the individual trade termination rates appear vastly different compared to bearish trades (Figure 2.7). The distinction is unavoidably noticeable.

In this graph, from one through ten bars, trade termination rates vary from about 5 to 10 percent. After that, the rates tail off considerably.

In the opposite case where the trade is bearish rather than bullish, the data shows that nearly 50 percent of all the trades that ended with success happened on the first bar—half of all trades.

WHAT IS THE TRADING SIGNIFICANCE?

Bearish trades are particularly difficult to execute successfully. To do so requires a trading plan that is extremely precise in its timing, is executed once the trend transition has begun, or is executed as repeated attempts to catch the turn, almost like a boxer continually jabbing at his opponent until he can land the big one.

When trading bearish trades, the one commonality of all such trades is that a market participant should expect extensions to the downside to come quickly when they occur. If a bearish trade is entered into but does not materialize quickly, then the timing is likely off to some degree and the risk of a failed trade rises. The data shows that bearish trades necessarily end much faster than long trades regardless of whether the outcome is a profit or a loss.

In bearish trades, a market participant needs to be decisive on the break of a swing point low. When the break comes, the market participant must pounce and the outcome should be almost immediate.

Note that the intermediate and long-term trends have the same characteristic as seen earlier on the short term. On the intermediate term the failure rate starts at 45 percent and drops immediately to 15 percent for two to three bars and then 7 percent for four to five bars. Likewise, on the long-term trend the percentages are even more pronounced, starting at 58.6 percent followed by a drop to 14.2 percent and then 7 percent, respectively.

Carrying these ideas farther, Figure 2.8 presents data for the same criteria as Figure 2.7, with the single difference that the trade fails and a loss is realized. Note that in this chart, like Figure 2.7, roughly 22 percent of all trades fail and a loss is realized within one bar as well. Within five bars, more than 50 percent of all trades fail. Clearly, when trading from the

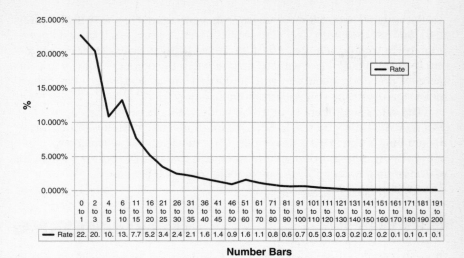

FIGURE 2.8 Trade Termination Rates for Bearish Trades Where Losses Are Realized for Short-Term Time Frames Using Anchor Zones for Target and Stop Criteria (2002 to 2011)

bearish side of the equation, profits or losses are typically realized rather quickly when utilizing anchored zones as the trade termination criterion.

WHAT IS THE TRADING SIGNIFICANCE?

Because bearish trades offer market participants both a fast decision and a higher degree of certainty with respect to the outcome (see Figures 2.7 and 2.8), the result is that a break of a swing point low (especially if confirmed) should immediately cause a market participant to make a large bet in the direction of the trend for a one or two bar trade because in more than 75 percent of the cases, the trade will be over in a single bar (win or loss) and the chance of closing the trade with profits is about 50 percent greater than losses after the one bar!

It is also worth noting that the intermediate-term time frame shows the same characteristic curve—just a little less pronounced. The first five values on the intermediate-term time frame are 20.5 percent, 15.3 percent, 8.34 percent, 14.9 percent, and finally 9 percent for 11 through 15 bars.

For the long term the first five values are a little more skewed with a much more pronounced bounce between 6 to 10 bars. Those numbers are 23.3 percent, 18.5 percent, 10.4 percent, 21.7 percent, and 10.9 percent.

Although most traders shy away from bearish trades, those trades offer fast opportunities with excellent probabilities for success if traded appropriately. In trading, a large part of the battle is to knowing when to pounce and to pounce large. You want to do that when the odds are heavily in your favor. It does not mean you will be correct on each attempt, but it does mean that over time you will profit handsomely.

The other significant point to be made with a bearish trade is that the trading window is very small. That is a huge advantage because the shorter the amount of time that a larger pile of money is at risk in the market, the better. Being able to make a large trade and to have it exposed for a short period of time is probably the most ideal trade you can make.

SUMMARY

Not only are all trends unequal, the entry and exit criteria that a market participant must utilize to increase their likelihood for success are not equal as well. Some trades have a much higher probability for success, and likewise, some have a much greater probability for failure and are to be avoided.

Although a qualified trend is an excellent provider of direction, in most situations, a trend's transition is not a great timing tool for both entry and exit. The break of a swing point and, to a lesser degree, the break of an anchor zone provide reasonable signals for trade entry in certain situations but not for exit. As we will see later, such a trade is referred to as *breakout trade*. A much better exit timing tool is the utilization of anchored zones constructed from anchor bars.

Anchor zones offer greater permanence because they are a much better measure of the supply and demand at varying price points. Classical technical analysis techniques of support and resistance lines as well as channel lines, unfortunately, cannot compete in this regard.

Although much more could be said about anchor bars and zones, this quick review offers a good sense of what they are and sheds some light on some of the more interesting data characteristics associated with a simplistic application of them for trade exits (both profit and loss targets).

In future chapters, anchor zones will play a larger part in the trading regimen but before jumping to those thoughts, there is the need to recognize that stocks do not trade in isolation. Because this is the reality of the stock exchanges, the recognition and respect of this fact can again be used to create an even more favorable situation for the data driven market participant. Chapter 3 tackles that idea next.

CHAPTER 3

Broader Influences Affecting Stocks

I n the preceding two chapters, stock direction and entry/exit timing were reviewed in the context of a neoclassical approach to technical analysis. The material reviewed was enhanced with the addition of some basic data analysis and comparisons showing how qualified trends that are confirmed do have a higher probability of trend continuance as compared to suspect trends. A distinction was made between trends and trades that led to trade failure analysis based on a differing exit criteria.

What was not considered was the larger picture—the broader influences that necessarily affect a stock. It has been said that 75 percent of all the stocks move in the same direction as the general market,[1] and though the data behind this number have never been published as far as I can tell, the research I have done seems to support the notion that the percentages are this high—if not higher.

In particular, every stock represents some company, and that company is engaged in the sale of either products or services or both. Unless the company is a complete monopoly in their industry, then there are other businesses that compete in the sale of the same goods and services. For the purposes of trading, companies that compete are categorically arranged into industry groupings which are in turn aggregated into larger groupings generally referred to as subsectors. Eventually subsectors are combined to form the broadest sector groupings—the major stock sectors. The finality

---

[1] William O'Neill, *How to Make Money in Stocks: A Winning System in Good Times or Bad*, 3rd ed. (New York: McGraw-Hill, 2002), 48.

of this arrangement is the general market, which is comprised from the major stock sectors.

For example, from a top down view, the NYSE is comprised of roughly nine major sectors ranging from energy to consumer durables, from financials to utilities. Within each of these major sectors you can find subsectors or industry groups. For example, the energy component can be neatly divided into integrated oil companies, drillers, and oil services companies.

To more easily view this added complexity, a visual convention first introduced in *Trend Qualification and Trading*[2] is offered. The tool is referred to as the Trading Cube, and its primary purpose is to provide the market participant with an intuitive and easy to grasp visual relationship between the qualified trends for a stock, the stock's sector, and the general market it trades in. Not only does it provide a snapshot view of the major influences affecting the price movement for a given stock, it also offers a visual of the qualified trends across the differing time frames for a stock, its sector, and the general market it is part of as well as the inherent relationships between these three related components.

Since all stocks are influenced, to some degree, by the product and service mix they sell, viewing a stock in isolation of the stock sector is necessarily limited. For example, there will be times when the auto parts industry may be in great demand while at other times there is simply is no pent up demand. The supply/demand curve is ever changing, and sectors fall into and out of favor. Even if you are the best of breed, if your sector is out of favor, it will be difficult to sell your products and services.

Similarly, the broad market is a reflection of all the sectors that comprise it and the sectors in turn are a reflection of all the individual stocks that make up the various industry groups. Thus, the logical deduction is that the broad market is, in the end, a reflection of all the individual stocks that trade, and the collective health of the market, when good, suggests that most stocks are doing well and, when bad, that most are doing badly. Although this is a bit of an oversimplification, it does broadly reflect the reality we find. Thus, just a single glance at the sector and general market trends in the Trading Cube quickly provides a market participant with an overall assessment of the broader set of qualified trends that are likely to have an influence on the individual stock under consideration.

As an example, Figure 3.1 is the Trading Cube for Chipotle Mexican Grill. Realize that the Trading Cube is a snapshot view, a point in time that reflects the qualified trends for the stock, its sector, and the general market. It is constantly evolving as these components evolve. The Trading Cube has

---

[2]L.A. Little, *Trend Qualification and Trading* (Hoboken, NJ: John Wiley & Sons, 2011).

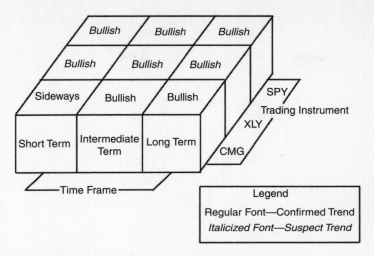

FIGURE 3.1   Trading Cube for Chipotle Mexican Grill (CMG)

nine squares presented across two dimensions that can each take one of six values:

- Confirmed or Suspect Bullish
- Confirmed or Suspect Sideways
- Confirmed or Suspect Bearish

These values are presented across the face of the cube for each of the three time frames as well as for the three components—the stock, stock sector, and the general market.

In the case of Chipotle, the stock was confirmed bullish on the long- and intermediate-term time frames at the time of the analysis—confirmed sideways on the short-term time frame. From a Trading Cube perspective, in isolation this is an excellent arrangement in the qualified trends since it essentially relays information to the market participant suggesting that the stock is trending very strongly on the long- and intermediate-term (confirmed bullish) time frames and is suffering what is likely to be a temporary setback on the short-term time frame.

The qualified trend assessment depicted in the Trading Cube is essentially gathered by examining each of the three charts for each time frame. For example, Figure 3.2 is the chart of Chipotle for the long-term time frame at the time of this snapshot. The qualified trend presented for the long-term time frame for Chipotle (confirmed bullish) is derived from an automated analysis of this chart's qualified trends.

FIGURE 3.2 Trading Cube for Chipotle Mexican Grill (CMG) (April 3, 2006 to April 1, 2011)

Similarly, the intermediate-term trend was drawn from analyzing the trend transitions for Chipotle using the weekly chart as shown Figure 3.3.

Finally, the short-term chart exhibits the currently expressed confirmed sideways trend for the same stock (Figure 3.4).

Now assume you need to look at 100 stocks. Would it be simpler and much faster to just scan the Trading Cube to determine if the stock required further investigation or to flip through 300 charts—one for each of the three time frames for all 100 stocks? Through the use of the Trading Cube, all but a few of the 300 charts can be dismissed and only those that are of the trading configuration that meets your current trading bias could be drilled down on so as to examine the individual stock charts.

But the Trading Cube is not just a time saver. It is a quality improvement as well. In Chapter 1, Figures 1.3 through 1.14 looked at the trend termination rates for bullish versus suspect trends *without* consideration of larger influences on the stock. In all of those studies, the trend of the sector and the broad market was ignored as part of the analysis. As has been suggested here, though, this is a somewhat short-sighted view of

FIGURE 3.3 Trading Cube for Chipotle Mexican Grill (CMG) (April 26, 2010 to April 25, 2011)

reality because it only stands to reason that the sector trend is likely to have some impact on the trend of a stock within the sector, just as the trend of the general market is likely to have an influence on all stock trends that comprise the larger market.

So how does that data compare when analyzed? Is there an influence? Is it measurable? Do confirmed bullish and bearish trends outperform even more so when the trends for the stock are congruent with the trends for the stock sector? To answer that question, the data from Chapter 1 was reanalyzed and examined with the additional constraint of sector congruence and then again for market congruence.

SECTOR CONGRUENCE

When seeking a trade, it behooves a market participant to seek out those trades with higher probabilities of trade success. As has been shown, qualified trends with confirmed attributes have a higher probability of trend

FIGURE 3.4   Trading Cube for Chipotle Mexican Grill (CMG) (January 28, 2011 to April 28, 2011)

persistence, which is definitely a large part of the equation when it comes to higher probabilities of trade success. The hypothesis suggested in the preceding paragraphs is that sectors influence the persistence of a stock's trend. To test this hypothesis, the same trend data that was examined in Chapter 1 was utilized once more, changing a single variable to note the effect of trend persistence when the trend of the stock and the stock's sector were congruent.

To accomplish this, each stock was associated with a sector ETF (exchange-traded fund) that was representative of the stock, and the relationship studied was the case where the stock and the stock sector were congruent—they both shared the same general trend. Essentially, the list of stock trends that were examined was filtered based on the following rules:

- Determine the qualified trend of the individual stock for each time frame.
- Determine the sector for the stock; then determine the sector's intermediate and long-term trends.
- For each stock trend encountered, check to see if the stock's trend is congruent with both the sector's intermediate and long-term trends. If

so, then use the data as part of the analysis; otherwise ignore this data instance.

- A trend termination occurs if either the sector's long- and intermediate-term trends transition or the stock's trend transitions.

The end result of this filtering resulted in an examination of only those stocks where the trend of the sector supported the trend of the stock being examined and it forced that consistency on both the intermediate and the long-term trends, which are less susceptible to intermittent trend change.

The results were consistent with the proposed thesis, namely, that there is a greater likelihood for a stock's trend to persist for a greater duration when the sector's intermediate and long-term sector trends are congruent.

Figure 3.5 is one of several figures examining this relationship between the stock and its sector. In this figure, the short-term trend is examined and the comparison is between the data presented in Chapter 1 for the same time period and trend type as compared to the case where the stock and sector trends are congruent according to the criteria specified earlier.

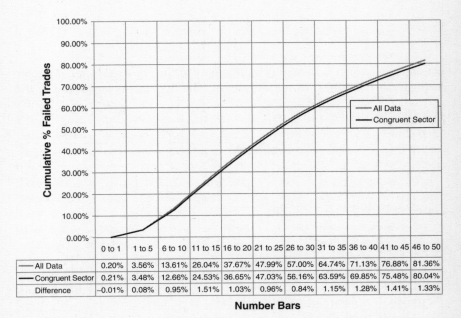

	0 to 1	1 to 5	6 to 10	11 to 15	16 to 20	21 to 25	26 to 30	31 to 35	36 to 40	41 to 45	46 to 50
All Data	0.20%	3.56%	13.61%	26.04%	37.67%	47.99%	57.00%	64.74%	71.13%	76.88%	81.36%
Congruent Sector	0.21%	3.48%	12.66%	24.53%	36.65%	47.03%	56.16%	63.59%	69.85%	75.48%	80.04%
Difference	−0.01%	0.08%	0.95%	1.51%	1.03%	0.96%	0.84%	1.15%	1.28%	1.41%	1.33%

Number Bars

FIGURE 3.5 Trend Failure Rate for All Confirmed Bullish Trends on the Short-Term Time Frame versus Only Congruent Sector Trends for Same Criteria (2002 to 2011)

Here are some notes on how to properly read this graph and those that follow:

- Each graph compares the same trend type (suspect or confirmed bullish, suspect or confirmed bearish)
- One line represents the trend failure rate for the *congruent* sector while the other line represents the trend failure rate for all data (both congruent and noncongruent)
- The difference between these two lines is represented at the bottom of the table and indicates the higher or lesser likelihood of a trend failure solely based on whether the stock's trend was, or was not, congruent with the trend for the sector

The data presented in Figure 3.5 shows that, for the short-term time frame where the trend was confirmed bullish, those stocks where the trend was congruent with the sector showed a slightly greater persistence probability than those where congruence was not a consideration.

Figure 3.6 is the exact same chart and time frame, but this time for suspect bullish trends rather than confirmed trends. Again, the data indicates

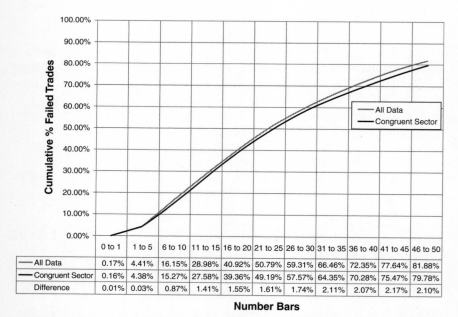

	0 to 1	1 to 5	6 to 10	11 to 15	16 to 20	21 to 25	26 to 30	31 to 35	36 to 40	41 to 45	46 to 50
All Data	0.17%	4.41%	16.15%	28.98%	40.92%	50.79%	59.31%	66.46%	72.35%	77.64%	81.88%
Congruent Sector	0.16%	4.38%	15.27%	27.58%	39.36%	49.19%	57.57%	64.35%	70.28%	75.47%	79.78%
Difference	0.01%	0.03%	0.87%	1.41%	1.55%	1.61%	1.74%	2.11%	2.07%	2.17%	2.10%

Number Bars

FIGURE 3.6 Trend Failure Rate for All Suspect Bullish Trends on the Short-Term Time Frame versus Only Congruent Sector Trends for Same Criteria (2002 to 2011)

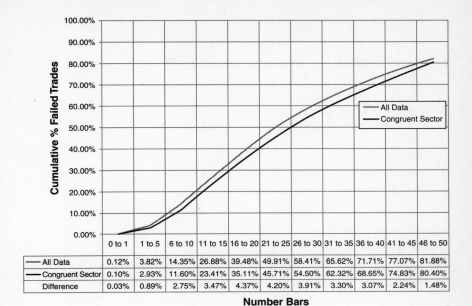

	0 to 1	1 to 5	6 to 10	11 to 15	16 to 20	21 to 25	26 to 30	31 to 35	36 to 40	41 to 45	46 to 50
All Data	0.12%	3.82%	14.35%	26.88%	39.48%	49.91%	58.41%	65.62%	71.71%	77.07%	81.88%
Congruent Sector	0.10%	2.93%	11.60%	23.41%	35.11%	45.71%	54.50%	62.32%	68.65%	74.83%	80.40%
Difference	0.03%	0.89%	2.75%	3.47%	4.37%	4.20%	3.91%	3.30%	3.07%	2.24%	1.48%

Number Bars

FIGURE 3.7 Trend Failure Rate for All Confirmed Bullish Trends on the Intermediate-Term Time Frame versus Only Congruent Sector Trends for Same Criteria (2002 to 2011)

that there is a greater likelihood for trend persistence when the sector's intermediate and long-term trend is congruent with the stock's short-term qualified trend. Note that in this graph, trend persistence is a bit more pronounced than it was in Figure 3.5.

When examining the longer term time frames, the relationship between trend persistence and sector congruence is, for the most part, more prominently correlated. The next four graphs (Figures 3.7 through 3.10) display that relationship, starting with the intermediate-term trends.

Again, the idea is the same here but with long-term bullish qualified trends.

WHAT IS THE TRADING SIGNIFICANCE?

When considering trade entry, there is a definite correlation between a stock and the stock's sector. If the sector's trend is congruent with the stock's trend, then the stock has a greater probability of persistence. Said another way, the likelihood of a stock's trend failing is greater if the sector doesn't support the stock.

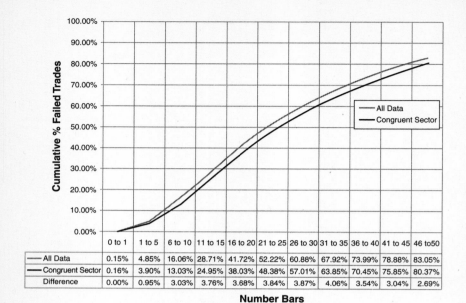

	0 to 1	1 to 5	6 to 10	11 to 15	16 to 20	21 to 25	26 to 30	31 to 35	36 to 40	41 to 45	46 to50
All Data	0.15%	4.85%	16.06%	28.71%	41.72%	52.22%	60.88%	67.92%	73.99%	78.88%	83.05%
Congruent Sector	0.16%	3.90%	13.03%	24.95%	38.03%	48.38%	57.01%	63.85%	70.45%	75.85%	80.37%
Difference	0.00%	0.95%	3.03%	3.76%	3.68%	3.84%	3.87%	4.06%	3.54%	3.04%	2.69%

Number Bars

FIGURE 3.8 Trend Failure Rate for All Suspect Bullish Trends on the Intermediate-Term Time Frame versus Only Congruent Sector Trends for Same Criteria (2002 to 2011)

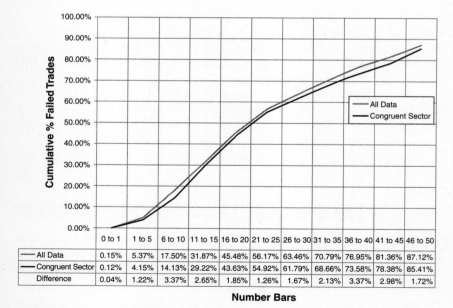

	0 to 1	1 to 5	6 to 10	11 to 15	16 to 20	21 to 25	26 to 30	31 to 35	36 to 40	41 to 45	46 to 50
All Data	0.15%	5.37%	17.50%	31.87%	45.48%	56.17%	63.46%	70.79%	76.95%	81.36%	87.12%
Congruent Sector	0.12%	4.15%	14.13%	29.22%	43.63%	54.92%	61.79%	68.66%	73.58%	78.38%	85.41%
Difference	0.04%	1.22%	3.37%	2.65%	1.85%	1.26%	1.67%	2.13%	3.37%	2.98%	1.72%

Number Bars

FIGURE 3.9 Trend Failure Rate for All Confirmed Bullish Trends on the Long-Term Time Frame versus Only Congruent Sector Trends for Same Criteria (2002 to 2011)

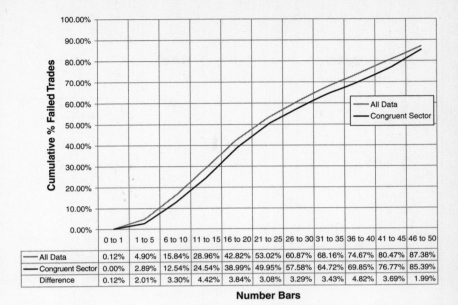

	0 to 1	1 to 5	6 to 10	11 to 15	16 to 20	21 to 25	26 to 30	31 to 35	36 to 40	41 to 45	46 to 50
All Data	0.12%	4.90%	15.84%	28.96%	42.82%	53.02%	60.87%	68.16%	74.67%	80.47%	87.38%
Congruent Sector	0.00%	2.89%	12.54%	24.54%	38.99%	49.95%	57.58%	64.72%	69.85%	76.77%	85.39%
Difference	0.12%	2.01%	3.30%	4.42%	3.84%	3.08%	3.29%	3.43%	4.82%	3.69%	1.99%

Number Bars

FIGURE 3.10 Trend Failure Rate for All Suspect Bullish Trends on the Long-Term Time Frame versus Only Congruent Sector Trends for Same Criteria (2002 to 2011)

By shifting the focus to bearish qualified trends, the short-term time frame provides the same sort of correlations as seen with bullish for trend persistence. In these graphs, the confirmed bearish trend shows a minor but still greater likelihood of persistence when considering sector congruence versus not (see Figure 3.11).

And, similar to what was seen for suspect bullish trends, suspect bearish trends show an increased persistence comparatively when congruent versus all data independent of congruence (see Figure 3.12).

However, when moving to the intermediate and long-term time frames for bearish trends, the relationships shown thus far appear to break down. The increased trend persistence correlated with sector congruence seemingly has less of a bearing for intermediate-term bearish trends (see Figures 3.13 and 3.14).

The natural question is why. Why would it be the case that bearish intermediate-term trends show less correlation when sector congruence becomes part of the calculation? To make matters more intriguing, the long-term trends show this same breakdown in an even more pronounced manner and in fact the correlation is mostly negative (see Figures 3.15 and 3.16).

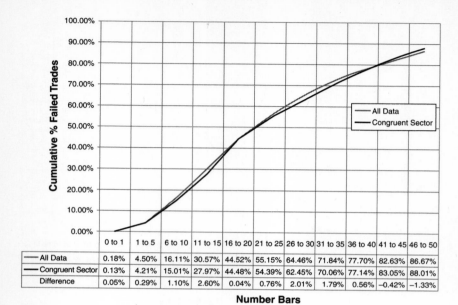

	0 to 1	1 to 5	6 to 10	11 to 15	16 to 20	21 to 25	26 to 30	31 to 35	36 to 40	41 to 45	46 to 50
All Data	0.18%	4.50%	16.11%	30.57%	44.52%	55.15%	64.46%	71.84%	77.70%	82.63%	86.67%
Congruent Sector	0.13%	4.21%	15.01%	27.97%	44.48%	54.39%	62.45%	70.06%	77.14%	83.05%	88.01%
Difference	0.05%	0.29%	1.10%	2.60%	0.04%	0.76%	2.01%	1.79%	0.56%	−0.42%	−1.33%

Number Bars

FIGURE 3.11 Trend Failure Rate for All Confirmed Bearish Trends on the Short-Term Time Frame versus Only Congruent Sector Trends for Same Criteria (2002 to 2011)

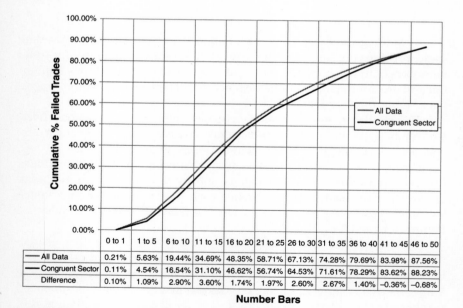

	0 to 1	1 to 5	6 to 10	11 to 15	16 to 20	21 to 25	26 to 30	31 to 35	36 to 40	41 to 45	46 to 50
All Data	0.21%	5.63%	19.44%	34.69%	48.35%	58.71%	67.13%	74.28%	79.69%	83.98%	87.56%
Congruent Sector	0.11%	4.54%	16.54%	31.10%	46.62%	56.74%	64.53%	71.61%	78.29%	83.62%	88.23%
Difference	0.10%	1.09%	2.90%	3.60%	1.74%	1.97%	2.60%	2.67%	1.40%	−0.36%	−0.68%

Number Bars

FIGURE 3.12 Trend Failure Rate for All Suspect Bearish Trends on the Short-Term Time Frame versus Only Congruent Sector Trends for Same Criteria (2002 to 2011)

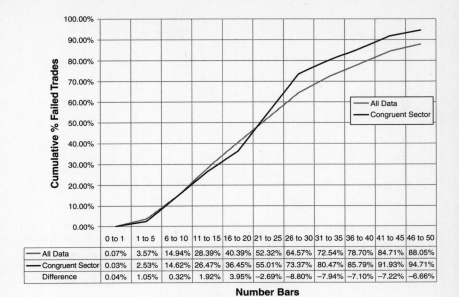

Number Bars	0 to 1	1 to 5	6 to 10	11 to 15	16 to 20	21 to 25	26 to 30	31 to 35	36 to 40	41 to 45	46 to 50
All Data	0.07%	3.57%	14.94%	28.39%	40.39%	52.32%	64.57%	72.54%	78.70%	84.71%	88.05%
Congruent Sector	0.03%	2.53%	14.62%	26.47%	36.45%	55.01%	73.37%	80.47%	85.79%	91.93%	94.71%
Difference	0.04%	1.05%	0.32%	1.92%	3.95%	−2.69%	−8.80%	−7.94%	−7.10%	−7.22%	−6.66%

FIGURE 3.13 Trend Failure Rate for All Confirmed Bearish Trends on the Intermediate-Term Time Frame versus Only Congruent Sector Trends for Same Criteria (2002 to 2011)

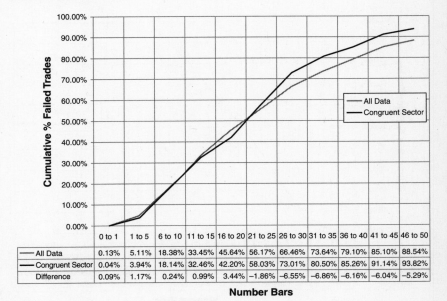

Number Bars	0 to 1	1 to 5	6 to 10	11 to 15	16 to 20	21 to 25	26 to 30	31 to 35	36 to 40	41 to 45	46 to 50
All Data	0.13%	5.11%	18.38%	33.45%	45.64%	56.17%	66.46%	73.64%	79.10%	85.10%	88.54%
Congruent Sector	0.04%	3.94%	18.14%	32.46%	42.20%	58.03%	73.01%	80.50%	85.26%	91.14%	93.82%
Difference	0.09%	1.17%	0.24%	0.99%	3.44%	−1.86%	−6.55%	−6.86%	−6.16%	−6.04%	−5.29%

FIGURE 3.14 Trend Failure Rate for All Suspect Bearish Trends on the Intermediate-Term Time Frame versus Only Congruent Sector Trends for Same Criteria (2002 to 2011)

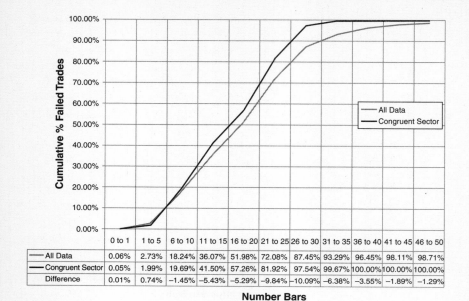

	0 to 1	1 to 5	6 to 10	11 to 15	16 to 20	21 to 25	26 to 30	31 to 35	36 to 40	41 to 45	46 to 50
All Data	0.06%	2.73%	18.24%	36.07%	51.98%	72.08%	87.45%	93.29%	96.45%	98.11%	98.71%
Congruent Sector	0.05%	1.99%	19.69%	41.50%	57.26%	81.92%	97.54%	99.67%	100.00%	100.00%	100.00%
Difference	0.01%	0.74%	−1.45%	−5.43%	−5.29%	−9.84%	−10.09%	−6.38%	−3.55%	−1.89%	−1.29%

Number Bars

FIGURE 3.15 Trend Failure Rate for All Confirmed Bearish Trends on the Long-Term Time Frame versus Only Congruent Sector Trends for Same Criteria (2002 to 2011)

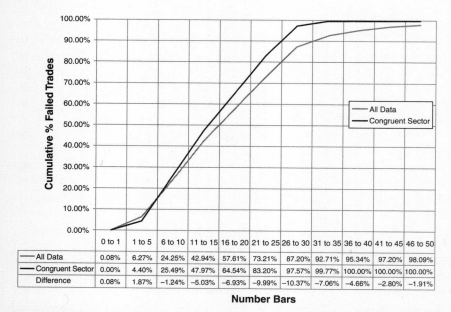

	0 to 1	1 to 5	6 to 10	11 to 15	16 to 20	21 to 25	26 to 30	31 to 35	36 to 40	41 to 45	46 to 50
All Data	0.08%	6.27%	24.25%	42.94%	57.61%	73.21%	87.20%	92.71%	95.34%	97.20%	98.09%
Congruent Sector	0.00%	4.40%	25.49%	47.97%	64.54%	83.20%	97.57%	99.77%	100.00%	100.00%	100.00%
Difference	0.08%	1.87%	−1.24%	−5.03%	−6.93%	−9.99%	−10.37%	−7.06%	−4.66%	−2.80%	−1.91%

Number Bars

FIGURE 3.16 Trend Failure Rate for All Suspect Bearish Trends on the Long-Term Time Frame versus Only Congruent Sector Trends for Same Criteria (2002 to 2011)

Upon a further and more detailed analysis, there are several factors at work here, a couple of which are important to grasp. The first fact is related to the data and time periods being analyzed. If you recall, in Chapter 1, the inversion of the correlation on the long-term time frame in the bearish case was determined to have a direct relation to the tremendous and rapid price declines experienced in 2008. Once more, this data suffers from the same issue but that is less of a factor here than before.

A point by point examination of the data reveals an interesting phenomenon—when a stock becomes weak, it has a greater tendency to stay weak for long periods of time. In fact some never recover and continue to spiral lower. The way the exchanges deal with such stocks is to simply remove them from the exchange. This is done through the exchange's minimum listing requirements policy. For the purposes of this analysis, this continual removal of weaker stocks creates a natural bullish skew to all the data. To note this behavior is not so much an indictment of the process as an observation of the practice and the effect it has on data analysis. Most any database one obtains (and the one used for the purposes of this analysis) consists of only those stocks that are currently listed on the respective exchanges. That results in a situation where the vast majority of weak stocks are no longer included in the data being analyzed. Similarly, merged stocks are not included. That has a direct effect on any analysis performed on the data and the conclusions reached.

Referring back to Table 1.1 (Occurrence Ratios for Trend Types for Differing Time Frames) from Chapter 1, bullish trends are about 11 percent more likely than bearish ones across all time frames. This natural bias for bullishness is at work on all time frames. Although it is recognized that wealth creation is not a zero sum game and that inflation also has a lot to do with the natural bias for price escalation over time, index scrubbing certainly contributes to the appearance of price appreciation as well.

When you look at a chart such as Figure 3.17 showing the venerable Dow Jones Industrial Index and its methodical and inevitable march northward, one has to wonder just how much of this price rise is the result of such index scrubbing. In fact, only 1 of the 30 original members of the Dow Jones Index remains today, and the other 29 have been replaced multiple times over the years.

Clearly there has been increased value over time, and the argument is not that this isn't the case—just that there is an inevitable bias toward an overstatement of the true valuations, and some measure of that is related to the removal and replacement of weakest stocks over time. This is true of all indexes in fact. How much of an illusion is created by this process is a question for another researcher to tackle if not previously quantified already.

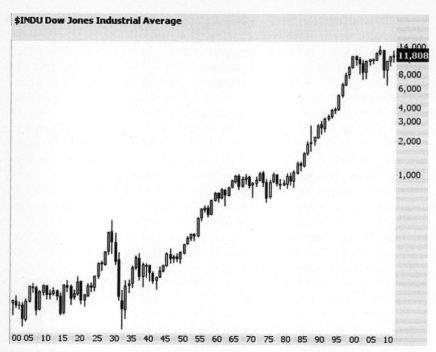

$INDU Dow Jones Industrial Average

FIGURE 3.17   Dow Jones Industrial Average (January 1900 to January 2011)

WHAT IS THE TRADING SIGNIFICANCE?

Although fanciful to think that the best trading methodology is to simply buy and hold the best stocks for extremely long periods of time, the reality is unlikely to match the performance displayed in Figure 3.17. Of the original 30 stocks in the Dow Jones Industrial Average, only one remains a component to this day, while to date, 125 have come and gone. This simple example shows that the probabilities are firmly against such a buy and hold strategy. Portfolios and positions have to be managed. Even the venerable Dow Jones Index is so managed.

Although the preceding two considerations are factors, they are minor compared to the final factor. The most important reason for the correlation inversion for sector congruency has more to do with how market tops and bottoms are made than anything else. In general, market tops are mostly domed shaped, while market bottoms tend to take the form of a more V-shaped move. The result is that, at market tops, because of the relative flatness of the top, both the stocks and the sectors tend to act in unison when bullish trends begin to terminate.

For bearish trends, however, this is not the case. With bearish trends, the end tends to be rather sudden and abrupt, and the turnaround is initially concentrated in larger capitalization stocks that dominate the sectors because they are most liquid, best known, and easiest to take down in larger quantities. Thus, while many of the stocks in a sector continue to show bearish trends, the sectors themselves begin to turn earlier due to the smaller number of larger stocks that dominate the price averages for the sectors. The fact is that almost all indexes and sectors are weighted by market capitalization. In other words, the larger stocks have a larger weighting. When a bear market begins to turn, it is the large money that causes the turn and the large money necessarily finds a home in the larger capitalization stocks because they are viewed as less risky and both large and liquid enough to purchase in size.

WHAT IS THE TRADING SIGNIFICANCE?

At the end of bear markets and, in general, all market sell offs where price reductions are significant and widespread, money first flows to the larger capitalization stocks, then to the smaller capitalization stocks. This sequence is important to understand for two reasons. First, market participants should focus their early purchases in the larger capitalization stocks right along with the institutions who are likely purchasing the exact same set of stocks.

Second, as the qualified trends begin to transition, the smaller capitalization stocks will begin to have larger percentage moves as they catch up. Again, knowing this allows a market participant to participate in the right equities at the right time.

After some tedious data analysis, the revelation is that the inverse and non-correlated results for intermediate and long-term bearish trends are due to the fact that sector trend terminations were *causing* bearish trend terminations. Since the algorithm utilized in this study specifically records a bearish trend as having ended if the stock *or* the stock's sector intermediate or long-term trend transitions, the apparent congruency inversion was realized for what it was—a premature end to a bearish trend due to the sector's rise, not the individual stock's recovery. When compared to all stocks independent of the sector trend, the apparent premature end for stock to sector congruency is not so much an inversion as much as an anomaly of how bottoms are made and how the comparison algorithm used for this analysis functioned.

This analysis reveals another important point—weak stocks have a greater tendency to stay weak for some period of time even after the general market and sector's trend begin to heal (the general market correlations also show this effect). For the market participant, selling weak stocks first when weakness develops in the general markets is a far better idea than holding them and hoping they will eventually recover. If the general market does in fact weaken further, then the weak stocks will become lead weights in your portfolio and will stay that way much longer than the average stock. Weak stocks almost universally recover after the strong thus they are doubly negative to your performance.

One more takeaway from this analysis is that sector weightings have a significant effect on sector congruency analysis, particularly during a bearish trend. The larger capitalization stocks typically are the stronger stocks, and given their size, their weighting in the sector is much greater. It is for this reason that a sector with a few heavily weighted stronger stocks can mask the weakness in many smaller sized companies and can lead to a turn in the sector's trend prior to a turn in most stocks that comprise the sector.

VIRTUAL INDUSTRY GROUPS—FUTURE DIRECTION

In the preceding section, the sectors used for sector congruence studies were comprised of the nine highest level sectors as defined by the Select Sectors SPDRs (www.sectorspdr.com). These SPDRs break the S&P 500 into nine major stock groups (see Table 3.1) and each ETF trades well in excess of several million shares daily. For this reason, they provide an excellent read on the broad sectors, but therein lies their weakness

TABLE 3.1 Select Sectors SPDRs

SPDR Sector Description	Symbol
Consumer Discretionary SPDR	XLY
Consumer Staples SPDR	XLP
Energy SPDR	XLE
Financials SPDR	XLF
Health Care SPDR	XLV
Industrials SPDR	XLI
Materials SPDR	XLB
Technology SPDR	XLK
Utilities SPDR	XLU

http://www.sectorspdr.com. The S&P 500® and Select Sector SPDRs are trademarks of The McGraw-Hill Companies, Inc.

as well—these ETFs are limited to the most broadly defined measure of goods and services.

For the purposes of the Trading Cube, as long as one is willing to not drill down any further, these nine major sectors work reasonably well in most cases as is borne out by the analysis in the preceding section. Ideally though, it would be much more advisable to drill down in order to get a more granular view of sector influences. It seems reasonable to expect that the more granular the sector view, the less likely that sector influences are misinterpreted.

For example, at the highest level, the technology sector includes everything from software companies to disk drive makers. It does not take much of an imagination to realize that a sector reading of confirmed bullish for the health of the Technology SPDR can be quite misleading for disk drive makers who may in fact be confirmed bearish at exactly the same time. Since the disk drive industry group is only 1 of the 31 industry groups that comprise the technology sector it is not uncommon to see the broad sector reflecting a qualified trend reading that is diametrically opposed to the qualified trend reading that might apply to one or more of the industry groups within the sector.

Given that most sectors are market capitalization weighted, trying to use these broad sectors as trend measures for the purposes of the sector influence as exhibited through the Trading Cube necessarily contains an error margin that would best be erased. For example, as of the end of September 2011, roughly 60 percent of the entire technology sector weighting (XLK) consisted of just 10 stocks—Apple Inc., IBM, Microsoft, AT&T, Google, Oracle, Verizon, Intel, Cisco Systems, and Qualcomm—although the sector is comprised of more than 220 stocks.

Looking back at the Trading Cube in Figure 3.1, the sector for Chipotle Mexican Grill is identified as consumer discretionary (XLY). Although true, the consumer discretionary sector is comprised of firms selling food products (such as Chipotle's fast food burrito menu) as well as those selling newspapers. Morningstar (www.morningstar.com) categorizes about 210 different industry groups,[3] of which the number of ETFs that trade and cover those industry groups can be counted on, at most, two hands and most of which simply do not trade enough shares to make their derived trends viable.

It is for this reason that it only stands to reason that the creation of virtual industry groups to replace the nine broad sectors in the Trading Cube would add significant value and reduce the error rate associated with the status quo. The key components for sector virtualization are as follows:

- Use an industry standard of industry groups such as Morningstar's categorization to associate each stock with an industry group.

---

[3] www.tradertrainingschool.com/indgrp.pdf.

- Determine market capitalization weighting of stocks within the virtual industry groups.
- Compute the sector weightings for each virtual industry group on each time frame for high, low, close, and volume statistics.

The result of this effort is likely to yield a much better measure of a sector's influence on a stock vis-à-vis the Trading Cube. At Technical Analysis Today (www.tatoday.com), we had already begun this process by tracking liquid ETFs for subsectors such as the Semiconductors Holders Trust (SMH), which tracks semiconductor companies within the larger technology sector. To move to virtual industry sectors is almost guaranteed to improve the correlations that were sought after in this section of the book and is likely to represent a significant improvement in the Trading Cube and its representation of the reality of influences for a given stock.

GENERAL MARKET CONGRUENCE

The value of considering sector influences was not as pronounced or as consistent as desired when utilizing high level sectors. Preliminary data from industry group virtualization offers the promise of a more valuable future direction for sector influences on individual stocks primarily because of the increased granularity. Although the work to both prove and utilize the industry group virtualizations remains to be done, this is not the case with general market influences.

Unlike sectors, the general market for domestic stocks is reasonably well defined with readily available data sets. There are three broad markets that comprise the vast majority of all stocks—four if you included the Dow Jones Industrial Average, which is more symbolic but widely quoted. Those three broad markets are the Standard and Poor's 500 Index (S&P 500), the National Association of Securities Dealers Automated Quotation (NASDAQ), and the Russell 2000, which is a broad measure of smaller capitalization stocks. The S&P 500 represents the 500 largest capitalization stocks, while the NASDAQ represents a vast number of large and smaller capitalization stocks that historically were primarily centered on technology.

Like sectors, each of these broad markets has associated ETFs although only two of the three are liquid. Since each market has both price and volume data readily available, it is a better practice to simply use the underlying index rather than the proxy ETFs.

So the question is, as before, what does the data indicate? Is the qualified trend for the general market an influence on the qualified trend for

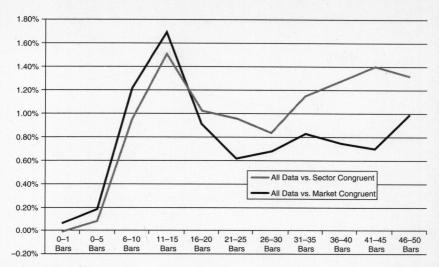

FIGURE 3.18 Trend Persistence for Sector and Market Congruency for Confirmed Bullish Trends on Short-Term Time Frame

individual stocks? Is there a higher persistence of trend if the general market is in congruence?

Although it would be reasonably simple to examine another set of 12 charts that are basically of the same presentation style presented in Figures 3.5 through 3.16, there is more to gain from viewing this data through a different lens. That lens considers three sets of data in one chart. Figure 3.18 is the first of these twelve graphs and can serve as an introduction to all of them.

In this figure there are two lines. The darkest line reflects stocks congruence with the general market. It is indicative of how much more or less persistent trend is when the general market trend (long- and intermediate-term time frame) is of the same trend type as the trend of the stock under examination. In this figure, between zero and five bars, trend persistence was about .20 percent greater for stocks where the general market shared the same trend at the same time versus all trends of this type and time frame where the congruency of the general market was ignored. If you recall, the data examined in Chapter 1 ignored general market congruency and are utilized again as the base data being compared to throughout the remainder of the figures in this chapter.

The second line takes the data analysis presented earlier in this chapter for sector congruency and repeats it here under this different microscope. Note that the market and sector congruency still display the anomaly

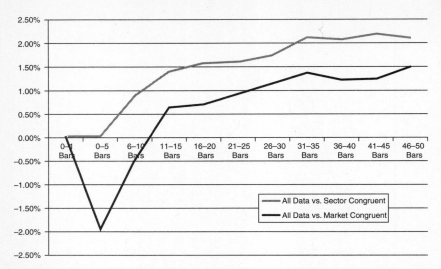

FIGURE 3.19 Trend Persistence for Sector and Market Congruency for Suspect Bullish Trends on Short-Term Time Frame

previous discussed regarding bearish intermediate and long-term trends. There is some value in looking at those charts as well because it shows the positive impact of market congruency.

Taking the data in order, Figures 3.18 and 3.19 display the analysis for short-term bullish (confirmed and suspect) trend comparisons. Figure 3.18 indicates that, for all samples of more than one bar, trends were more likely to persist if the sector or the market were of the same qualified trend type when compared to the case where no congruency was considered. On this time frame the difference is not overly significant and in a large portion of the cases, sector congruency actually increased trend longevity more so than market congruency.

For suspect trends, again sector trends proved more valuable and for all trends lasting more than 10 bars, both sector and general market congruency added value to trend persistence.

Continuing on, once the intermediate-term time frame is encountered, trend persistence increased to more than 8 percent for trends examined that were confirmed bullish and the general market was bullish as well. For those data points where the sector and stock met this criterion, the trend persistence still topped 4 percent at the peak. Unlike the short-term time frame, the more stable intermediate-term time frame shows a marked increase in trend continuation due to sector and market congruency as seen in Figure 3.20.

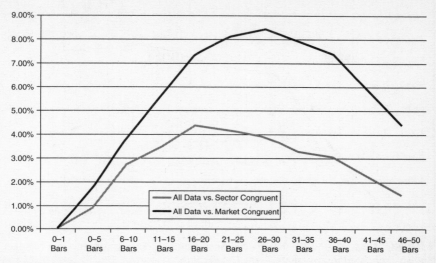

FIGURE 3.20   Trend Persistence for Sector and Market Congruency for Confirmed Bullish Trends on Intermediate-Term Time Frame

WHAT IS THE TRADING SIGNIFICANCE?

The impact on the trend persistence for a stock is clearly enhanced as a result of the general market's trend and it is significant. Old sayings such as "In a bull market everyone is a genius" and "A rising tide lifts all boats" are borne out by this relationship—especially for suspect trends as shown in Figures 3.21 and 3.23, which show that suspect trends tend to persist much longer due directly to general market congruency.

In the suspect case, Figure 3.21 shows that the increased persistence curve is much flatter for both sector and market congruency but still reasonably significant.

Finally, on the long-term time frame we see an explosion of significance when requiring that the market be congruent with the stock. It peaks at slightly more than 18 percent trend longevity that is directly the result of being in synchronization with the general market's trend.

Figure 3.22 extends this huge advantage to just over 20 percent increased trend persistence solely because the stocks trend is synchronized with the general market's trend.

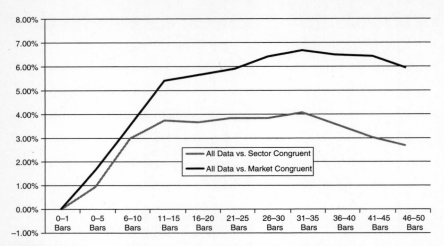

FIGURE 3.21   Trend Persistence for Sector and Market Congruency for Suspect Bullish Trends on Intermediate-Term Time Frame

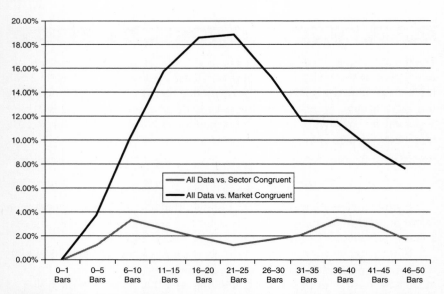

FIGURE 3.22   Trend Persistence for Sector and Market Congruency for Confirmed Bullish Trends on Long-Term Time Frame

WHAT IS THE TRADING SIGNIFICANCE?

An investor should always seek to trade with the prevailing general market trend, which, as has been shown, is more often up than down. Trading with the market's trend is the dominant determinant of success on the long-term time frame.

The fact that the market trend is such a determinant on the longer term time frames is seen in Figure 3.23, where even suspect bullish trends benefit greatly from the positive market trend. It is why everyone looks like genius in a bull market.

Turning the focus to bearish trends, in those graphs the short-term time frames show a reasonably large increase in the trend persistence when the market is congruent as compared to when it is not. It eclipses the sector congruence persistence numbers easily for both confirmed and suspect bearish trends as seen here in Figures 3.24 and 3.25.

The bearish intermediate-term time frames begin by showing the same correlations seen in previous graphs and then fall victim to the same issue witnessed with sector congruence, namely, that market tops and bottoms

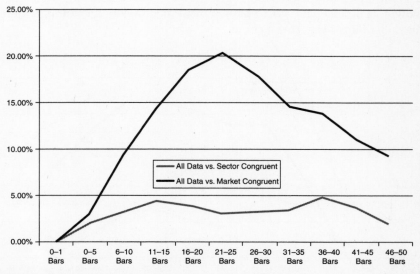

FIGURE 3.23 Trend Persistence for Sector and Market Congruency for Suspect Bullish Trends on Long-Term Time Frame

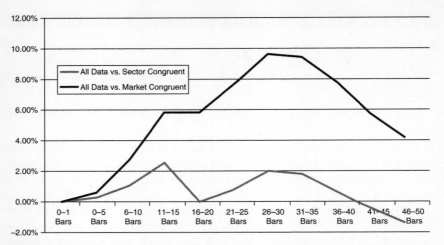

FIGURE 3.24   Trend Persistence for Sector and Market Congruency for Confirmed Bearish Trends on Short-Term Time Frame

do not share the same characteristics with respect to how they form. The result once more is that for bearish trends, on the longer term time frames, the abrupt turnarounds typically witnessed at the end of bearish trends result in trend failure as a result of the market trend transitions while many individual stocks have yet to have transitioned. Again, an examination of the data points bears this fact out.

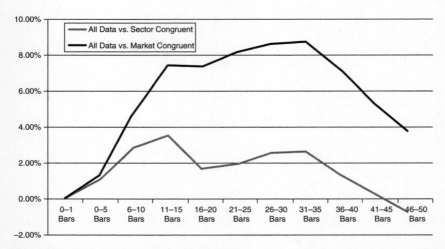

FIGURE 3.25   Trend Persistence for Sector and Market Congruency for Suspect Bearish Trends on Short-Term Time Frame

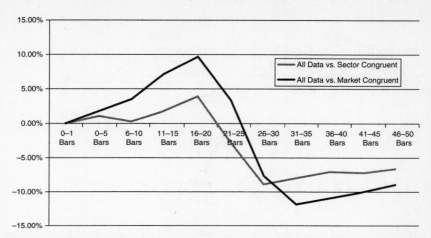

FIGURE 3.26 Trend Persistence for Sector and Market Congruency for Confirmed Bearish Trends on Intermediate-Term Time Frame

Figures 3.26 and 3.27 are for the intermediate-term bearish trends while Figures 3.28 and 3.29 are for the long-term bearish trends (suspect and confirmed).

SUMMARY

Although intuitively expected, the data supports the notion that the relationship between the general market trend and its effect on the individual

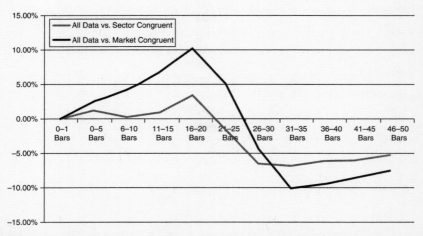

FIGURE 3.27 Trend Persistence for Sector and Market Congruency for Suspect Bearish Trends on Intermediate-Term Time Frame

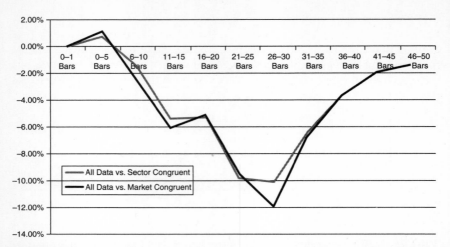

FIGURE 3.28 Trend Persistence for Sector and Market Congruency for Confirmed Bearish Trends on Long-Term Time Frame

stock's trend where trend is defined in the neoclassical manner. The same is true for sector influences. Although the data presented in this chapter is the beginning rather than the end of such an examination, it does shed light on the subject and reveals the significance of the impact. It does this for qualified trends and for varying time frames, which shows a definite and differing impact across these different views.

For the record, the data set examined is a reasonably representative set of data spanning from January of 2002 through the middle of 2011. During

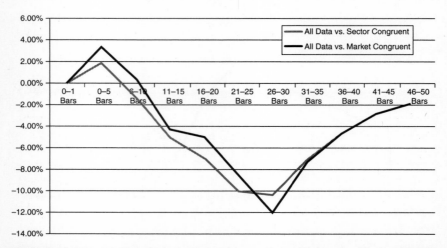

FIGURE 3.29 Trend Persistence for Sector and Market Congruency for Suspect Bearish Trends on Long-Term Time Frame

that time span the stock markets witnessed the end of a great bear market that began in 2000 and was centered in the NASDAQ; the rise of a bull market that persisted from 2003 through 2007; one of the worst bear markets in the history of the venerable NYSE in 2008 and early 2009; and a remarkably unloved bull market that began in March of 2009 and continued to press on through the summer of 2011. Though somewhat restricted in terms of time, the data analyzed has been rich in ups and downs and well representative of both bullish and bearish trends and, if anything, is probably a more extreme data set than any other period that could be examined save the 1930s.

This analysis underscores the need to synchronize individual stock trades with the sector's trend and, to a much greater degree, with the trend of the general market. The use of nine major broad sectors in the sector analysis pointed out the weakness in not having sufficient sector granularity to make sector correlation more significant. The idea of creating virtual industry groups seems to be a promising methodology going forward to address this deficiency and to improve the correlation of trend persistence between individual stocks and stock sectors or, in this case, stock industry groups.

The Trading Cube was introduced as a fast and simple visual representation of these correlations between the stock, the sector, and the general market with respect to qualified trends across the three primary time frames. With the data presented in this chapter, one can envision improvements to the Trading Cube that would provide some increased recognition of trend termination probabilities. Taking the same Trading Cube shown in Figure 3.1, what if the probabilities of trend persistence were added to show the current probability for trend failure? An example of such a Trading Cube is displayed in Figure 3.30.

By compiling and maintaining live trend failure probabilities, the Trading Cube can be extended to offer even more valuable insights to a market participant—and do so at a glance.

WHAT IS THE TRADING SIGNIFICANCE?

Trends have a life cycle, as shown throughout these first three chapters. In that respect they can be treated in the same way that you would any appliance or device. They exhibit a mean time to failure rate (MTTF), and given that the data of the entire population set can be examined, that MTTF can be constructed in a rather precise manner independent of small samples. Knowing the life cycle of a trend is a powerful tool that provides the market participant with enhanced knowledge and the ability to tie time to price and volume. MTTF rates provide a systematic method of knowing when a trend is nearing failure from a time perspective or just getting underway.

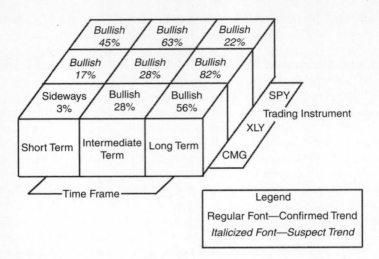

FIGURE 3.30 Trading Cube for Chipotle Mexican Grill with Trend Failure Probabilities Included (CMG)

In this chapter, some underlying tendencies were also noted such as the tendency for bearish trends to plunge much more quickly than for bullish trends to rise and the fact that the topping pattern in a bull market is very much different in terms of formation and timing when compared to a bear market's bottoming process.

Other useful observations were highlighted, including the fact that weak stocks tend to get weaker and stay weaker longer than the average stock and the fact that the exchanges scrub their indexes periodically, causing a natural upside bias.

All are interesting and useful to know, but the real thing a market participant needs and desires is a systematic method for finding and participating in the best trades that are available. What is the definition of the best trade and how can it be found? Is it always the same or constantly changing? Is one trading methodology better than another? In general, how can a market participant consistently make money over time? That's what all market participants are aiming for.

To answer that ultimate question, a market participant needs to have a fundamentally sound trading plan and the knowledge of and ability to find the best trade set-up opportunities. Chapter 4 addresses the trading plan while the remaining chapters in Part II considers trade set-ups—which are best and what are their defining characteristics. Although trading is probably one of the most difficult jobs one can undertake, it can be extremely rewarding—both mentally and monetarily. If you do not know what you are doing, it can be equally unrewarding—and in some ways even more so!

*R*eductionism is a simple word. It was born in eighteenth-century philosophical thought and introduced to the world through the writings of David Hume. It can be most elegantly thought of as the process of reducing the whole into its component parts—of moving from the complex to the simple. There are few systems more complex than the stock market with all the various avenues that one can approach it from. To reduce the market to just its core components might seem like an impossible task, yet the first three chapters reflect such reductionism.

In an unfettered marketplace, supply and demand are the simplest parts, and the construction and tracking of qualified trends allows one to measure both the direction of and enthusiasm in a stock. That enthusiasm or lack thereof is evident and available to all who care to look. It is expressed across all freely traded instruments and is best studied by artificially segmenting and examining the data across multiple and relative consistent sized time frames. As long as prices are associated with volume and time, a trail of evidence is left for the technician to work with.

Carrying the idea a bit further, with trend there are areas of conflict where both sides (buyers and sellers) find great significance. Those price points are typically found near the highs and lows of recent pricing activity, but not always. They denote significance, and as such, they reflect another source of knowledge regarding supply and demand. In the simple yet holistic model first introduced in *Trend Qualification and Trading*,[1] these

---

[1]L.A. Little, *Trend Qualification and Trading* (Hoboken, NJ: John Wiley & Sons, 2011).

price areas typically can be denoted as anchor bars and when combined with other anchor bars became anchor zones.

With this knowledge and with the appropriate tool set, a trader can both locate and evaluate the *very best trading opportunities* in the market no matter what the general market trend. Since traders are offered the opportunity to profit in both up and down markets, direction is not important as long as you understand what the direction is and have a methodology for exploiting it.

By understanding the trend along with those price points where buyers or sellers are likely to materialize, a trader has reduced the complex to the simple and has the basic knowledge needed to capitalize and profit. All that is left is to add a few more pieces to the puzzle, and the picture that puzzle paints is often referred to as a *trading plan*. For every trade you make, you should formulate a trading plan. The following list is not exhaustive as much as it is critical.

- Trend direction and strength for stock, sector, and general market
- A clear understanding of time frames and which one or ones you are trading
- Timing for entry and exit
- Planned trading size and scale trading percentages
- Probability of trade success
- Reward versus risk for the trade

Most of these bullet items you have heard before. None are really new. Probably the least familiar item on the list is the concept of time frames and the need to fully understand which one or ones you are trading. A lot more is said about that a bit later. The next least likely item on the list is the idea of scale trading. It is not new but it is grossly underutilized. It is critical to your success. When viewed in time frames, markets are not unidirectional—they all revert to the mean eventually and as such, they ebb and flow. The need to use this underlying market rhythm to your advantage cannot be overstated.

Without a trading plan that considers each of these concepts and assigns reasonable and realistic assumptions for each, the probability of being consistently profitable over time is likely a pipe dream. In trading you need a reasonably well thought out trading plan for each trade you make. That does not mean that each trade requires endless hours of assessment; quite the contrary. But it does require some thought, otherwise you are simply flipping coins.

With a reasonable trading plan template, what is left is to find trading set-ups that are to your liking, plugging the numbers into the trading plan, and deciding if the success probability quotient is high enough to pursue. A success probability quotient is just a fancy way of asking, "Is the trade worth making?" Its computation is not that difficult and is tackled in Chapter 4, "Formulating a Workable Trading Plan."

With a workable and realistic trading plan, the stage is set to tackle what every trader finds satisfaction in—trading. Chapter 5 reduces trade set-ups to their most simplistic form then once more looks to the data to ask, "What are the highest probability trade set-ups?"

You might be wondering, exactly what is a trade set-up? Essentially a trade set-up is the fulfillment of a set of factors that make the probability of a trade succeeding favorable, as well as its potential profitability. Trade set-ups exist for classical technicians just as for the neoclassical. For the former, a triangle is a common example of a trade set-up. When a triangle forms on a chart, it tells the trader that a break of either the top or bottom of the triangle formation is likely to see price carry in the direction of the break for the foreseeable future. A triangle formation also suggests that the higher probability outcome is for the break of the triangle to be to the upside if the trend is bullish or to the downside if the trend is bearish.

In neoclassical trading, the numerous patterns that technicians have become familiar with in classical technical analysis literature no longer exist. The focus is much more on price levels—not patterns. There are qualified trends, anchor bars, and the resultant anchor zones, and that is just about it. Simplicity is the cornerstone of the neoclassical method. It eschews complexity and releases the trader from numerous rules and all the variations that inherently end up accompanying those rules. It focuses instead on time frames to provide trade context and utilizes the same rules across all time frames.

The result of this more simplistic approach to trading is that it removes what many professions and professionals seek—to make the material appear more complex than it has to be. Whether by coincidence or design, complexity always seems to go hand in hand with most professions. Trading is difficult—make no mistake about that—but it need not be overly complex. It is difficult because of the emotions that accompany the decisions when money is on the line. There certainly isn't a good reason to make it any harder than it already is.

With Chapter 5 under your belt, it is time to consider the trades. Chapter 6 eases into that with range trade set-ups—how to identify them and trade them. Chapter 7 follows with retrace and breakout trade set-ups. Once more, identification and executions are detailed. Although the trade set-ups are presented in isolation for simplicity, to effectively trade warrants a top down approach. A critical component for individual stock trading success is a clear understanding of the qualified trends as well as the anchored support and resistance zones for both the general market and the sector across all three time frames. It does not matter if you are going to trade one stock or twenty—a complete understanding of these items for the general market and sector is required in order to pursue the highest probability trades. Without doing so you are trading in a vacuum and the ideal of pursing the best trade set-up is lost.

Despite all the complexity that trading entails, once you have finished these final chapters you will appreciate the fact that it is possible to reduce the complex into the simple—or at least as simple as it can be—and it is in this vein that the empirical embodiment of reductionism is applied to the world of trading.

CHAPTER 4

Formulating a Workable Trading Plan

O n the surface trading can seem very complicated and while the details are no doubt messy, at the highest levels trading is reasonably simple—something is bought and something is sold. That is about as basic as it gets.

The concept of a trading plan is not all that difficult either. It does not have to be overly complex, and in some ways the plan is part checklist and part plan. What is most important is to understand what each step means and how to effectively execute it. As outlined in the prelude to Part II, a trading plan must, at a minimum, necessarily address these six items:

1. Trend direction and strength for stock, sector, and general market
2. A clear understanding of time frames and which one or ones you are trading
3. Timing for entry and exit
4. Planned trading size and scale trading percentages
5. Probability of trade success
6. Reward versus risk for the trade

One could argue that other factors deserve consideration as well and that may be true, but at a minimum, the preceding six items are necessary to consistently trade successfully, so the remainder of this chapter addresses them as part of a trading plan decision template. It is important to note that the first four items in the list are the inputs to the final two. The probability of a trade being successful is highly dependent on each of the first four items just as the reward-to-risk ratio for the trade is critically dependent on items 2 through 4.

To illustrate this fact and to more concretely demonstrate a viable trading plan, the stock of a widely followed technology giant (Intel Corporation) is analyzed for each of the preceding attributes and a conclusion is reached as to whether a trading plan supports the purchase for the stock. The time frame considered was for the short- and intermediate-term time frames and the analysis was performed on October 26, 2011, after Intel had released earnings and its stock had increased substantially in value as a result of the earnings release.

Finally the clock is moved forward and the trade success or failure is examined. In this way, the trading plan can be brought to life and shown for what it is—a decision template as to whether a trade should or should not be made based on these critical information inputs available to the market participant at that particular point in time.

TREND DIRECTION AND STRENGTH

The process of trend qualification was covered in Chapter 1 and more extensively in *Trend Qualification and Trading*,[1] so the assumption is that this material is reasonably well understood at this point. Qualified trends are critical to trading and that is true regardless of how you tend to trade.

Figure 4.1 is a snapshot view of the qualified trends for Intel as of October 26, 2011, its sector, and the general market that it trades in as viewed through the Trading Cube.

Through this snapshot view you can see that Intel is more bullish than both the sector and the general market on the intermediate-term time frame. What you cannot see from the Trading Cube is how Intel arrived at this current state of qualified trends. That is true also of the sector and the general market. To know that the current trend for the short-term time frame is suspect bullish really does not tell you anything about how it got to that state. Was it sideways before? If so, has it strengthened? What if the prior trend state was confirmed bullish? In that case, the trend has weakened rather than strengthened. Having the context of where a trend was previously adds color to where it is and where it might be heading.

When a swing point breaks, either a trend transitions or is reaffirmed. Reaffirmation means that the same trend applies after a swing point breaks that applied prior to it. In such a case, the strength remains the same. In all

---

[1]L.A. Little, *Trend Qualification and Trading* (Hoboken, NJ: John Wiley & Sons, 2011).

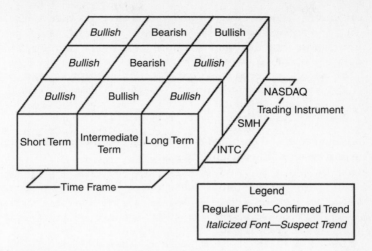

FIGURE 4.1 Intel Trading Cube (INTC) (Snapshot as of October 26, 2011)

other cases, the resultant trend either grows stronger or weaker. One way to measure qualified trend strength is to place a value on the strength based on how the transition occurs. To accomplish this, one can assign a relative measure of strength ranging from $+3$ to -3 where the value $+3$ is the strongest bullish trend while -3 is the strongest bearish trend. Zero would imply neutrality. An algorithm to assign trend strength is as follows:

```
If swing point low breaks then
        If the (prior trend was confirmed or suspect bullish) and
               the (current trend is suspect sideways) then
               Trend Strength = 1
        Else if current trend = confirmed bullish then
               Trend Strength = 3 ## this is the reaffirmation
               case
        Else if current trend = suspect bullish then
               Trend Strength = 2 ## this could be reaffirmation
               or transition
        Else if current trend = suspect sideways then
               Trend Strength = 0 ## this could be reaffirmation
               or transition
        Else if current trend = confirmed sideways then
               Trend Strength = 0 ## this could be reaffirmation
               or transition
        Else if current trend = suspect bearish then
               Trend Strength = -2 ## this could be reaffirmation
               or transition
```

```
        Else if current trend = confirmed bearish then
                Trend Strength = -3 ## this could be reaffirmation
                or transition
Else if swing point high breaks then
        If the prior trend was confirmed or suspect bearish and
                the (current trend is suspect sideways) then
                Trend Strength = -1
        Else if current trend = confirmed bullish then
                Trend Strength = 3 ## this is the reaffirmation
                case
        Else if current trend = suspect bullish then
                Trend Strength = 2 ## this could be reaffirmation
                or transition
        Else if current trend = confirmed sideways then
                Trend Strength = 0 ## this could be reaffirmation
                or transition
        Else if current trend = suspect sideways then
                Trend Strength = 0 ## this could be reaffirmation
                or transition
        Else if current trend = suspect bearish then
                Trend Strength = -2 ## this could be reaffirmation
                or transition
        Else if current trend = confirmed bearish then
                Trend Strength = -3 ## this could be reaffirmation
                or transition
```

The value in having a strength measure associated with a qualified trend is to extend the notion of the Trading Cube from a simple snapshot to include historical information. Once computed it provides a simple visual method that lets a market participant quickly ascertain if a qualified trend is getting stronger or weaker at a glance. One way to present this is via a trend transitions table where strength of trend in either direction is displayed as up (↑) and down arrows (↓). For Intel, as of October 26, 2011, the trend transition history is presented in Table 4.1.

Table 4.1 shows that on the short-term time frame, Intel has moved from reasonably weak to reasonably strong. Table 4.2 is the same exercise, but this time on the intermediate-term time frame showing that Intel has been as strong as it can be on this time frame for a good six months.

TABLE 4.1   Short-Term Trend Transition Table for Intel as of October 26, 2011

Date	Trend	Time Frame	Strength
October 11, 2011	Suspect Bullish	Short Term	↑↑
September 13, 2011	Confirmed Sideways	Short Term	
August 19, 2011	Suspect Bearish	Short Term	↓↓

TABLE 4.2 Intermediate-Term Trend Transition Table for Intel as of October 26, 2011

Date	Trend	Time Frame	Strength
October 17, 2011	Confirmed Bullish	Intermediate Term	↑↑↑
October 10, 2011	Confirmed Bullish	Intermediate Term	↑↑↑
April 25, 2011	Confirmed Bullish	Intermediate Term	↑↑↑

Carrying the exercise one step further, Table 4.3 is the long-term trend utilizing the same methodology. It shows that Intel has moved from very weak during the 2008 stock market crash to reasonably strong as of the beginning of October 2011.

Given that all of the preceding computations can be easily accomplished algorithmically, time is not an issue and the color it adds to a stock's transition history is valuable. With one glance at the previous transition histories, a market participant can quickly surmise that holding a bearish stance on Intel is not a high probability trading option as the trends are definitely bullish and Intel has shown increasing trend strengthening for the majority of 2011 from an intermediate-term time perspective.

The same exercise can and should be performed for the sector and the general market since they exert a direct influence on the success or failure of a trade on the individual stock as shown previously in Chapter 3. Rather than detail this in six additional tables, the summary of those states are as follows.

The sector has shown increasing strength for the past month moving from confirmed bearish to suspect bullish on the short-term time frame. On the intermediate-term time frame it is struggling, moving from confirmed sideways to suspect bearish and on to confirmed bearish in August of 2011. Long term, it is not nearly as grave and mimics the long-term qualified trends of Intel.

The general market is confirmed bullish on the long term and was suspect bullish previously. On the intermediate term it mimics what is seen for the sector with degradation from a confirmed sideways trend to a confirmed bearish trend. This occurred on August 1, 2011. The confirmed

TABLE 4.3 Long-Term Trend Transition Table for Intel as of October 26, 2011

Date	Trend	Time Frame	Strength
October 1, 2011	Suspect Bullish	Long Term	↑↑
April 1, 2011	Confirmed Sideways	Long Term	↑
August 1, 2010	Confirmed Bearish	Long Term	↓↓↓

bearishness was reaffirmed on August 15, 2011, as well. That tells you a lot of damage was done with the selling that occurred in August 2011 for both the general market and the sector.

In summary, by looking at the history of the stock, the sector, and the general market, it is clear that the company (Intel Corporation) is stronger than the sector and the general market; particularly on the intermediate term. The short-term sector and general market trends favor a purchase of Intel, but the intermediate-term trends for the sector and general market are in opposition to the strength seen in the stock. Long-term trends are bullish for all instruments—suspect for the stock and the sector; confirmed for the general market.

TIME FRAMES

The preceding discussions interleaved time frames with qualified trends for the various instruments so there is no need to rehash that material again. A different but related consideration for the trading plan is whether a single time frame will be traded or multiple time frames. There are no rules stating that only one time frame can be traded at a time. In fact, when the general market conditions are supportive of such a trading proposition, then it is advantageous to a market participant to do so. A simple example of trading multiple time frames in the case of Intel would be to consider a bullish trade for both a short and intermediate or long-term time frame.

If multiple time frames are to be traded, then the ideal way to do so is to construct separate but complementary trading plans for the stock—one for each time frame. The reason for this is that each time frame has its own particulars and they are most likely not the same.

For example, the entry and exit criteria based on anchored support and resistance zones are almost certainly different for the differing time frames. The same is true for how and where you would scale into and out of the position. Furthermore, the probability of success is almost certainly different as are the reward-to-risk ratios based on entry and exit points. To try to trade the long-term time frame with a short-term trading plan, as an example, is tantamount to asking for failure. They are different. They almost certainly have differing entry and exit criteria at a minimum and to treat them the same is not an advisable strategy.

Having separate but complementary trading plans is the answer. Having complementary trading plans implies that certain aspects of the trading plan might be slightly modified to complement the other trading plan. As an example, the size of the overall trade for the two time frames and the scale in and scale out methods might be modified if two time frames are traded for the same instrument. Since the two trades are meant to complement each other, they should not be viewed in isolation even though certain aspects will necessarily be different.

ENTRY AND EXIT TIMING

In Chapter 2, the fact that qualified trends provide direction while anchor zones provide timing was emphasized. In neoclassical technical analysis, the complications and numerous rules that accompany all the various indicators that classical technical analysis professes to use are eschewed. They are not needed. That is not to say that they cannot be mastered; it is just that to do so is more complicated than it has to be. They are replaced with the simplicity of qualified trend and anchored support and resistance zones—technical constructs that have a dearth of rules for construction and execution.

These replacements are predicated on the notion that qualified trends provide a higher probability for understanding the solidity of a trend, while anchor bars identify true price points where supply and demand can be measured. When a certain price area has seen excitement from both buyers and sellers, then that price area has significance. It denotes conviction by either the buyers or the sellers or both and as such is a flash point for future price activity. A revisit to that area of the chart has a greater probability of finding either support or resistance and thus supplying additional information to the market participant with respect to trade entry and exit.

Minimizing risk and maximizing reward is the most basic concept in trading, and it plays out again and again. Anchor bars, when combined, create anchor zones, and zones offer a view of where price *stickiness* is likely to occur in the future. If the anchor zone is above the current price point, then it is resistance; if below, then support. *For Long Position*

Figure 4.2 is the chart of Intel Corporation for the short-term time frame and is a continuation of the example begun in preceding paragraphs. In this chart, the stock turned from a confirmed sideways trend to a suspect bullish trend in early October and immediately performed a retest and regenerate sequence on the very next bar to confirm that it has an increased probability of rising even higher despite being a suspect trend.

A lot more will be said about retests and regenerate sequences in Chapters 5 and 7, but let it be said that they are the way suspicion is cast aside for the time being. When a stock rises and transitions to a trend that is suspect, it is indicating uncertainty. For a suspect bullish transition as

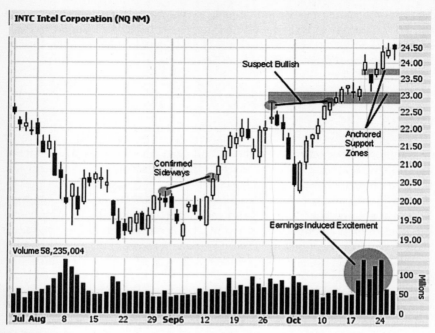

FIGURE 4.2　Daily Chart of Intel Corp. after Earnings (INTC) (July 26, 2011 to October 26, 2011)

seen in Figure 4.2, buyers were unsure of their footing. Will price hold and move higher? That question is answered when a stock retraces back into and tests the swing point bar that was broken. That is the time that the buyers and sellers have the opportunity to step up and indicate their real stance. Do they abandon the move and sell their stock? Do large short sellers see an opportunity and begin to sell the stock, looking to profit on a subsequent fall, or do the sellers step aside and/or new buyers come in and support the higher prices? That is the litmus test after all—is there more demand for shares than there is supply? If so, prices will hold and will work higher. That is what happened on the retrace, and that led to the regenerate.

In the case of Intel, once the successful retest and regenerate sequence played out, prices stumbled along for a few days more until they spiked higher on some earnings and induced excitement that hit the shares on October 19, 2011. On that day, a wide price spread and high volume anchor bar was created. Subsequent anchor bars and the prior swing point are combined to create the anchor zones as shown in Figure 4.2. Both anchor zones are below the current closing price as of October 26, which is $24.48. The higher of the two support zones combines the low of the gap up day with the low of the high volume day that occurred three days later. The lower of the two support zones combines the prior swing point high with the low of the day after earnings. These zones are price areas where, for this time frame, any price retraces should find support. Unlike trend lines and countless other classical technical constructs, they reflect supply and demand and thus they have a higher probability of actually supporting price once it begins to retreat.

Moving to the intermediate-term time frame and performing the same uncomplicated methods reveals a support zone that ranges from just shy of $23 to roughly $23.60 (see Figure 4.3).

For this chart, the current trend is confirmed bullish given the escalating volume on the break of the prior swing points. The overlap between the lower anchored support zone from Figure 4.2 and the one denoted in Figure 4.3 is a positive for all buyers of Intel stock for it says that, on both time frames, buyers most likely will step up and continue to buy the stock.

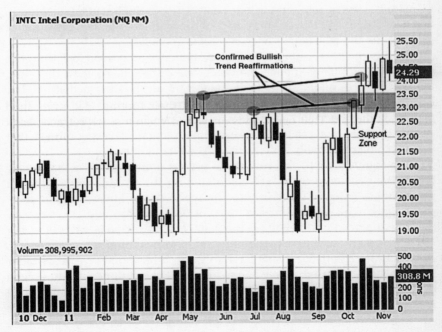

FIGURE 4.3 Weekly Chart of Intel Corp. after Earnings (INTC) (November 15, 2010 to November 14, 2011)

The demand at that price level has been shown to favor buyers, not sellers. Knowing that increases the probability that this price area should contain any selling that might materialize as price retreats—especially on the first retrace. Let's consider that statement a bit farther.

It is almost always the case that the first revisit to an area where either buyers or sellers have flexed their muscle will find an attempt to break back through that area most difficult. It is just simple math. In the case of the Intel charts in Figures 4.2 and 4.3, do you really believe that at this particular time there are many sellers left in the $22.80 to $23.50 price range (the support zone on the intermediate-term time frame)? It is unlikely. It is certainly less likely that there will be more sellers there than buyers. It may be that sector or general market influences could temporarily overrun the strength in Intel, but that would most likely be an opportunity.

If weakness in the general market were to tug the price of Intel lower, then that would simply offer the opportunity to buy the stock at lower prices than otherwise might be possible in the near term. The same is true of anchored resistance, just the other way around.

Knowing this provides the market participant with ideal entry points for a long trade in Intel on a retrace buy set-up, which will be covered in detail in Chapter 7. For the purposes of the trading plan, identification of the support and resistance zones is what is needed.

At this juncture, support zones are understood reasonably well, but for the trading plan you need the other side of the equation. In this case, the trading plan under study is to trade Intel on the intermediate and/or the short-term time frame. What are missing are resistance zones. When looking at the short- and intermediate-term time frames, none are evident. Pulling the chart back to the long-term time frame reveals one, though, and it looks to be reasonably significant, as shown in Figure 4.4.

The significance of this resistance zone is underscored by the anchor bar at the beginning of 2008 as annotated on the chart. That bar has all the characteristics of significance. The width of the bar is extreme as is the volume expansion. Almost all buyers between May and December of 2007 were placed into losing positions in January of 2008, and it is highly likely that many of them remained mired in losses for all the years since. Now that price is finally rising back to those levels some five years later, they are likely to be extremely happy to be able to exit for even—to escape their paper losses. The top of that bar is $23.67 and the resistance zone extends to the swing point high above at $25.16.

Clearly there are many who will say that price points from four years ago are nonsense; that stock holders do not wait around for years to get even. My experience says to think again. One of the more dominant forces in trading is the desire to get out for even when wrong, and many times it

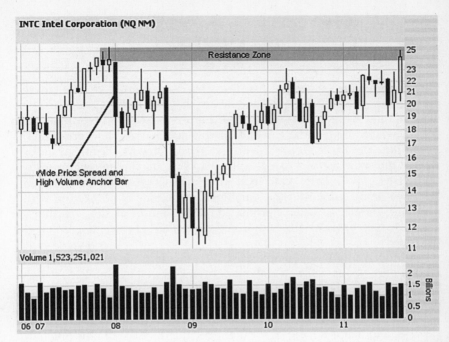

FIGURE 4.4 Monthly Chart of Intel Corp. after Earnings (INTC) (October 2, 2006 to October 3, 2011)

takes a very long time; thus, it will likely take some time to work through this natural supply of sellers.

WHAT IS THE TRADING SIGNIFICANCE?

Locating anchor bars and creating anchor zones across each time frame provides the context needed to understand supply and demand across all the time frames. These inputs are critical to understanding a potential trade's probability of success, as well as its reward-to-risk characteristics. Both are critical to being consistently profitable in trading.

From a trading plan perspective, understanding the optimal entry and exit price points is not only used to actually enter and exit the trade but also provides critical inputs for the evaluation of the trade. Without reasonably well-defined entry and exit criteria, how can market participants evaluate the reward-to-risk of the trade? They cannot!

TRADING SIZE, SCALE TRADING, TRADE SUCCESS PROBABILITIES, AND REWARD-TO-RISK RATIO

For every trade, a conscious decision is required of the market participant—how much capital should be placed on a given trade. An abundant amount of literature exists that addresses how to determine trade size of which the general calculation was summarized and presented in *Trade Like the Little Guy*.[2] The bulk of the trading size formulas revolve around the same factors, namely, portfolio size, maximum risk for a given trade, trade entry, stop, and target price. These variables are all reasonably well understood and the numbers can be simply plugged in with a resultant number of shares produced as the output of the computation given the risk one is willing to take and the reward-to-risk expectations for the trade.

Although a bit more complicated, the same formula can be utilized if a market participant scales in and out of trades as well by simply calculating the average price of the purchase and sell. Given the abundance of material on this subject, I will forgo yet another reprint of this information.

What is not as easily understood, however, is the probability of trade success, and that is a huge factor in the overall decision of how much capital to allocate to a given trade. The formulas discussed previously treat every trade the same. There is no qualitative difference. That is like saying all trends are created equal, and we know that is not true. Neither is the probability of trade success. The problem is finding a way to effectively evaluate it.

WHAT IS THE TRADING SIGNIFICANCE?

Knowing when the probabilities for success are significantly greater than failure affords the market participant the luxury of making comparatively outsized trades in such situations. Money is made in the market in bundles most of the time. It does not just arrive day in and day out. In fact, it usually leaks out rather than leaks in. Being able to make a larger bet when the probability for success is greater while at the same time the reward-to-risk of the trade is quite favorable is the Holy Grail of trading.

---

[2]L.A. Little, *Trade Like the Little Guy*, 2nd ed. (Charleston, SC: BookSurge Publishing, 2009), 180–183.

To begin to appreciate and estimate the probability of trade success, reflect back for a minute on the two criteria used to identify a potential trade—the qualified trend and the anchored support and resistance zones. Those two items are the critical components to trading. They provide trade direction, entry and exit timing, the reward versus risk for the trade, and even the probability of the trade's success.

In the ongoing Intel example, the qualified suspect bull trend for the short-term time frame has been in place for 11 bars. Looking back at Figure 1.3 in Chapter 1, the probability of the suspect trend failing for Intel is approaching 30 percent at this juncture.

Not overwhelmingly bad odds but they are nearing that point because within five bars the probabilities of trend failure will approach 45 percent, which is just slightly removed from a coin flip.

Hypothetically speaking, consider the following possibility. What if Intel were to retrace in price and transition to a short-term sideways trend while remaining within the support zones identified previously?

Referring back to the probability of a trend failure as detailed in Chapter 1, Figure 1.12 indicates that a short-term sideways trend fails at the rate of 36 to 40 percent within 5 bars and 60 percent to 62 percent within 10 bars. Thus, a retrace that holds support yet transitions is likely to transition again quickly—either up or down. In the case where the stock retraces but does not break below anchored support zones, the strength in the stock is undeniable and strongly suggests that it will most likely continue to try to work higher on that time frame.

With this knowledge and the fact that less than 10 percent of intermediate-term trends fail at this particular juncture in their life cycle (again refer to Chapter 1, Figure 1.4), the probabilities of a failed trade in Intel appears reasonably low.

WHAT IS THE TRADING SIGNIFICANCE?

A patient market participant typically can increase his probabilities for success by waiting for a particular trading set-up to unfold. Having the tools to constantly search for trade set-ups that are ready offers a market participant the greatest opportunity to continually deploy scarce capital to the best trades that are at their optimal entry points rather than entering or remaining in positions that are not optimal.

With known support and resistance zones and a reasonable assumption that the probability of a trade success may end up better than average if the set-up evolves correctly, a market participant can begin to formulate a strategy of when to make purchases and how large or small those purchases should likely be. By doing so, the reward-to-risk calculation can be calculated, which is the final piece of the trading plan puzzle.

In the Intel example, there are three general price points where the stock could be purchased if prices retreat. The first area is somewhere in the higher of the two support zones. Let's assume $23.70 as the first targeted purchase price. The weekly chart has $23.42 as the top of its support zone so a second scaled purchase could be made in that price area. The final price area where a planned purchase might be made is the bottom of the support zone, which is $22.96.

Scale purchases, when done as part of a trade set-up that is buying a retrace in the opposite direction of the trend being traded, are necessarily constructed so that the larger purchases occur at more favorable prices. In the Intel example, assume a total of $10,000 of capital is allocated to the trade. A general rule of thumb when scale purchasing with three scales in price points is to purchase 25 percent of the desired total on the first scale in price point, 35 percent on the second, and 40 percent on the final purchase. In this way, the average price point is at the "best" possible price.

For Intel this would amount to buying 105 shares at the highest price of $23.70, which is approximately in the middle of the highest support zone. Another 150 shares would be purchased at $23.42, which is just inside the weekly anchor zone (the high volume weekly bar from May 2, 2011). The final 174 shares would be bought at $22.96, which is the bottom of the weekly anchor zone. Scaling in at this pace and price points would make the average purchase price $23.31.

At this juncture, the average price point is known but what is not computed yet are the other main factors that are needed to understand the reward-to-risk, which is the target stop loss if wrong and target exit if right.

As will be explained thoroughly in Chapter 6, there are many ways to calculate stop loss percentages but a rational person should consider placing a stop loss order at some point beyond where they expect support to be located for a bullish trade or resistance for a bearish trade. Similarly, an exit target price should be placed just shy of where resistance is expected for a bullish trade or support is anticipated in a bearish trade.

As discussed already, the supply and demand is best understood to be located where anchor zones are found, and thus it would seem natural to use that knowledge to place the exit orders, just as the entry orders have been based on the same knowledge. The only question remaining is how far.

One reasonably consistent and unbiased method for doing this is to determine the average true range of the stock and then multiply that number by some percentage to create and offset. I personally like to use 20 percent or 25 percent. That yields a value that is then used as an offset of the anchor zone and is the place to put the stop loss order.

For Intel, the average true range on the daily chart as of October 19 is $.47 and when multiplied by the more conservative 25 percent, that yields a figure of roughly $.12 to use as an offset. For a bullish trade on Intel where the bottom of the lower support zone is used as the final measure of support, the stop would be placed $.12 below the low of the support zone, which is, in this example, $22.66 ($22.78 − $.12). This establishes the stop at roughly 1 percent lower than the high volume breakout bar on the intermediate-term time frame. With these price points, the risk is $.65 per share or $650 plus commissions.

The exit target for profits is the beginning of the resistance zone for a portion of the position and then near the top of the resistance zone for another portion or all of the remaining position, depending on how the resistance zone is pushed into. If the trend remains young (higher probability of continuing), volume expands, and the bars are wide in their price spread, then it may be advisable to hold on for more with a reduced position size. If not, then the profits should probably be reaped. Since in the trading plan you want to be conservative rather than optimistic, just assume that all shares are to be sold at the lower bounds of the resistance zone. That price point is $23.84. Thus, the reward if the trade succeeds will be minimal; just $530. As can be seen, the risk is greater than the reward and this trading plan is a non-starter.

When such a situation develops, the market participant has to back up and reevaluate the entry points (never exit points). For example, an entry point at the lower two price points could be considered using a scale approach of 40 percent and 60 percent. In this case, the average cost is now $23.13, reducing the risk on the trade to $.47 and increasing the reward to $.71—thus $710 worth of reward versus $470 worth of risk—not ideal, but workable if the probability of success is high. If the scenario described were to occur, then this reward-to-risk ratio when combined with the probability of success, which would elevate to reasonably high given trend failure probabilities, makes the trade favorable enough to consider. Note that this is by no means a trade with the potential for greatness but since the objective of this chapter is to walk through the formulation of a viable trading plan we will continue on with the example. Whether a trade is taken depends on what other trades are available at the time and what kind of reward-to-risk characteristics and success probabilities they carry. As suggested earlier, the trades that carry the potential for greatness come about rarely. It is highly unlikely that you will wake up each morning to find one.

EVALUATING AND ACTING UPON THE PLAN

In the Intel example, the details of the trading plan have been gathered and the computations made. The idealized plan is to buy the stock on the short-term time frame scaling in at two price points as the short-term trend transitions to sideways. The exit decision is to scale out at the lower end of the resistance zone and then again near the higher end of the resistance zone unless the assumptions stated above require modification.

The size of the trade is probably average to below average because this is not the kind of trade where a larger than average size should be taken. The probability of a success is better than average, but the reward-to-risk is below average.

Figure 4.5 is the daily chart of Intel almost one month later.

In this example Intel does almost exactly what is desired. Prices retrace to price zone where the first purchase is targeted and, for two days, hit that price area. Note that both days end up closing higher than the swing point low (SPL) and thus no trend transition occur. Although this did

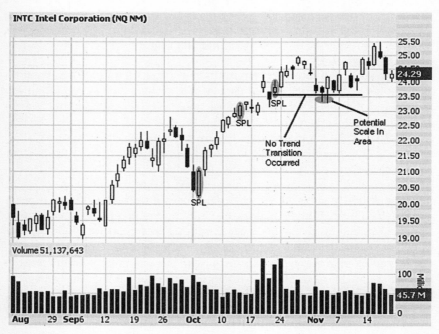

FIGURE 4.5 Daily Chart of Intel Corp. after Earnings (INTC) (August 19, 2011 to November 18, 2011)

provide the opportunity to purchase the stock at a low risk entry point with favorable reward-to-risk characteristics without a reset of the short-term trend, the probability of a trend failure in the near future increases and thus decreases the probability of success factor. In fact, on a short-term trend basis, in Figure 4.5, Intel has reached the coin flip state with about a 50 percent chance of trend failure.

For this reason, the astute trader should begin to look for an exit and book his or her profits. The trend is becoming too old and time is a critical element in trading strategies.

WHAT IS THE TRADING SIGNIFICANCE?

With the probability matrixes associated with qualified trends, time can be incorporated as part and parcel of a trading strategy. When the probabilities of trend failure grow too large, full or partial profits should be taken or some sort of hedging strategy considered to minimize the impact of a sizable retrace. The same is true for losses. If the probabilities are increasingly growing against the trade, cutting losses short is a lot better than waiting for the increasing likelihood of a stop loss order triggering a full loss.

SUMMARY

There are three critical elements to trading: price, volume, and time. Price and volume have received a tremendous amount of press since the practice of technical analysis began. Time, on the other hand, has always been most difficult to incorporate. W.D. Gann is probably the most famous technician associated with the study of time. His work concentrated primarily on time cycles though, not time relative to trend failure probabilities. Understanding the probabilities associated with trend failure leaves a market participant with the enviable task of using that knowledge to profit in the markets.

The task of finding market profits does not occur by chance. It results from a methodical assessment of trade potential—not just some trades but all trades. The focus on trend and the trend's strength across all time frames for not only the stock, but also the sector and the general market, sharpens the focus as to what time frame(s) the trading plan should incorporate. The discovery of anchored support and resistance zones provides the reward-to-risk parameters and contributes to the evaluation of trade success probabilities. Trend failure probabilities is considered essential to properly evaluating trade success probabilities and breathes new life into the desire to incorporate time as a constraint on the trading plan. Most important, a trading plan always defines risk, planned trading size, and scale in and out percentages as key elements to the trading plan.

In the end, risk is the only thing that a market participant can really control. Everything else is up to the market and the events that drive it. Once that fact is accepted, trading is no longer a mystery but instead a series of probabilities. Not all trades will succeed. That is a given, and they do not all need to succeed for you to be successful. The task at hand is to evaluate each trade with the most complete set of facts available at that particular point in time and then to decide, given all potential trades available at this particular time, is this trade the best to be had and if so, just how good is it? If the answer is yes and "how good" is above average, then the trade should be taken and the size determined. Larger-than-average trade size is regulated to only those occurrences where both the reward-to-risk ratio and the success quotient are better than average. If both are less than average and there's nothing better to be had, then a less than average size should be used if any trade is to be made, and in many cases, simply waiting is best. A trader can churn his or her account quickly pursuing less than average trades. Anything else results in an average size trade. It really is that simple.

At this juncture the tools are in place. Trend, trend transition histories, support and resistance zones, and a trading plan have all been discussed. What remains are the trade set-ups. Although seemingly complicated, trade set-ups typically fall into either one of two categories. Either you trade breakouts or you trade retraces. Chapter 5 considers the fact that every trade set-up results from a test, and just as probabilities for success and failure were ascertained for qualified trend and trade failures, retrace and breakout trade set-ups can also be qualified and considered in terms of a probability matrix.

The Data behind Trend Trade Set-Ups

There are few absolutes in trading but of the few that exist, one unavoidable fact is that everything in trading is based on tests. There are tests of swing points, anchor bars, and anchor zones. For those who dabble in classical technical analysis, there are tests on most all patterns there as well, such as flags, triangles, moving averages, and so forth. All technical analysis is premised on the idea of a test and, in fact, is continually defined by the unending series of tests that is always present and repeating in the market.

For neoclassical technical analysis, with the emphasis being on keeping it simple yet holistic, tests of swing points that succeed result in trend transitions and reaffirmations as identified through swing point breaks. Those tests that fail lead to retraces. Similarly, tests of anchor bars lead to retraces (failure) and breakouts (success). The same is true of anchor zones which many times serve to define trading floors and ranges and are themselves the object of tests.

Test . . . test . . . test is what the market does on a continual basis. Testing is the market's way of discovering the correct price for securities, and it is a constant process since price discovery is never final. Price and value are continually shifting, and it is through testing that the market discovers it. The process is referred to as *efficient*, though the use of such a term is somewhat debatable. Without question though, it is workable and it does yield concrete value even though that value resembles the shifting desert sands rather than some concrete and immovable object. Value in a free and unencumbered market is constantly shifting and necessarily so since value is, to a great degree, a mental concept founded on both current assumptions and future expectations. Those assumptions and expectations are grounded in little more than perception, and perception is anything but concrete.

Tests are best understood as having a result, and the result of a test is either a success or a failure, but these terms are void of meaning unless viewed in the context of price direction and the particulars of the test. In trading, and over time, price either moves up or it moves down; that movement does not occur in isolation but instead in relation to prior price action. This forms either sideways or directional movement and is the foundation for the concept of trend. For the purposes of test success and failure, think of bullish and bearish trends and tests that occur within the context of that mental framework.

THE ONLY TWO TYPES OF TRADE SET-UPS

Probably the greatest mental complexity foisted upon the trader is the idea that there are multitudes of trade set-ups—a plethora of possibilities for entering into and exiting from equity trades. In reality, there are but two fundamental trade set-ups: breakouts and retraces. All other trade set-ups really are an extension of these two basic trade types, which can be viewed as building blocks. All the countless patterns and various indicators are but variations off these two basic trade set-ups and, as you have already probably surmised, both involve a test.

For both bullish and bearish trends, there are two distinct situations where a test may occur during a trending process. Both test situations happen in both bullish and bearish trends and are simply mirror images of one another.

To illustrate, take the case of a bullish trend. In such a situation, price can either be pushing higher or drifting lower in the context of the overall bullish trend. When price pushes higher and resistance is encountered, for the purposes of this book, this is referred to as a *bullish breakout test*. In the case where a previously rising price drifts lower to the point where support is encountered, for the purposes of this book, this is as a *bullish retrace test*.

Figure 5.1 provides an example of the success or failure of a bullish breakout test.

In the same vein, Figure 5.2 provides an example of the success or failure of a bullish retrace test.

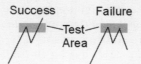

FIGURE 5.1   Bullish Breakout Test Success and Failure Examples

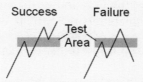

FIGURE 5.2   Bullish Retrace Test Success and Failure Examples

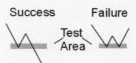

FIGURE 5.3   Bearish Breakout Test Success and Failure Examples

Flipping the tests upside down yields the mirror images, which are the bearish cases. Figures 5.3 and 5.4 illustrate bearish breakout and retrace success and failures.

Each of the preceding figures is purposefully centered on the notion of a test. Tests are a special area on a chart because the result of a test releases information to market participants. The tests outlined in Figures 5.1 through 5.4 are the totality of test types that take place in the market each and every day. It is not any more complicated than that. These tests happen all the time on whatever time frame you wish to investigate.

FIGURE 5.4   Bearish Retrace Test Success and Failure Examples

The tests shown in the prior figures appear to be swing point tests, but they are not intended to be isolated to only swing points. The same pattern appears when anchor bars and anchor zones are tested, for example.

Because there are only two ways for the market to directionally travel (up or down—bullish or bearish), the only possible tests that can occur are tests that happen as prices rise or as they fall. Sideways price activity is covered in the preceding four figures as well since these same tests continually take place for the duration of the sideways range trade. It is just that in a sideways range trade, as long as the sideways range holds, the result of the test is always a bullish or bearish breakout failure. When the range trade breaks, then it has to be the result of a bullish or bearish breakout success.

As an aside, this idea of just four test types is not how most textbooks present technical analysis, and in fact, the act of making it appear so rudimentary likely runs the risk of turning off some readers who would rather it appear more challenging. Trading is most assuredly challenging, not because it is complicated but because it is difficult to execute. The risk of loss or the fear of missing out can certainly make the decision process more difficult. Nevertheless, there is value in reducing the seemingly complex to the simple and elegant when and where that is possible. That is the essence of understanding, and reductionism is at the core of that process. It is a travesty if that simplicity is not projected to the nonprofessional in order for him to understand the essence of the discipline he seeks knowledge about.

Returning to the idea of a test, when any one of the four test types occurs, regardless of the outcome, information is released to those willing to observe. Using the bullish or bearish breakout test as an example, if such a test is successful the obvious informational release is the creation and qualification of trend when a swing point is involved. If no swing point is involved, the breakout still retains the same qualitative measure of confirmed or suspect as a result of the breakout beyond the resistance or support zone. Though not explicitly noted elsewhere, if a resistance zone is punctured, then clearly the resistance was not sufficient to contain price— at least not at that time and on that time frame. Qualitatively, such a move through resistance is certainly more "believable" if it simultaneously occurs with volume expansion as compared to what is being broken, versus it occurring on even lighter volume than the resistance zone's anchor bars. These principles of trend qualification are not narrowly applicable to only swing points, but likewise apply to anchored support, resistance breakouts, and retraces as well.

Information is not limited to a successful breakout, however, as it is also released in failure cases as well. For bullish and bearish breakout attempts, for example, if volume expands while a test is in process, even if the test fails, it increases the probability that the test will eventually take place again. Tests on increasing volume that fail are likely to be retested at some point in the future, for the increase in volume is unlikely to have randomly occurred. For whatever reason there was an increase in buying and selling intensity, and the battle is unlikely to have concluded. It is only when the interest in the price of the stock no longer excites that an observer can conclude that the battle over price has likely concluded. Until then, though, one has to expect repeated retests until the fate of price is definitively decided, with one side winning and the other losing.

The repetition of a test also can be telling. Again using the example of a breakout test, if such a test is repeated, the odds of a successful breakout increases with each attempt as long as the testing process does not extend past four or five attempts. Beyond that, the testing process begins to lose its informational power.

Although not as obvious, information release also occurs even when an actual test fails to materialize. Similar to a failed test on greater volume, if price moves near a test price point or price zone, a measure of the comparative volume can be informative. Does volume expand into that price zone or decrease? If it expands, yet price retreats away from the test, the probabilities are greater that price will regroup and try again within a few bars. If volume dries up and withers on the vine, then the market is telling you that, for whatever reason, there is not enough desire on the part of market participants to even get price to the test point or test area. That is a pretty clear indication that test may not even occur. That too is useful to know.

TRADING BREAKOUTS AND RETRACES

As shall be seen in Chapters 6 and 7, when tests occur they are releasing information as they occur. The information release involves price, volume, and time, and these three fundamental technical constructs allow a trader to make an informed decision as to whether to make a trade or not. Tests, irrespective of their outcomes, create both an opportunity and a risk. It cannot be any other way. The opportunity is that the unfolding trade set-up works as expected while the risk is that it does not. The fascinating part of all trading is that the death of one trade set-up typically eventually gives birth to a different yet tradable trading set-up.

Buy the breakout or

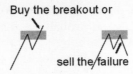

sell the failure

FIGURE 5.5   Bullish Breakout Trade Set-Up Possibilities

Trading is but a series of tests with resultant opportunity and risk. The success or failure of one test simply leads to the next. The demise of one trade set-up simply births another.

In life there is an abundance of opposing forces: hot and cold, dry and wet, black and white. In trading it is no different. There are breakouts and breakdowns; test failures and successes; profits and losses; rewards and risks. The key success in the trading game is to limit the risk while maximizing reward for trades that have a higher probability of success.

Glancing back at Figures 5.1 through 5.4, a trader can easily visualize the trade set-ups that emanate from these few test patterns that represent the totality of what the market can and will throw at you. There are only two possibilities per figure. Do you see them?

Figure 5.5 shows the corresponding trade set-ups that emanate from the bullish breakout tests depicted in Figure 5.1 It is pretty simple. You either buy the breakout (test success case) or not. In the case of a test failure, you can short sell the failure or simply pass on the trade.

That is as complicated as it gets. Figure 5.6 shows the corresponding trade possibilities based on the bullish retrace tests from Figure 5.2

Again, the possibilities are limited to just three outcomes. You buy the retrace when it holds (succeeds), you sell the retrace test failure, or you do not trade the set-up.

The bearish breakout and retraces are the exact same yet opposite situation, as shown here in Figures 5.7 and 5.8 Again, there is not anything complicated in these trading dynamics, and that is exactly as it should be.

Though simple in thought, trading is far from simple in practice, for the information released on a test is not always accurate and will, at times,

Buy the retrace or

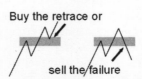

sell the failure

FIGURE 5.6   Bullish Retrace Trade Set-Up Possibilities

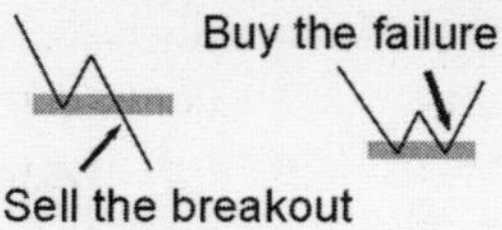

Buy the failure

Sell the breakout

FIGURE 5.7 Bearish Breakout Trade Set-Up Possibilities

be untrustworthy. A breakout trade set-up can have all the characteristics to suggest it should succeed yet still fail. There is never a sure bet. There are probabilities, and knowing those probabilities is critical to the trader if he or she is to pursue the best trade set-ups with the highest probabilities for success.

There are an untold number of outside influences that the trader cannot escape, whether it is friends, trading buddies, or news sources of every imaginable kind. To block out this noisy chatter and somehow trade just the technical picture is next to impossible, which further complicates the job, but that is another subject for another day. This chapter's topic is limited to the analysis of the possibilities and probabilities associated with these two basic trade types—breakouts and retraces. Armed with this information, a trader can deploy capital in the wisest manner and at the most opportune time. It is a sea change in approach.

BREAKOUTS VERSUS RETRACE TRADE PROBABILITIES

As described previously, there are four basic test scenarios and each has a potential corresponding trade set-up that emanates from it. For the trader, the primary focus of any trade should center on the question of what constitutes the highest probability trade set-up. Since not all trade set-ups have the same probabilities for trade success, this quest is critical. Once determined, however, and combined with the potential reward versus risk for a particular trade, the overall best trade available at any given time is ascertainable.

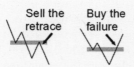

Sell the retrace

Buy the failure

FIGURE 5.8 Bearish Retrace Trade Set-Up Possibilities

As a reminder, stocks do not trade in a vacuum; thus, the probabilities governing an individual trade's success are, to a varying extent, dependent on broader technical aspects of the sector and general market. The following data were greatly influenced by those outside factors and thus constitute the broader influences that prevailed for the duration of the sampled data. That period was from the beginning of 2002 until the summer of 2011—a period of time that saw significant rises and falls in equity prices. For this reason, it is believed that this data represents a favorable population sample and the probabilities derived from it are both valid and representative of true underlying trend and test probabilities.

As stated in various forms already, the decision to enter a trade always is dependent on two factors: the probability that the trade will succeed, which should be greater than a coin flip, and the reward-to-risk ratio, which should be 2:1 at a minimum but more preferably 3:1 or 4:1. If a trader scales into trades, the initial reward-to-risk ratio may be less but the entire trading plan should yield something between 2:1 and 4:1 ratios. The probability of trade success is, to varying degrees, tied to entry timing. Trade entry usually defines trade success or failure. A bad trade with a good entry will many times allow a trader out of the trade at little to no cost. A bad trade with a bad entry is typically unforgiving.

To illustrate this more clearly, consider the bullish breakout trade set-up depicted previously in Figure 5.5 and the bullish retrace trade set-up depicted in Figure 5.6 When viewed as a time sequence, Figure 5.6 is simply a continuation of Figure 5.5 with the retrace being the subsequent pull back after the breakout. These two trade setups present a plethora of questions, such as, is it better to buy the breakout or the retrace, and how does a trader decide? Do the probabilities differ depending on if the breakout is a bullish or a bearish trend? What if breakout is suspect versus confirmed? How does time factor into the decision?

These types of questions are at the heart of trading and trade setups and need to be considered to understand the parameters governing trade entry. They are what enable a trader to maximize the known probabilities.

To address these types of questions, a vigorous analysis of the data was performed. The frame of reference taken was to consider two possible points of entry for a trade—either on the breakout or on a retrace back to a prior support or resistance area. Since breakouts and retraces are part and parcel of swing point tests, trend transitions were used to key the analysis. It is noted and accepted that there are breakout and retrace tests that do not involve a swing point, with the most obvious being a breakout and/or retrace to an anchored zone. The limitation of this study, if viewed that way, is duly noted. Had the time and resources been unlimited, a study of both would have been preferable but alas, time and resources are always limited. Therefore, given the choice, it was deemed much more preferable to focus breakout and retrace trade set-ups involving swing points versus those that don't because swing points are such a pivotal part of contested price levels and thus supply and demand.

Given the above, the methodology employed is that each trend transition (price) was analyzed with respect to breakout quality (volume) and in terms of the number of bars that transpired prior to a retrace (time). In this way, the three fundamental technical analysis building blocks are each incorporated.

For the breakout and retrace set-ups, seven possible and related scenarios were identified. These scenarios were carefully chosen in order to shed light upon and yield useful information about the most pressing questions facing all traders. It turns out that these seven scenarios are tightly coupled around another idea first presented in *Trend Qualification and Trading*,[1] and that is the concept of *retest and regenerate.* As it turns out, after further analysis, the concept has broader applicability than first envisioned. In fact, its impact is felt far more often and in ways not appreciated at the time of its initial recognition.

The term *retest and regenerate* was first coined to describe the common and repetitive situation where a swing point is broken and a suspect trend created (volume does not expand on the break). In the ebb and flow that accompanies most markets and stocks, it is overwhelmingly probable that when a stock breaks out under such conditions it will, after some period of time, retrace back to the area where it broke out to retest.

A more comprehensive analysis of the data shows this to be true of both confirmed and suspect trends, which wasn't fully appreciated previously. This has far reaching application that has, until now, escaped attention.

More about this shortly, but for now refocus your attention to the seven test scenarios that are outlined in Table 5.1. For each scenario, a description is offered along with the failure and success criteria associated with the scenario. Note that these seven scenarios yield probability matrixes for each of the possible breakout and retrace trade set-up outcomes previously depicted in Figures 5.5 through 5.8 This tight coupling enables a market participant to consider and formulate high probability trading strategies and plans for each scenario.

To address Table 5.1 in a bit more depth before presenting the probability data for each of the bullish and bearish retest and regenerate scenarios, recognize that Scenarios 1 and 2, as well as Scenarios 3 and 4, are essentially the same scenarios save for a difference in the number

---

[1]L.A. Little, *Trend Qualification and Trading* (Hoboken, NJ: John Wiley & Sons, 2011), 97–105.

TABLE 5.1 Retest and Regenerate Scenarios and Failure/Success Criteria

Retest and Regenerate Scenarios	Failure (Stop Out) Criteria
Scenario 1—A retest/regenerate sequence occurs within six bars of the breakout. Price violates the stop without moving back beyond the original swing point breakout price. In this case, volume on the retrace has not necessarily increased as compared to the breakout bar. This is a failure on the first attempted retest/regenerate sequence.	A retest failure occurs if price exceeds the far side of the swing point bar that was broken as part of the breakout. For a bullish breakout this would be the low of the swing point bar broken. For a bearish breakout, this would be the high of the swing point bar that was broken.
Scenario 2—A retest/regenerate sequence occurs after more than six bars have passed since the breakout. Price violates the stop without moving back beyond the original swing point breakout price. In this case, volume on the retrace has not necessarily increased as compared to the breakout bar. This is a failure on the first attempted retest/regenerate sequence.	A retest failure occurs if price exceeds the far side of the swing point bar that was broken as part of the breakout. For a bullish breakout this would be the low of the swing point bar broken. For a bearish breakout, this would be the high of the swing point bar that was broken.
Scenario 3—A retest/regenerate sequence occurs within six bars of the breakout, but excessive volume occurs as compared to the breakout bar, which eventually leads to a price stop out. Volume expansion provides the early warning for trade exit or avoidance and is treated as a stop out based on volume rather than price.	In this case the volume action is not favorable behavior and should be interpreted as a reason to exit the trade. Price has not violated the far side of the swing point, but volume expands as compared to the breakout bar on the retrace.
Scenario 4—A retest/regenerate sequence occurs after more than six bars have passed since the breakout, but excessive volume occurs as compared to the breakout bar. This is treated as a stop out based on volume rather than price.	In this case the volume action is not favorable behavior and should be interpreted as a reason to exit the trade. Price has not violated the far side of the swing point, but volume expands as compared to the breakout bar on the retrace.
Scenario 5—After the first successful retest/regenerate sequence, price violates the stop out area. This occurs after at least one or more retest/regenerate sequences succeed. In this case, volume necessarily has not increased as compared to the breakout bar.	A retest failure occurs when price exceeds the far side of the swing point bar that was broken as part of the breakout. For a bullish breakout, this would be the low of the swing point bar broken. For a bearish breakout, this would be the high of the swing point bar that was broken.

TABLE 5.1 (*Continued*)	
Retest and Regenerate Scenarios	**Failure (Stop Out) Criteria**
Scenario 6—After the first successful retest/regenerate sequence, excessive volume occurs as compared to the breakout bar, which eventually leads to a price stop out. Volume expansion provides the early warning for trade exit or avoidance and is treated as a stop out based on volume rather than price. Note that this occurs after at least one or more retest/regenerate sequences succeed. A successful retest/regenerate sequence implies that price moved back beyond the original swing point breakout.	In this case the volume action is not favorable behavior and could be interpreted as a reason to exit the trade. Price has not violated the far side of the swing point, but volume expands as compared to the breakout bar on the retrace.
Scenario 7—A retest/regenerate sequence never occurs.	For the duration of the data examined, a retest of the swing point that was broken never occurred. A portion of these instances is related to the fact that the analysis must stop at some point, but some of the cases were actual breakouts that still had not retested and regenerated over an extended period of time.

of bars that occur prior to the retest and regenerate. Scenarios 1 and 3, as well as 2 and 4, are also the same with the exception of volume characteristics.

The reason for examining the data in this manner is that the characteristics of time and volume are closely related to trade set-up success and failure. In the original work on this subject presented in *Trend Qualification and Trading*,[2] it was postulated that the general principals governing the area to be retested are tied to time and volume. If a retest occurs relatively quickly (within five or six bars), then the test is likely to involve either

- The opposite side of the broken swing point bar *or*
- The prior and opposite directional swing point

---

[2]L.A. Little, *Trend Qualification and Trading*, 99.

If, however, the retest comes after more than six bars then most of the time a successful retest and regenerate sequence is limited to a test of the breakout area and not much more. Excessive volume as compared to what is being tested tended, more often than not, to result in a failure of the retest.

The stop out criteria presented in Table 5.1 originally considered two different stop out areas based on the time duration between a breakout and the occurrence of the subsequent retest and regenerate sequence. This was consistent with the original thoughts as described earlier. After detailed analysis, however, it was determined that conservative stops should always be used in all four scenarios (Scenarios 1 through 4), which specifically implies a retest and regenerate sequence fails (stops out) only if

- The closing price of a subsequent retest and regenerate sequence closes beyond the opposite side of the broken swing point bar *or*
- When price trades back into the broken swing point bar, volume expands to an amount greater than the broken swing point bar

Another possibility for stop out criteria was to utilize anchor zones for the stop loss. Back testing was completed for that criterion as well, and though it yielded differing results, the outcomes were not nearly as desirable as expected because of the difficulty in algorithmically separating anchor zones exhibiting significance versus those that did not. Clearly, this is an area for potential future refinement but for now, the data as is yields value and the analysis presented proceeds in this manner.

Continuing on with the specifics of how the probability data, as presented in Table 5.2, is constructed, the analysis was also segmented into four possible qualified trend breakout types of confirmed and suspect bullish as well as confirmed and suspect bearish. Furthermore, percentages are supplied based on each of the three time frames (short-, intermediate-, and long-term) as well as a composite for all combined time frames.

Finally, for readability, each scenario detailed previously in Table 5.1 is reprinted as part of Table 5.2 and accompanied by the likely trader impact had a trader taken the trade. In all cases, the impact statement considers both an entry in the breakout case as well as on the retrace.

As for the actual probabilities, they are all presented from the perspective of failure (as before in all previous analysis). For example, in Table 5.2, for Scenario 1, the probability that a confirmed bullish trend will fail (stop out based on price as described in Table 5.1) when a retest and regenerate sequence occurs within six bars of the breakout is 19.86 percent for all time frames and across all scenarios. For a suspect bullish trend, the probability is 11.35 percent and so forth.

TABLE 5.2 Retest and Regenerate Probabilities on All Qualified Trends for All and Individual Time Frames

Criteria and Trader Impact	Time Frame	Confirmed Bullish	Suspect Bullish	Confirmed Bearish	Suspect Bearish
Scenario 1—A retest/regenerate sequence occurs within six bars of the breakout. Price violates the stop without moving back beyond the original swing point breakout price. In this case, volume on the retrace has not necessarily increased as compared to the breakout bar. This is a failure on the first attempted retest/regenerate sequence.	All Time Frames	19.86%	11.35%	22.44%	13.69%
	Short Term	20.44%	12.10%	23.66%	14.11%
	Intermediate Term	15.16%	9.26%	22.01%	11.61%
Trader Impact: If a trader enters a position on the breakout, then this is a guaranteed loss. If a trader waits for the retrace test, he/she will never enter the trade.	Long Term	12.53%	6.31%	18.26%	10.93%
Scenario 2—A retest/regenerate sequence occurs after more than six bars have passed since the breakout. Price violates the stop without moving back beyond the original swing point breakout price. In this case, volume on the retrace necessarily has not increased as compared to the breakout bar. This is a failure on the first attempted retest/regenerate sequence.	All Time Frames	5.55%	3.00%	5.84%	3.27%
	Short Term	5.89%	3.22%	5.10%	3.43%
	Intermediate Term	4.91%	2.00%	4.62%	2.50%
Trader Impact: If a trader enters a position on the breakout, then depending on how the trade is managed, this may or may not result in a loss as there is a reasonable chance to exit before losing. If a trader waits to buy the retrace, then money is not tied up in the interim but it is not clear from this data sampling whether money could have been made on the breakout and then again on a retrace entry.	Long Term	3.89%	2.03%	4.74%	2.41%

(continued)

119

TABLE 5.2 (Continued)

Criteria and Trader Impact	Time Frame	Confirmed Bullish	Suspect Bullish	Confirmed Bearish	Suspect Bearish
Scenario 3—A retest/regenerate sequence occurs within six bars of the breakout but excessive volume occurs as compared to the breakout bar, which eventually leads to a price stop out. Volume expansion provides the early warning for trade exit or avoidance and is treated as a stop out based on volume rather than price.	All Time Frames	5.98%	19.67%	8.98%	22.22%
	Short Term	5.71%	19.61%	8.93%	22.30%
	Intermediate Term	8.15%	20.19%	8.93%	21.84%
Trader Impact/Probable Result: If a trader enters a position on the breakout, then this is a guaranteed loss if she exits due to heavy volume on the first retrace.	Long Term	10.11%	17.96%	10.69%	21.62%
Scenario 4—A retest/regenerate sequence occurs after more than six bars of the breakout but excessive volume occurs as compared to the breakout bar, which eventually leads to a price stop out. Volume expansion provides the early warning for trade exit or avoidance and is treated as a stop out based on volume rather than price.	All Time Frames	1.82%	2.79%	2.13%	4.07%
	Short Term	1.81%	2.88%	2.11%	4.06%
	Intermediate Term	1.88%	2.55%	2.27%	4.24%
Trader Impact: If a trader enters a position on the breakout, then, depending on how the trade is managed, this may or may not result in a loss as there is a reasonable chance to exit before losing. If a trader waits to buy the retrace, then the position likely would not be entered into.	Long Term	1.93%	1.46%	2.16%	2.97%

Scenario 5—After the first successful retest/regenerate sequence, price violates the stop out area. This occurs after at least one or more retest/regenerate sequences succeed. In this case, volume necessarily has not increased as compared to the breakout bar.

Trader Impact: If a trader enters a position on the breakout and sticks with the trade through the first retest/regenerate sequence, then profits are likely realized. If a position is entered on the first retrace, then profits are likely realized.

All Time Frames	28.67%	9.57%	28.12%	9.53%
Short Term	30.11%	10.25%	28.71%	9.66%
Intermediate Term	22.14%	5.90%	25.96%	8.68%
Long Term	13.80%	3.88%	22.33%	10.09%

Scenario 6—After the first successful retest/regenerate sequence, excessive volume occurs as compared to the breakout bar, which eventually leads to a price stop out. Volume expansion provides the early warning for trade exit or avoidance and is treated as a stop out based on volume rather than price. Note that this occurs after at least one or more retest/regenerate sequences succeed.

Trader Impact/Probable Result: If a trader enters a position on the breakout and sticks with the trade through the first retest/regenerate sequence, then profits are most likely realized. If a position is entered on the first retrace, then profits are likely realized.

All Time Frames	34.96%	51.06%	30.19%	45.62%
Short Term	33.40%	50.00%	29.68%	45.21%
Intermediate Term	42.48%	55.63%	32.28%	48.05%
Long Term	47.79%	57.09%	34.10%	44.77%

Scenario 7—A retest/regenerate sequence never occurs.

Trader Impact/Probable Result: If a trader enters a position on the breakout, then profits are guaranteed. If a trader waits for the retrace to enter a position, it never happens.

All Time Frames	3.16%	2.56%	2.30%	1.60%
Short Term	2.64%	1.94%	1.81%	1.23%
Intermediate Term	5.28%	4.47%	3.93%	3.08%
Long Term	9.95%	11.27%	7.72%	7.21%

Given all of the preceding notations, Table 5.2 displays the probability tables for each of the seven scenarios for the qualified trend types across all time frames and for each qualified trend type.

Although having the raw probability data is critical and is therefore supplied, it is realized that its true usefulness comes when massaged and grouped to answer useful questions such as, "What is the probability that a trend transition (breakout) will eventually retrace for a retest and regenerate sequence, and how quickly is such a retrace likely to occur?"

It is only when such critical questions are answered that the data transforms into valuable information. The remainder of this chapter sets about to do just this for those scenarios that hold the greatest promise. Note that all data for the remainder of this chapter is pulled from Table 5.2 and in particular from the "All Time Frames" row. For the most part, the divergence between all time frames and particular time frames is reasonably insignificant except for a few scenarios.

PROBABILITIES FOR TRADE SET-UP SCENARIOS

Before digging into more detail it is best to once more remind the reader that all the data presented here is abstracted in "bars" rather than days, weeks, or months. This is purposefully done because the data is applicable to all time frames. There are insignificant differences noticed across the time frames, and it is believed that these probabilities likely hold to other time frames as well, such as quarterly bars or, on the other extreme, five-minute or one-hour bars.

Returning to the data, a critical question in trading is whether a trader is better served to enter a trade on a breakout or wait for a retrace. Figure 5.9 sheds some light on this question, exhibiting the probability that a trend transition (breakout) will eventually retrace for a retest and regenerate sequence. A few words are needed in preparation, however.

The raw data shows that roughly 97 to 98 percent of all breakouts eventually retrace into the retest and regenerate zone, but there is a reasonably significant standard deviation attached to the numbers when considering just how many bars it takes for the retrace to occur.

From a trading perspective, if a retrace takes more than roughly 60 bars to retrace, then it probably has little value. Most important, since time frames are viewed as a sequence of roughly 60 bars per chart, a retrace that takes longer than 60 bars will not even be witnessed in most cases.

A second issue is that the longer it takes, then the less value it likely has. More work needs to be done to determine if a delay of greater than

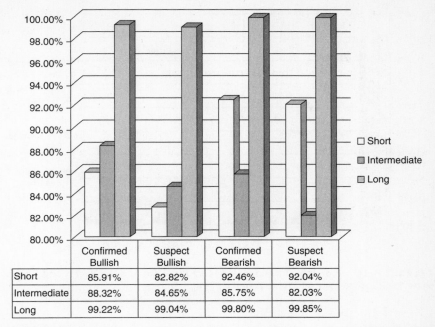

	Confirmed Bullish	Suspect Bullish	Confirmed Bearish	Suspect Bearish
Short	85.91%	82.82%	92.46%	92.04%
Intermediate	88.32%	84.65%	85.75%	82.03%
Long	99.22%	99.04%	99.80%	99.85%

FIGURE 5.9 Percentage of All Breakouts That Retest and Regenerate within 60 Bars

60 bars has a higher probability of failing on a retest and regenerate sequence versus one that occurs in less time, but a cursory look through the data tends to support that assumption.

Given these two items, Figure 5.9 addresses the question of just how many breakouts retrace to the retest and regenerate zone within 60 bars of having broken out.

As seen, the probabilities of a retest approach 100 percent for long-term trend, while bearish trends tend to retest and regenerate or fail at a higher rate than bullish trends in general. The takeaway is that if you feel you must chase a breakout, then bullish trends would be where you would concentrate your efforts. Even so, realize that even in the worst case, more than 82 percent of all bullish breakouts will retest and attempt to regenerate within 60 bars.

Although one could leave the analysis at that, there is actually more to be gained from further scrutinizing the data. The data shown in Figure 5.9 can be further broken down in smaller time slices, and that is what Figure 5.10 does, incorporating more time granularity into the retrace probabilities (Table 5.2 does not contain this granularity), and finds that

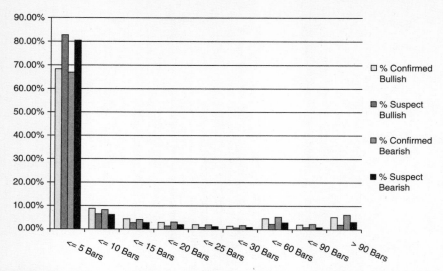

FIGURE 5.10 Probable Duration between a Breakout and the Retest and Regenerate Sequence across All Trend Types and Time Frames

roughly two-thirds of all trade breakouts typically retrace within five bars of the breakout (<= 5 bars).

Looking more closely at this figure, one can see that suspect breakouts (both bullish and bearish) witness a much higher retrace probability as compared to confirmed breakouts—on the order of 10 to 15 percent more.

WHAT IS THE TRADING SIGNIFICANCE?

Suspect breakouts should almost never be bought (the only exception is noted in Chapter 7 for breakout trade set-ups). The odds of a reasonably quick retest and regenerate attempt are extremely high (80 + percent) overall. It is far better to let it retrace and see how it retraces and then decide whether to enter a trade.

In general, even buying confirmed breakouts should be done with the idea of a quick trade (with the exception of those trades that fit the breakout trade set-up contained in Chapter 7) as the retrace probabilities are almost 70 percent.

Although the information presented in Figure 5.10 is eye-opening, more can be gleaned by viewing the data in a slightly different form. Figure 5.11 displays the same data on a cumulative basis.

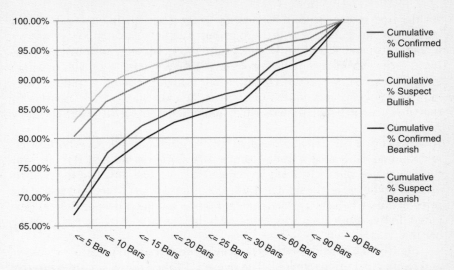

FIGURE 5.11 Cumulative Probable Duration between a Breakout and the Retest and Regenerate Sequence across All Trend Types and Time Frames

When viewed cumulatively, it is easier to see that the bulk of breakouts retest and regenerate within 15 bars. Fully 90 percent of all suspect bullish trends do so, and more than 80 percent of all confirmed trends do so as well.

Note the significant increase in probabilities for a retrace of both bullish and bearish suspect breakouts as compared to confirmed breakouts. Chasing suspect breakouts is generally not a good idea.

WHAT IS THE TRADING SIGNIFICANCE?

With the probabilities heavily favoring a retrace within 15 bars for all breakout qualified trend types, longer term traders/investors should almost always await the first retrace off a breakout rather than chase the move higher. In general, it is hard to justify a breakout trade unless it meets the set of criteria defined in Chapter 7.

Given the fact that almost all breakouts eventually retrace and that most do so rather quickly, the next question to ponder has to do with the probability of a failure when a retrace does occur. Just how likely is it for the first retrace to fail? Is it more likely if the qualified trend type is suspect versus confirmed? Is there useful knowledge available that allows a trader to more intelligently pick and choose which trades to take during the retest and regenerate process? Clearly, buying a bullish or short selling a bearish suspect breakout is not a high probability trade as previously demonstrated, unless one moves quickly on the trade relative to the time frame being traded. But should the retrace be used to enter a position?

Answering this question is slightly more difficult because both price and volume can cause a trader to exit a position on the first retrace, and these two stop out factors are both dependent on just how fast the retrace occurs. To be clear, the data in Table 5.2 assumes that a stop out based on price occurs when the retrace ends up retracing much deeper than anticipated. In this study, that was assumed to be the far end of the swing point bar that was broken.

Figure 5.12 considers the case where the retrace in price is extensive and results in a price stop out. The figure is broken down according to the qualified trend type and segmented into two groups: retraces that occur within six bars and those that occur after six bars.

Although the probabilities are not heavily skewed toward failure on the first retest and regenerate sequence due to a price stop out, the failure rate is not insignificant. It ranges from 11.3 to 22.5 percent, depending on the qualified trend type.

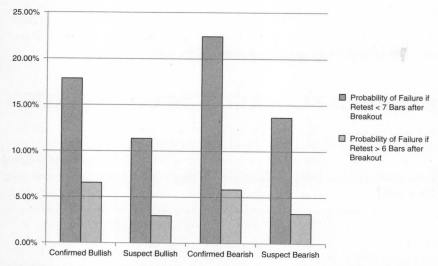

FIGURE 5.12   Probability of First Retest and Regenerate Sequence Trading beyond the Far Side of the Broken Swing Point Bar

Interestingly enough, suspect trends show up as less susceptible to a price stop out versus the confirmed trends, which is somewhat of a mystery. In looking through a random number of data points in an attempt to resolve this apparent discrepancy, the failure commonalities noted suggest that using the far side of the broken swing point bar many times results in a premature failure because the width of the swing point bar is miniscule. An alternative price stop out mechanism would be to use anchored support or resistance zones as discussed previously but that too carries its issues. As discussed in Chapter 4, the Average True Range (ATR) when combined with anchored support or resistance offers the greatest promise. Further research should concentrate on optimizing some combination of the far side of the breakout bar and anchor zone violations or ATR based percentages complementing anchored zones, where the zone has significance. As with most things, improvements can almost always be made, but in life and trading you continue on making decisions with the best knowledge that is available at the time.

WHAT IS THE TRADING SIGNIFICANCE?

When trading, if the broken swing point bar's extreme opposite price point is reasonably close (1 or 2 percentage points) to the breakout bar's closing price, then the price stop out when entering a trade either on the breakout or the first retrace (when that retrace occurs within six bars) should ideally be based on anchored support or resistance combined with the ATR, as described in Chapter 4, rather than the far side of the breakout bar. This greatly increases the probability of a trade success. If the reward-to-risk parameters do not align with this more conservative stop loss order, then the potential trade should be skipped. From a trading plan perspective, this argues strongly for scale in techniques when establishing a position so that the average entry price is more favorable.

Switching from price to volume stop outs, the same type of analysis was performed as with price. As part of that investigation, it became clear that comparing volume on the retrace to the swing point bar is a mistake if the retrace occurs reasonably quickly. First elaborated on in *Trend Qualification and Trading*,[3] this implied assumption appears to have missed the mark.

---

[3]L.A. Little, *Trend Qualification and Trading*, 105.

Given the data presented in Figure 5.10, we now know that a quick retrace is overwhelming likely. Taking this to its logical conclusion, the data clearly indicates that a fast retrace on a swing point break where volume expands significantly increases the likelihood of volume being heavier than the swing point when the retrace occurs. In fact, the increased probability of volume being heavier on the retrace if compared to the swing point bar as compared to the breakout bar approaches 25 percent, and it is reasonably independent of the qualified trend type. Note that this is a *false failure* because further analysis reveals that comparing volume of the retrace to the breakout bar does not appreciably increase the occurrence of price stop outs.

WHAT IS THE TRADING SIGNIFICANCE?

When assessing the probability of a failure as price retraces, always compare volume to the breakout bar as the acid test. If volume expands on the retrace as compared to breakout bar, then the trade should be avoided as the probability increases that a price stop out will occur as well. From a trade entry perspective, a retrace that shows lighter volume when compared to both the breakout bar and the swing point bar has the highest probability for success. For those cases where volume is lighter than the breakout bar but heavier than the swing point bar, the trade is still viable and should not necessarily be avoided if the reward-to-risk parameters are convincing since the probabilities do not favor an immediate price stop out without first offering the opportunity to profit.

Figure 5.13 examines the probability of a volume based stop out in the same way that Figure 5.12 considered a price based stop out. The figure is broken down according to the qualified trend type and segmented into two groups: retraces that occur within six bars and those that occur after six bars.

Figure 5.13 highlights the fact that in both suspect trends (bullish and bearish) where the retrace happens quickly, the volume stop out failure rate is around 20 percent, while for confirmed trends it is under 10 percent. The larger take away from this chart is that, like price stop outs depicted in Figure 5.12, if the first retrace and retest sequence comes after more than six bars have transpired, the failure rates for the retrace are extremely low, comparatively.

Taking this analysis one step farther, Figure 5.14 combines Figures 5.12 and 5.13 to get a cumulative look at failure based on price or volume on the first retrace. This is the complete picture for the probability of a failure on the first retrace based on how quickly that retrace transpires.

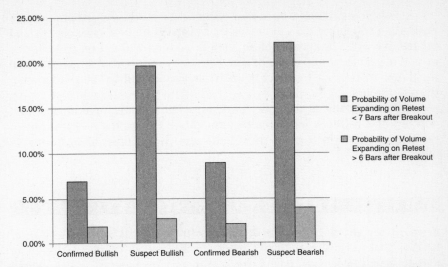

FIGURE 5.13 Probability of First Retest and Regenerate Sequence Seeing Volume Expand Compared to the Breakout Bar

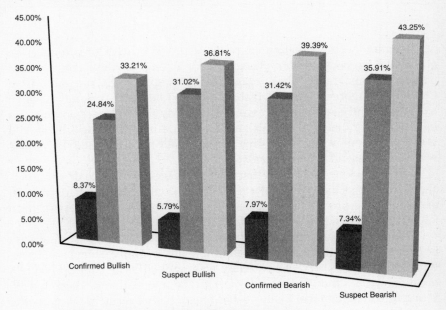

FIGURE 5.14 Cumulative Probability of the First Retest and Regenerate Sequence Stopping Out Based on Price or Volume

A few points should be noted about Figure 5.14 before continuing. First, the probability data indicates that even in the best case (confirmed bullish), roughly 25 percent of all such breakouts will fail on either price or volume on the first retrace if that retrace comes within six bars of the breakout. Worst case (suspect bearish) breakouts will fail more than one-third of the time.

A second point is that the cumulative failure rate for both fast and delayed first retraces indicates that roughly 33 percent to 40 percent of the retraces end in a price or volume stop out. Those are reasonably high numbers.

WHAT IS THE TRADING SIGNIFICANCE?

When 33 percent to 40 percent of all first retraces fail, it is a pretty clear indication that to consistently make money in the market a trader and even an investor needs to consider taking partial profits if a breakout trade was entered into and the market rewards the trader in the short run.

Another observation is that retraces off of bearish breakouts have about a 6 percent greater probability of failing on their retrace than confirmed breakouts. When combining this data with the data from Chapter 2 (Figures 2.7 and 2.8) that indicated bearish breakouts have an extremely high likelihood of extending quickly to profit targets, one can only conclude that if a bearish breakout trade is taken it will likely end very quickly one way or the other. If the trader does not take the money when price extends, the market will.

Figure 5.14 also indicates that a stop out based on price or volume is significantly less likely to trigger if the retest comes after six bars. In such a situation, the probabilities diminish significantly to between 6 percent to 8.3 percent, depending on the qualified trend type.

Continuing along this same path, probably the most revealing data point is that an overwhelmingly high probability of experiencing a successful trade is tied to a trader patiently waiting for the first retrace once a breakout occurs that has some legs to it. The implication of "having legs" is that the breakout most likely pushes higher before retracing because the retrace transpires only after more than six bars have printed.

Looking again at the raw data in Table 5.2 as well as the graphical representation of that data in Figures 5.12 and 5.13, the probability of a stop out occurring after more than six bars have printed is minimal for a first retrace. Viewed from the opposite angle, there is roughly a 65 percent to 85 percent probability of trade success if a trade is entered into on the first retest and regenerate sequence that comes only after six bars have transpired.

A trader can further increase the probabilities by paying close attention to volume characteristics of the retrace for the retrace and regenerate sequence prior to entering the trade. In this case, a trader can push her probabilities of trade success into the 95th percentile since the failure rate is reduced to the probabilities indicated in Figure 5.12 for retests after six bars.

WHAT IS THE TRADING SIGNIFICANCE?

When price retraces for the first time following a breakout, if the retrace comes after more than six bars have transpired since the breakout occurred, a trader can almost blindly enter a position in the direction of the breakout since the probability of failure rate averages less than 8 percent across all qualified trend types. By examining volume characteristics, though, the probability of a winning trade can be pushed into the 95th percentile.

Clearly, the first retrace that comes after the first six bars is something a trader should pay careful attention to when staking out potential trades, but what about subsequent retraces? Assuming that the first retest and regenerate sequence does not fail, then how does the eventual failure materialize? Does volume on a subsequent retrace provide a tip off to exit a trade or to avoid entry/reentry, or does the retrace occur on lighter volume and a price stop is triggered?

Figure 5.15 considers those possibilities graphically by mapping Scenarios 5 and 6 from Table 5.2. What this reveals is that there is a huge difference in how the eventual failure materializes. The distinguishing characteristic is tied to—what else—the quality of the trend type. Suspect trends are about 50 percent more likely to stop out some time after the first successful retest and regenerate sequence due to volume escalation on a subsequent retrace.

The most salient takeaway from this chart is that the market is usually kind enough to provide information that the end is near, and it does so with volume expansion. This is true of bullish and bearish trends alike but clearly more so for suspect trends. Before price stops out, volume expands and provides the early warning sign.

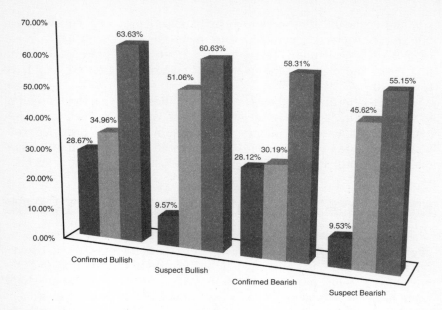

FIGURE 5.15 Failure Probability Characteristics after One or More Successful Retest and Regenerate Sequences

■ Probability of a stop out based on price after initial successful retest and regenerate

■ Probability of a stop out based on volume expansion after initial successful retest and regenerate

■ Cumulative probability of stop out based on volume and price after intitial successful retest and regenerate

WHAT IS THE TRADING SIGNIFICANCE?

A trader should always monitor volume on subsequent retraces for an early tipoff that price has a higher probability of failing the subsequent retest and regenerate sequence. This is even more necessary when the breakout was suspect to begin with. Suspect trends, as we know, have a greater probability of earlier failure as compared to confirmed trends, and it turns out that like the coal miner's canary, volume provides the early warning sign that something is awry.

Note that this opens the possibility of preparing for a trade in the opposite direction as well, for the death of one trade creates the birth of another in the opposite direction.

Finally, what does the distribution look like for multiple retests and regenerate attempts? How do the failures occur and what does the

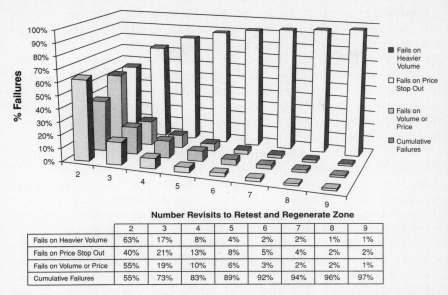

	2	3	4	5	6	7	8	9
Fails on Heavier Volume	63%	17%	8%	4%	2%	2%	1%	1%
Fails on Price Stop Out	40%	21%	13%	8%	5%	4%	2%	2%
Fails on Volume or Price	55%	19%	10%	6%	3%	2%	2%	1%
Cumulative Failures	55%	73%	83%	89%	92%	94%	96%	97%

FIGURE 5.16 Failure Frequencies for Subsequent Visits to the Retest and Regenerate Zone

distribution look like? How high is that failure rate? Does it happen because of volume swelling on the second revisit, or is it because price stops out? On the first revisit that ended in failure, volume swelled. Is that true of the second? How about the third and fourth?

Figure 5.16 considers subsequent retraces after that first successful retrace has occurred and the failure rates that show up there. What you find is that volume swells on subsequent retests as well, which leads to failed retest and, on average, all retraces that did not fail on the first retrace do so by the fifth, where 90 percent of all breakouts are done. The odds of getting through three successful retests of the retrace and regenerate zone are heavily stacked against a trader, with fully 73 percent of all those failing.

As with most things in trading, the first test is almost always the best test. If there's one rule to remember, file that one away as worth its weight in gold.

SUMMARY

For a trader, the most important time in the market is the time tied to a test. It does not matter what time frame one uses, a test is the time when the market is forced to release information about its intentions. It is the point in time when the collective consciousness of all traders is brought to bear in terms of price and volume. It is the time when decisions have to be made, one way or the other. If the buying pressure is greater than the selling pressure at the time of a test, price will move higher. If not, then lower. The fact that a test results in price moving higher or lower is not the most significant item of information released once the test is complete. The real informational nugget has to do with how the test unfolded as compared to what was being tested. That is where one's focus should lie.

It has been shown that there really is not an abundance of test types but instead just a handful. There are breakout tests and retrace tests, and those two test types occur in both directions. The results of these two test types yield only four possible outcomes: either a breakout test succeeds in trading beyond what is being tested, or it fails and stays within the boundaries of what was tested. The same is true of retrace tests.

If viewed in this way, then probabilities regarding these possible outcomes can be examined. Such an examination does not happen in the vacuum of just price, however, but within the context of volume and time as well. In this holistic view, true probabilities can be associated with real outcomes and can guide traders in their quest for profits. It is only with this backdrop can higher probability trades be recognized for what they are—having a greater probability of a successful outcome.

At this juncture an abundance of data has been uncovered and related to you—the potential trader/investor. So far the data analysis, though detailed, probably remains somewhat abstract, so the next chapter takes the groundwork laid here and in previous chapters and begins to apply it to actual trades. The desire is to take actual charts and show how these nuggets of information can be used to both uncover and capitalize on the higher probability trading possibilities.

In each case, the conditions supporting trade entry are outlined, charts are marked up clearly demonstrating those conditional set-ups, and example trading strategies are outlined. They are example trading strategies because in the end, the amount of risk you or the next trader takes is a personal preference. What are not personal are the probabilities that apply to the trade.

As has been emphasized so far, the best trades have the highest trade success probability that, when combined with a sufficiently high reward-to-risk ratio, creates an excellent trading opportunity. In the end, my friends, recognizing that and acting upon it is what separates the good traders from the great ones.

CHAPTER 6

Sideways Range Trades

E ach of the preceding chapters was, in a way, simply the preparation for the actual trade set-ups. Although an oversimplification, there are nevertheless basically two ways to trade. A market participant trades either breakouts or retraces, which happens to demarcate most traders because one typically falls into one camp or the other.

For all trade set-ups, the basic data that is always available and at the market participant's disposal are price, volume, and time. From this basic data the market participant creates information. Over the years, the information created from these basic elements ranges from the simple to the complex. This book argues to keep it simple. In terms of derived information, it strongly suggests that all a market participant truly requires to trade profitably are qualified trends and anchored support and resistance bars and zones. There are a few additional technical constructs utilized during trading, but they are not actually derived information but instead existing data elements such as price magnets, two bar reversals, and AB = CD constructs. Each of these constructs was identified and explained in *Trend Qualification and Trading*,[1] and though I am not the originator of the concepts, I find value in their use. In the trade set-ups that follow, their existence is pointed out where useful and applicable.

---

[1]L.A. Little, *Trend Qualification and Trading* (Hoboken, NJ: John Wiley & Sons, 2011), 167–187.

By adding in the notion of time, additional information is possible as demonstrated through the probability matrixes displayed in Chapters 1 through 3 based on trend and trade failure probability rates. That work suggests that market participants can and should incorporate expected failure probabilities into their trading decisions.

Thus, the remainder of this book weaves all these concepts together using qualified trends to recognize preferred trade direction and all the other data constructs and derived information to actually trade the trade set-ups as identified and illustrated. Note that all the trade set-ups presented are available across all time frames ranging from one minute to yearly bars. The concepts are the same independent of the time frame.

TRADE SET-UP CONDITIONS AND CATEGORIZATIONS

An important and significant point that is many times overlooked in trading is that the same trade set-up does not provide the same value or success/failure percentages over time. The reason for this is that each and every trade set-up does not trade in a vacuum. For example, a trade set-up of "Retrace to swing point after a breakout" operates differently in terms of the success characteristics if the general market trend has strength in the direction of the breakout versus if it does not. This is one example of an obvious influence, but there are others that are particular to the stock itself, as shown in Table 5.2 in Chapter 5.

To aid the presentation and understanding of each trade set-up, a matrix is utilized and presented at the beginning of each trade set-up section consisting of what can be thought of as preconditions that outline the ideal conditions that increase the odds for trade success. The matrix consists of the following elements:

- Definition—This defines the characteristics and objectives of the trade.
- Alignment Conditions—Unless you are trading the highest level instrument (the general market), there are technical influences on the success of the trade that are outside the instrument itself. Although there are undoubtedly others, the technical influences considered here are the general market and sector qualified trends. Those broader influences are used to form a trading bias for a given time frame. The trading bias can be confirmed or suspect bullish, bearish, or sideways.
- Trade Triggers—Trades are triggered when certain conditions are met. The trade triggers specify those conditions.

TRADING SIDEWAYS TRENDS

There are three types of trends: sideways, bullish, and bearish. Bullish and bearish trade set-ups are somewhat similar and more numerous. Sideways trading set-ups are limited because a sideways trend essentially denotes a range. There is not a lot that can be done with a sideways range other than to sell the top of the range and buy the bottom. Sometimes both trades are possible (buying range bottoms and selling tops). Other times they are not.

Two other trade possibilities for a sideways trend occur when the sideways range meets its demise. One possibility is to trade the breakout while the other is to let the breakout occur, then trade the retrace back to the breakout area. Trading the breakout or the retrace off the breakout overlaps with breakout and retrace trades in general for bullish and bearish trends; thus, it is not covered separately here but instead in Chapter 7.

When considering trading a sideways trading range, it is important to realize that although sideways trends tend to fail reasonably quickly (as was shown in Figures 1.12 through 1.14 in Chapter 1), that does not mean that sideways trading ranges will necessarily fail quickly. The fact that sideways trends fail quickly does not equate to the assumption that sideways trading ranges will fail as quickly and thus cannot be traded. To better understand this statement, Figure 6.1 illustrates the thought graphically.

In this chart it is easy to see the sideways range trade that has developed, yet a close examination shows the qualified trend to have remained bearish through this entire period for this long-term time frame.

The fact that sideways range trades do not require a trend transition to a sideways trend clearly delineates the difference between the concepts of sideways trends and sideways range trades. They are separate and distinct. What typically happens is that most sideways range trades contain a sideways trend at least for some portion of the sideways trading range. There are many examples of sideways range trades consisting of sideways trends mixed with trend transitions to and from both bullish or bearish trends (and sometimes both). This happens frequently if the sideways trading range is broad (top to bottom range) and especially if the time frame being traded is reasonably shorter term in duration.

A market participant might ask if there are any significant markers that alert a market participant to the potential development of a sideways trading range, and there are. In trading literature, sideways trading ranges are many times referred to as *consolidation ranges* and for good reason because sideways trading ranges generally result as a need to consolidate gains or losses after a fast price appreciation or depreciation (large percentage move in a relatively short period of time) which eventually exhausts itself.

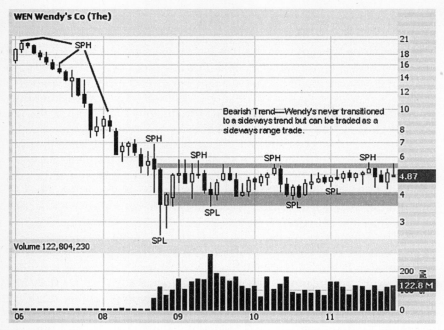

FIGURE 6.1 Wendy's Sideways Trading Range (WEN) (November 1, 2006 to November 1, 2011)

WHAT IS THE TRADING SIGNIFICANCE?

Reasonably early recognition of a trade set-up is a critical element to trade success. For a sideways trading range set-up, the key is to realize that the sideways range is under construction, and the most prevalent signal is a fast price appreciation or depreciation over a relatively short period of bars that witnesses one or more (clustered) anchor bars (wide price spread and/or high volume) at the apex of the fast move.

Finally, range trades come in two flavors—those that allow a market participant to exploit each side of the range and those where the market participant should limit his trades to just one side of the range. The terminology used for the purposes of discussing these are a *one-sided range trade* and for the former a *two-sided range trade*.

Like most things in trading, general definitions and rules are applicable, but the target is moving. As a pattern unfolds, each bar that prints can change the character of the trade set-up. For example, a range trade may begin as a two-sided range trade, but as it develops, it may turn into a one-sided range trade set-up because the conditions change. All trading and trade set-ups require constant monitoring because *trades are evolutionary—not static.*

The determination of whether both the tops and bottoms of the range can be traded is primarily conditioned upon three factors:

1. The alignment conditions for the general market and sectors as compared to the instrument being traded for the duration of the trade.
2. The strength of the tests. Each test of the edge of the trading range (as identified through anchored support and resistance zones) must be examined in the context of the strength of the current price and volume as compared to the anchor bars that form the anchor zone. Test failures that occur on lighter volume support the notion that the range trade remains valid.
3. The number of tests that occur over time. Ranges, like trends, have a life cycle and though no data analysis has been performed to justify and quantify this observation, generally speaking, four or five tests on each side of the range is about all that one can expect to occur prior to a breakout occurring.

In the trade set-up examples that follow, more elaborations are included to try to remove any ambiguities that may exist.

One- and Two-Sided Range Trade Set-Ups

For the one-sided range trade, the trade set-up conditions exhibited in Table 6.1 apply.

As described previously, almost all sideways range trade set-ups come off of a fast price thrust (relative to the time frame being examined) that creates a higher probability for consolidation to take place. Figure 6.2 is a chart of Las Vegas Sands Corporation and exhibits this behavior surging almost 100 percent in price in just two short months. The thrust higher exhibits the wide price spread and high volume anchor bars clustered together at the apex of the move.

The resistance zone initially sets up as a result of the wide price spread anchor bars (four of them) that all exhibit high volume at the time of their creation. A market participant grows more confident that it is indeed a resistance zone because the zone begins to contain subsequent price rise attempts.

The support zone, however, takes a very long time to set up. It was not until February and March of 2011 that prices began to cascade lower,

TABLE 6.1   Ideal One-Sided Range Trade Set-Up Conditions

Definition	In a one-sided range trade set-up, a market participant purchases near the perceived bottom of the range with the intent of selling those positions near the perceived top of the range *or* short sells near the perceived top of the range with the intent of buying those positions back near the perceived bottom of the range.
Ideal General Market and Sector Alignment Conditions	For a stock that exhibited bullishness prior to the sideways range trade set-up, the ideal case is a bullish sector and general market trend.
	For a stock that exhibited bearishness prior to the sideways range trade set-up, the ideal case is a bearish sector and general market trend *or* a sideways sector and general market trend.
Ideal Stock Trade Triggers	Consolidation sideways trading ranges typically begin at the conclusion of a wide price spread and/or high volume bar that marks the end of a relatively fast price appreciation or depreciation.

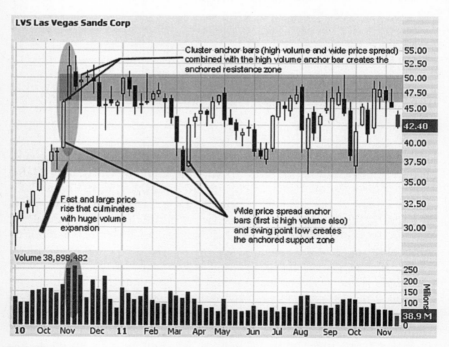

FIGURE 6.2   Las Vegas Sands—The Potential Set-Up of a Sideways Trading Range (LVS) (November 1, 2006 to November 1, 2011)

eventually reaching the bottom of the hammer candle bar that immediately preceded the huge escalation of price back in late October and early November. That dark candle from the week of March 14 ended up marking the bottom. The sideways range became recognizable when price gapped higher the next week and proceeded to run straight back up.

If Las Vegas Sands had been on a trader's watch list as a possible buy candidate on the retrace, the reversal off the dark candle was the signal. At this juncture a trader who recognizes the need for consolidation is probably thinking about a one-sided sideways range trade, but this could easily double as a retrace buy trade set-up as well to the more untrained eye. Either way it becomes a buy on the reversal. The trader thinking one-sided range trade has the advantage of realizing she will need to take profits into resistance, however, whereas the retrace buy trade set-up trader probably will not.

If a market participant did not catch the trade to get long as the support zone was finally formed, then he would have to wait for a subsequent visit to the support zone in order to get long because the general market bias is bullish as well and, thus, did not support shorting the stock at the top of the range. The general market trend that prevailed at this point in time makes this a one-sided trade (see Figure 6.3).

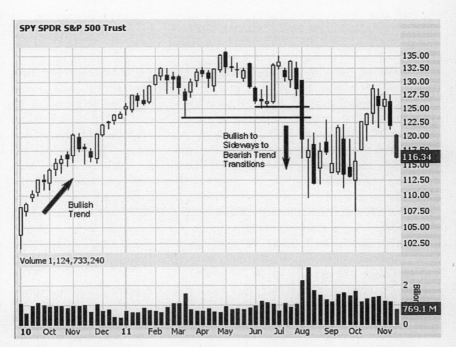

FIGURE 6.3   SPDR S&P 500 ETF Supporting a One-Sided Trade Set-Up (SPY) (August 30, 2011 to November 21, 2011)

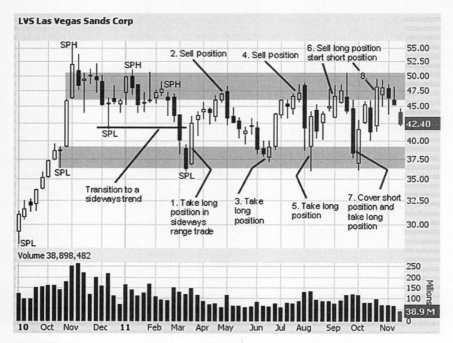

FIGURE 6.4 Las Vegas Sands—Trading the Sideways Trading Range Set-Up (LVS) (November 1, 2006 to November 1, 2011)

As can be seen, the general market remained in a bullish trend until August of 2011. With the general market exhibiting a bullish bias that is congruent with the trend that prevailed for Las Vegas Sands prior to the sideways trading range developing, a market participant cannot assume that the sideways range trade will remain a sideways trading range and risk shorting the stock near the top of the trading range. That simply is not a prudent high probability trade. Short trades when the general market bias is bullish are simply too difficult to win at. That is also true of shorting a sideways range.

Figure 6.4 outlines how trading a one-sided sideways trading set-up works, assuming a market participant was nimble enough to get in at the price area labeled as 1. After the price rises to the anchored resistance zone, the trade would be to sell the position previously purchased and to wait again for a decline (see 2 on the chart).

A long position could be entered into again at point 3 and sold once more at 4. The long position is taken because all the criteria are still met, including the fact that as price declines, volume does not increase to a level that is equal to or exceeding that of the anchor bars it is testing. Those anchor bars are the two bars that define the anchored support zone. Compare the volume there with the volume at point 3. No comparison implies a higher probability that the trade will succeed (price will turn and head the other direction once more).

The final purchase during the one-sided trading scenario comes again at 5, and though volume has increased, once again it is not nearly as significant as that witnessed on the anchor bars. After this trade (5), conditions change because the general market condition changes. A look back at Figure 6.3 shows the general market bias shifting when the time arrives to sell the long position (6). Given that general market bias shift, a market participant can likewise shift his or her thinking and modify the trading strategy to accommodate short sells as well as just purchases at support. In the case of Las Vegas Sands, when the long position is sold at 6, a short position is also entered making it a two-sided range trade rather than just a one-sided one. Again, volume is considered on the price rise as compared to the anchor bars anchoring the support zone. This is true for both the sale of the long position as well as the initiation of the short sell position.

Consider for a moment an alternate case where a market participant is long Las Vegas Sands as it reached the resistance zone, and rather than seeing comparative volume less, volume instead begins to swell to as much or even greater levels than the anchor bars supporting the zone. What should a market participant do then?

Since a range trade will eventually end, the astute market participant should either hold the position until a test of the top of the resistance zone occurs and fails or conservatively sell just a portion of the position rather than all of it. Ideally a market participant would want to wait to see if a breakout higher may be in the offing. When volume begins to expand as the far side of the range is tested, there is an increased probability that price will break out of the sideways trading range because, for whatever reason, greater and greater numbers of shares are being purchased at higher prices. That is the gauge. The same would be true for the support side of the range on a short sell trade.

Keeping with this thought and assuming that a market participant sold shares short at 6 only to see price rise further over the next couple bars, should the market participant remain short? In this example, the answer is clearly yes and for two reasons. First, volume is not swelling to levels equal to or greater than the anchor bars that form the resistance zone. Second, stop placement should be above the resistance zone—*not within it*, as first discussed in Chapter 4. How far above is a great question so let us consider stop loss and profit exit orders next. This discussion is not limited to just this example but to all trades where a defined support and resistance zone are used for stop loss decision making.

Stop Loss and Profit Exit Order Placement A constant issue with trading is the placement of protective stops and profit exit orders. Stops are required because risk is the only thing you can control in trading (and even then only partially as there is overnight risk when the markets are closed). An order to exit a position once a target profit is realized is just the flip side of the same coin. Without consistently booking profits in your trading and investing, you will find it very hard to consistently profit over time because eventually the market will take the paper gains away from you.

Order placement for stop loss and profit exit is always a difficult and critical question, so the stop loss calculations used for this first trade set-up are an example for all trade set-ups considered in the remainder of this book.

Remembering back, anchored support and resistance zones were described as ideal for timing for entry and exit because they exhibit verifiable significance. Trade exit can be triggered for both winning and losing trades by utilizing support and resistance zones. Both stop loss and profit exit orders are based on the same concept—it is just their placement that is different.

Where to place both stop loss and profit exit orders is critical. The general rule is that stop loss orders are always placed *beyond* where the anchored support zone is for long trades and the anchored resistance zone is for short sell trades. Profit exit orders are always placed at the nearest edge or somewhere inside the zone. The latter is straightforward but the former is not. Just how far is "beyond"?

As any market participant knows, the markets are not precise and for them to turn exactly at a particular price point is simply too much to ask for. It will almost never occur. Zones are constructed because they provide a price range to work with—a range that the market has indicated as having relevance. They simply are a better window to view the market through because price discovery is not exact. It never has been and never will be.

In Figure 6.4, the top of the anchored support zone is $39.15 while the bottom of the zone is $36.49. The corollary resistance zone has a top of $50.43 and a bottom of $46.28. From the trading examples described earlier, for the trade labeled 1, assume the purchase price was made at the top of the support zone at $39.16. Given the purchase price, where should the stop loss order be placed?

The primary consideration for how close a stop should be placed relative to the entry price should be related to how volatile the stock is. A very volatile stock is more likely to trigger a stop loss order than one that is not as volatile. One way to measure volatility is via the average true range (ATR). ATR is a measure of the average volatility of a trading instrument over some period of time. The concept of average true range was introduced in the late 1970s by Welles Wilder in his book *New Concepts in Technical Trading.*[2] His computational formula was as follows:

```
The true range indicator is the greatest of the following:
- Current high less the current low.
- The absolute value of the current high less the previous close.
- The absolute value of the current low less the previous close.
```

The formula takes the greatest of three possible ranges—a single bar's high/low range or the broader range created if a gap down or up in price occurs from one bar to the next. This is a good measure of a stock's volatility. When you sum these ranges over some period of time and then divide them by that same periodicity, you end up with the average. Wilder used a 14 bar periodicity. My experience is that, when used in conjunction with support and resistance bars as a stop out calculation, a periodicity of 10 bars yields a better volatility measure because it is slightly more reflective of the more recent price action, and that price action is what a market participant really cares about when trying to decide where a stop should be placed.

Once more, turning back to the Las Vegas Sands example, Figure 6.4 is a weekly chart thus the "bars" are weekly bars and the ATR over a period of 14 bars yields $6.03, while a 10 bar ATR is $6.44. Using the 10 bar ATR, the average range of the stock for each trading bar (in this case a weekly range) is roughly 15 percent if the bottom of the support zone is considered as the price point, or almost 11 percent if using the high of the anchored resistance zone. Any way you look at it, this is a volatile stock. For trading a sideways range, that is what you would prefer, though.

Assuming that the resistance zone is properly constructed, then at least one-fifth (less conservative) and, at most, one-fourth (more conservative) of the 10 bar ATR percentage can be used as an adequate guide as a stop out. Taking the calculations from the previous discussion, stop placement when purchasing Las Vegas Sands would have the less conservative stop placed at $36.40 while the more conservative stop would be placed at $36.13 using the following general formula:

```
Less Conservative stop placement for anchored support zone
Bottom of Anchored Resistance Zone - (Average True Range over
   10 bars * .2)

More Conservative stop placement for anchored support zone
Bottom of Anchored Resistance Zone - (Average True Range over
   10 bars * .25)
```

---

[2]J. Welles Wilder Jr., *New Concepts in Technical Trading* (Greensboro, NC: Trend Research, 1978).

For stop placement over an anchored resistance zone the formula is as follows: *To Stop out Short*

```
Less Conservative stop placement for anchored resistance zone
Top of Anchored Resistance Zone + (Average True Range over
   10 bars * .2)

More Conservative stop placement for anchored resistance zone
Top of Anchored Resistance Zone + (Average True Range over
   10 bars * .25)
```

In both cases (support and resistance zones), the stop is *always* placed on the other side of the zone. The assumption is that the zone should contain price as it presses into the area.

For profit exit, profits should be taken either at or into the anchored support (for short sell trades) and resistance zones (for long trades). Again, since anchored zones should serve to slow down and reverse price, taking profits once the zone is reached is the logical place to do so. How quickly profits are taken is a function of two things: the volume characteristics of the bar(s) when the test of the anchored zone occurs as compared to the anchor bars that comprise the anchored zone and how the stock's sector and general market are behaving simultaneously. If the stock sector and/or the general market begin to weaken while the stock being traded is trying to work higher, taking profits at the beginning of an anchored resistance zone would be wise. If stock sector and/or the general market are generally supporting the stock's move and if the volume characteristics are positive, then waiting until price moves into and toward the opposite edge of the zone is reasonable.

The calculation of stop loss and profit exit targets is not only about risk and money management, it is also a key component a market participant uses to decide if a trade should or should not be entered into, because unless the trade can yield at least two but preferably three times as much potential profit as it does potential loss, it probably is not worth taking. When combining this with the probability of a trade's success, then a market participant can make additional decisions with respect to position sizing and how aggressively or passively to scale in and out of a position. An introduction to those thoughts is considered next.

Entry and Exit Strategies   The typical entry and exit strategy is all in and all out. This is not the ideal strategy in most situations. Scaling into and out of positions offers the opportunity to both establish a position and to have the average price point where the entry price is lower than just jumping in all at once.

In Figure 6.4, take a close look at point 3. The top of the support zone is \$39.15 and the bottom is \$36.49. That is a spread of \$2.66. Assume that a market participant decides this one-sided range trade set-up is a good one and wants to start a position. In such a situation, a market participant does not know where price will stop declining once the support zone is reached. It could occur right at the top or bottom of the zone or anywhere in between, so why not scale into the trade with multiple orders placed at various intervals somewhere in this zone? Doing so offers a huge advantage that buying at one price level does not. The most significant advantage is that such a practice offers you the opportunity to start a position and then monitor whether or not the price and volume behavior support adding to that position. In this particular example, purchasing at the very start of the support zone and then again somewhere near the middle of the zone and finally once more near or at the bottom of the zone, if done properly, would actually provide a more favorable average price than just purchasing all the shares at the middle of the zone. Let us examine that statement more carefully using Figure 6.4 and the specific purchase made at the trade labeled as item 3.

In this particular example, assume price retreats with lighter volume as compared to the anchors and that a market participant both intends to and does scale into the position at 25, 35, and 40 percent scale ratio on the successive entry point suggested previously (top of the zone, the middle, and the bottom). This procedure in this example would provide two entries (25 percent at \$39.15 and 35 percent at \$37.82) at an average price of \$38.72. The competing strategy to buy everything at once would take the entire position at \$38.72. In this particular case, given the way things worked out, the all or nothing strategy would have performed better, because a full position was entered into and a profit exit was reached rather than a stop loss. In the scale in case, only the first two buys trigger so a lesser size is purchased as a result.

Now consider the same scenario for item labeled 5. In that case, the scale in method would create a better overall entry price, scaling in at \$39.15, \$37.82, and \$36.49 for an average price of \$37.62 rather than the \$37.82 price point for the all in method. Again, it can only be emphasized that the strength of the scale in approach is that it allows the market participant to measure how price comes into the areas where positions are being considered in order to make a real time decision as to whether the overall success of the trade continues to have a high probability. If it does not, then the market participant forgoes further purchases/short sales. If it does, then he or she proceeds. This many times results in smaller losses because the behavior of the stock is not conducive to further entry.

The disadvantage is that in many cases, a full sized position will not be reached. That could be viewed as a negative, but it really should not be and here's why. First off, if a full sized position is not achieved, what does that mean? It means one of two things—both of which are advantageous:

1. The trade is *necessarily succeeding* because the stop cannot be reached unless the position is full sized.

    Or

2. You have decided that the position should not be added to because the probability of trade success has deteriorated.

In both cases, isn't this desirable? If the position was made full, then the money that would have been put into this trade is simply allocated to another trade. If the position was not made full even though the opportunity to do so was available, then that says that the conditions have changed, which, in that case, you really do not want a full sized position in place as the odds are higher that the stop loss will be triggered. That is the very definition of a win-win trading plan.

Two-Sided Range Trade

Table 6.2 exhibits the trade set-up conditions for a two-sided range trade.

TABLE 6.2   Ideal Two-Sided Range Trade Set-Up Conditions

Definition	In a two-sided range trade set-up, a market participant purchases near the perceived bottom of the range with the intent of selling those positions near the perceived top of the range followed by a short sell near the perceived top of the range with the intent of buying those positions back near the perceived bottom of the range. The exchange of positions is generally performed either simultaneously or in close price and time proximity.
Ideal General Market and Sector Alignment Conditions	For a stock that exhibited bullishness prior to the sideways range trade set-up, the ideal case is a bearish or sideways sector and general market trend.
	For a stock that exhibited bearishness prior to the sideways range trade set-up, the ideal case is a bullish or sideways sector and general market trend.
Ideal Stock Trade Triggers	Consolidation sideways trading ranges typically begin at the conclusion of a wide price spread and/or high volume bar that marks the end of a relatively fast price appreciation or depreciation.

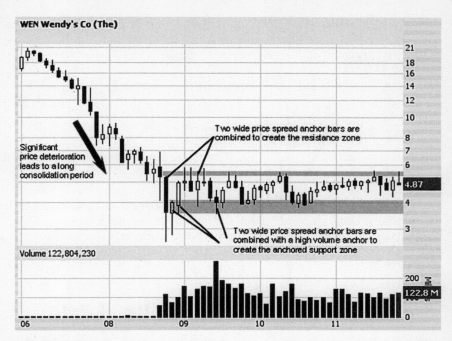

WEN Wendy's Co (The)

Volume 122,804,230

Significant price deterioration leads to a long consolidation period

Two wide price spread anchor bars are combined to create the resistance zone

Two wide price spread anchor bars are combined with a high volume anchor to create the anchored support zone

FIGURE 6.5   Wendy's Two-Sided Trading Range Set-Up (WEN) (November 1, 2006 to November 1, 2011)

The previous trade set-up example with Las Vegas Sands offered a good preview of a two-sided trade toward the end of the range since the conditions of the general market and sector changed. In the first chart displayed in this chapter (Figure 6.1), Wendy's exhibited a reasonably good two-sided sideways trading range set-up on a monthly time frame. As was indicated previously, the principles are the same across all time frames. In this case, significant price deterioration led to an exhaustion move at the end of the decline creating a huge wide price bar. Figure 6.5 is a repeat of Figure 6.1 with differing annotations showing the support and resistance zones.

The trade set-up is two-sided because by the time the range sets up in the middle of 2009, the general market has turned from decidedly negative to positive, as seen in Figure 6.6, while Wendy's has not.

Using the same thoughts presented in the one-sided trading example, once the anchored support and resistance zones can be constructed for Wendy's, the trade set-up produces six trading opportunities (four short sells and two longs), but only five had their full potential realized because the next to the last short selling opportunity never retraced far enough to

FIGURE 6.6 SPDR S&P 500 ETF Supporting a Two-Sided Trade Set-Up (SPY) (November 1, 2006 to November 1, 2011)

cash in and get long again. Each trade in this sideways trading set-up would have offered good scaled entry attributes, and using the ATR for stop loss order entry, all trades would have successfully concluded (except the last one, which has yet to complete).

Figure 6.7 is another example of a two-sided sideways trading range set-up, this time on a weekly time frame for eBay Inc. The set-up is defined by a fast price rise (a 30 percent rise in five weeks) that culminates with two wide price spread bars before a candlestick doji top forms.

The support zone is obvious from the prior swing point high, which roughly coincides with the high volume breakout bar near the middle of the chart ($28.37 and $28.44) that pushed into that swing point and broke it on the next high volume bar (middle of October 2010). Once the highs are in, and a subsequent retrace and spike higher occurs that fails, a resistance zone forms, creating the boundaries for the sideways trading range.

Figure 6.8 extends the time frame and is annotated with all the swing point highs and lows apparent on the chart. Trades into the resistance zone are short sells (only one occurs once the resistance zone is

FIGURE 6.7   eBay—A Two-Sided Trade Set-Up (EBAY) (March 15, 2010 to March 06, 2011)

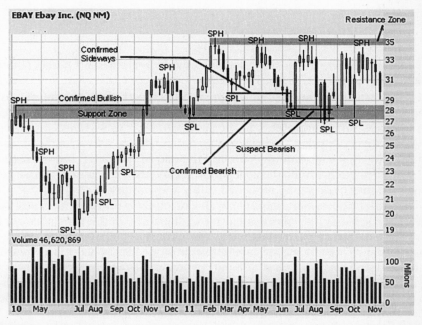

FIGURE 6.8   eBay—A Two-Sided Trade Set-Up Showing Qualified Trends (EBAY) (March 15, 2010 to March 06, 2011)

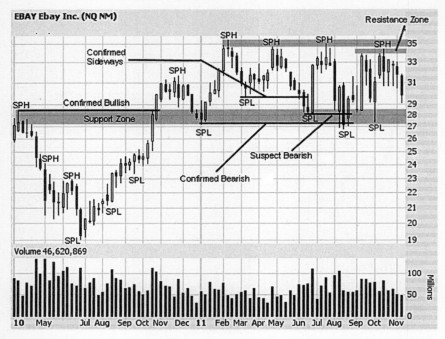

FIGURE 6.9 eBay—Evolution of the eBay Chart for a Two-sided Trade Set-Up (EBAY) (March 15, 2010 to March 06, 2011)

confirmed), while trades into the support zone are purchase points (three of these exist).

In a sideways range trade set-up, as indicated before, the trend need not remain sideways and may or not be sideways at all. The Wendy's chart was bearish the entire time, but it provided a sideways range trade set-up. For eBay the sideways trade set-up did occur when the qualified trend turned to confirmed sideways around the end of May 2011, but in August the trend actually turned to suspect bearish and then confirmed bearish yet the sideways trade set-up remained viable and workable.

As describe earlier, only two trades reach their potential because the final two sell and then short sale trades fall just shy of the resistance zone (toward the right side of the chart). This brings up an interesting point— support and resistance zones are not set in stone. Every chart is a work of art that is in progress. It is continually evolving and shifting as time passes. Figure 6.9 demonstrates how, given the information available at the time, a trade market participant would be justified in constructing a lower resistance zone as compared to the original one shown in Figure 6.8.

Given the way eBay had traded toward the end of the displayed time frame, it could easily be argued that the top tick of the wide price spread bar and the subsequent potential swing point high (the last bar annotated as SPH) created a smaller but valuable resistance zone for eBay and that full or at least partial profits should be taken into that resistance zone going forward.

WHAT IS THE TRADING SIGNIFICANCE?

Charts are not static—they evolve. They must be monitored continually because they are continually painting the picture that gives the market participant the knowledge needed to make wise trading decisions. To ignore the picture that they paint on a bar-by-bar basis is tantamount to asking for your money to be taken away.

Range trades are typically thought of as buying the bottoms and selling the tops of some defined range. Most market participants assume that the range is a constant that, from a trend perspective, is depicted by a sideways trend. Neither is necessarily true. That is one potential depiction of a sideways trading range, but it is not the only possible set-up as demonstrated in the preceding charts and examples.

Range Trade Breakdown

Eventually there will come a time where the range breaks down. It is inevitable. When that happens, there are a couple of trade set-ups that are possible, and they are described in Chapter 7 since they represent bullish or bearish breakouts or retrace buy set-ups after a breakout.

Conflicting Sector and General Market Qualified Trends

The ideal set-up in trading is rare. It is almost always a compromise. The trade set-up conditions outlined for one and two-sided range trades suggest the ideal. For a one-sided range trade, for example, the alignment conditions presented in Table 6.1 and repeated in Table 6.3 were for a bullish sector and general market trend immediate prior to the sideways trading range for the stock.

Figures 6.3 and 6.4 show the general market sector and the stock. The qualified trends for the sector were glossed over. Figure 6.10 displays the

TABLE 6.3 Ideal One-Sided Range Congruency Conditions

General Market and Sector Alignment Conditions	For a stock that exhibited bullishness prior to the sideways range trade set-up, the ideal case is a bullish sector and general market trend. For a stock that exhibited bearishness prior to the sideways range trade set-up, the ideal case is a bearish sector and general market trend *or* a sideways sector and general market trend.

sector chart, which, in this example, happens to provide an almost identical picture as the general market view.

In most situations, this is what a market participant will find—complementary trends for both the general market and the sector of which the stock is part. When the trends are not complementary, the general market tends to have a greater influence on the stock than the sector as was

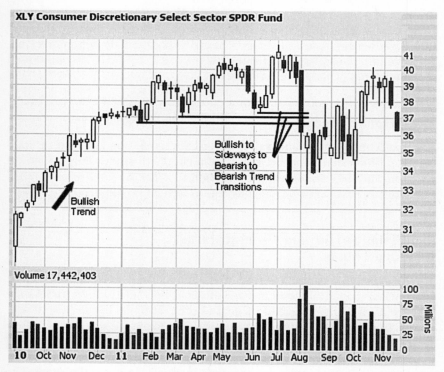

FIGURE 6.10 Consumer Discretionary Select Sector Fund (XLY) (August 30, 2011 to November 21, 2011)

demonstrated in Chapter 3, but the overall probabilities of the trade diminish because the sector influence is tugging in a different direction than the general market's influence. In the sideways trading range situation, this conflict can actually serve to support the continuation of a sideways trading range and is considered as such in the alignment conditions cited for a two side trading range set-up (see Table 6.2).

SUMMARY

Sideways trading ranges, as shown, are not necessarily part and parcel of a sideways trend, though many times a sideways trend is a major component of such a set-up. Independent of the trend, sideways trade set-ups almost always occur as the result of a fast extension of price in a short period of time that forces a period of price consolidation. In the classical technical literature, that consolidation is assumed to eventually break in the direction of the prevailing trend, but one need not trade a sideways trading range unidirectionally because of that. As was shown, the decision of whether to trade a sideways trading set-up in only one direction or two is dependent on the alignment factors associated with the general market and sector in which the stock trades.

Sideways trading ranges repeatedly appear in the charts for stocks, sectors, and the general market itself. When they become apparent, strategies that assume a continuation of an up or down trend are not profitable strategies to pursue. If the sideways trading range develops on the general market, then most stocks will be trapped in a sideways trading range set-up as well.

WHAT IS THE TRADING SIGNIFICANCE?

When a sideways trading range set-up is apparent in the general market, divergent strength and weakness in individual stocks and sectors becomes acutely visible. The same is true to a lesser degree of a sideways trading range in a sector and divergent strength in individual stocks. A market participant can use this knowledge to find and build a watch list containing the best of the best or the worst of the worst stocks and use that to her advantage in future trades.

Sideways trading strategies are generally limited to buying and selling the tops and bottoms of the range. They can represent high probability trades but are unlikely to provide the market participant with the rarer *great* trade. Sideways range trades have to eventually break out of their ranges to realize the greatness potential.

Fortunately, sideways trading set-ups are not the dominant trading strategy, just as sideways trends are not the dominant qualified trend. As shown in Chapter 1, the dominant trend is the bullish trend, and it is followed by the bearish trend and then the sideways trend; thus, the bulk of a market participant's trading is typically concentrated on bullish and bearish trend trading strategies.

Those strategies are described in the following chapter.

CHAPTER 7

Breakout and Retrace Trade Set-Ups

In Chapter 5, Table 5.2 considered the various probabilities surrounding breakout and retrace trades. Although the original intent was to focus just on the failure probabilities associated with the various retrace and breakout situations, as with any probability data, there is a mean as well a variance and thus outliers. Unlike many studies, the outliers in this study actually ended up being quite useful because they were representative of potential trading opportunities that hold great promise.

For example, it was shown that most swing point breakouts tend to come back quickly for a retest and regenerate sequence. Given this observable fact, one could ask if there is something in common for those cases that do not retrace within a few bars. If so, that would represent opportunity, and indeed the material below considers slow retrace trade set-ups and breakout trade set-ups as a result of studying the similarities within those data points.

The central thesis to this book was a promise to deliver a set of trade set-ups that were the *best* set-ups. *Best* was more or less defined as a trade where the reward outweighed the risk by at least 2:1, but more preferably 3:1 or 4:1, *and* the probability of the trade resulting in success was significantly greater than the probability of failure. To that end, the data analysis performed and detailed in Chapters 1 through 5 provided the framework to accomplish this grand goal. Having a good reward-to-risk ratio is great but does little for a trader if the failure probability of the trade is heavily skewed against the trade. Is it better to have a lower reward-to-risk payout with a 70 or 80 percent chance of the trade succeeding, or a higher reward-to-risk payout with a 20 or 30 percent chance of having a winning trade? That is the real question and the answer is obvious in my mind.

The first task in uncovering great trade set-ups is to recognize a common set of characteristics that increases the probability of trade success to nosebleed levels. Once understood, the task is to search for such set-ups on a regular basis, examining each to find those that offer the greatest reward-to-risk. With a high probability trade success outcome and a high reward-to-risk characteristic, you will enter those trades that hold great promise. This chapter focuses on those common high probability characteristics as they apply to the two basic trade set-up categories: retraces and breakouts.

In Chapter 6, these principles were applied to the trade set-up described as a sideways range trade. It was a good place to introduce the concept of trade triggers and ideal general market and sector alignment conditions to enable a trade to be taken. That same mind-set is followed here in Chapter 7 to describe and illustrate the *best* breakout and retrace trade set-ups. It is not as if there are an plethora of trade set-ups. Chapter 5 makes that clear. There are really only two types of trades, yet within those two trade types, there are a handful of excellent trade set-ups and that is what this chapter focuses upon. It is not quantity—its quality!

RETRACE TRADE SET-UPS

Retrace trades, as previously defined, are trades where a stock breaks through a defined support or resistance zone or swing point and, at some point in the future, retraces back to that breakout area. Although the data examined in Chapter 5 were limited to swing point breakouts, experience and some preliminary data analysis indicates that it is likely that the principals surrounding swing point breakouts and retraces are equally applicable to resistance and support zones. Future data analysis is needed to confirm this but the assumption for the trade set-ups presented in this chapter expects that relationship to hold. The trend direction can be bullish or bearish and generally they are traded in a similar manner. The primary difference is that bearish trades tend to exhaust themselves much faster comparatively.

Table 5.2 outlined seven scenarios of which the first four concerned retrace failure rates. Those retest and regenerate sequences were divided into two categories—those that retrace within six bars and those that retrace after more than six bars. The distinction of more than six bars and six bars or less was based on earlier work that indicated that retraces exhibited different testing characteristics depending on how long it took to retrace. Unbeknownst at the time, the success and failure characteristics for the retrace and regenerate sequence differs significantly depending on if the retrace is fast versus slow.

Fast Retrace into a Retest and Regenerate Sequence for Bullish Trends

Fast retraces into a retest and regenerate sequence are defined as those retraces that occur within six bars of the breakout. The trade success rate is not the highest available to a trader but, as was shown in Table 5.2, given the right trade triggers, the rate of success is enough to warrant serious consideration from a market participant.

Figures 7.1 and 7.2 illustrate a fast retest and regenerate sequence for a bullish breakout. As with all trading patterns, the time frame can be intraday, daily, weekly, or longer.

In Figure 7.1, McDonald's is an illustration of a fast retrace to perform a retest and regenerate sequence. In this example, McDonald's broke above the prior swing point high, then retraced back into the retest and regenerate zone three bars later. Note that this was a breakout on heavier volume

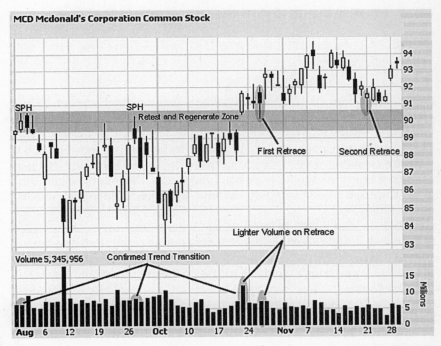

FIGURE 7.1 McDonald's Corporation—Short-Term Time Frame (MCD) (August 29, 2011 to November 29, 2011)

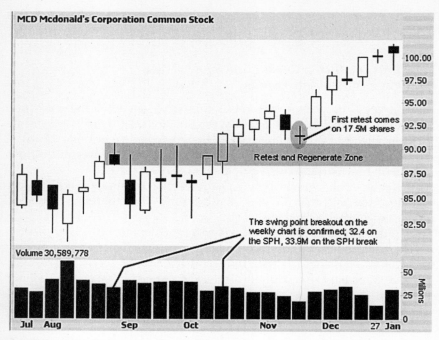

FIGURE 7.2 McDonald's Corporation—Intermediate-Term Time Frame (MCD) (July 18, 2011 to January 3, 2012)

and thus a confirmed breakout and trend transition—not suspect. As indicated in Chapter 5, there is a significantly high probability that confirmed breakouts retrace into retest and regenerate zones just as suspect trends. This fact was previously underappreciated. In fact, the entire retest and regenerate sequence was so termed because the expectation was that it applied to suspect breakouts—not confirmed ones. Clearly, the significance of a retrace and retest condition was not fully appreciated in prior qualified trend studies.

After the initial retrace to retest and regenerate, buyers of the retrace were able to get an extension higher to take partial profits into if so desired. A month later McDonald's retraced once more into the same retest and regenerate zone, which would mark the last time this would happen on this time frame.

Figure 7.2 is the same stock but on a weekly time frame, which reveals how differing time frames can be quite complementary and can add significantly to the analysis.

The second retrace on the short-term time frame seen in Figure 7.1 is the first retrace on the intermediate-term time frame shown in Figure 7.2, and here, as in Figure 7.1, the trend transition was confirmed on the breakout and the subsequent fast retrace (five bars) was a successful retest and regenerate sequence since volume was lighter on the test sequence as compared to both the breakout bar and the prior swing point bar.

As described in Chapter 5, this is an ideal case for a retest and regenerate sequence—lighter volume on the retrace as compared to the breakout bar. For further confirmation, volume on the retrace is compared to the prior swing point bar that was broken as well. This is applicable to both fast and slow retraces as shall be witnessed below.

Another important and previously unrealized fact is that these two charts lay witness to the concept of trend transitions being witnessed on multiple time frames simultaneously. In the case of McDonalds, both short and intermediate-term time frames transitioned trend and did so with confirmation. There's not much more one could ask for with respect to a high probability retrace trade set-up, as detailed in Table 7.1.

Recall from Figure 5.14 in Chapter 5, the cumulative probability of a failed retest and regenerate sequence averages out to a little less than one-third of all qualified breakout types if the retrace comes quickly. Confirmed breakouts show noticeably fewer failures comparatively, and in those situations where volume expanded on the retrace as compared to the breakout bar and the prior swing point bar that was broken, the failure rates were much higher. Given all of this, if a trader focuses on complementary signals across two or more time frames and pays close attention to volume comparisons on the retrace, suspect trends can be traded rather than ignored.

WHAT IS THE TRADING SIGNIFICANCE?

It is preferable to include suspect trends as tradeable trends rather than to simply ignore them as untradeable, since it was shown in Chapter 1 (Table 1.2) that suspect trends account for roughly 40 percent of all trends across all time frames. The caveat to the trader is that suspect trends will necessarily fail sooner (see Figure 1.4 in Chapter 1), so they are meant to be traded, not invested in for the long haul.

Figures 7.1 (second retrace) and 7.2 demonstrated an almost ideal trade set-up with respect to the stock trade trigger for a fast retrace trade. In these figures, the trends were confirmed; they were not extended and susceptible to trend failure yet, the volume on the retrace was light as compared to the breakout bar, and the intermediate-term time frame complemented the short-term time frame. Furthermore, the general market trend was also supportive although less than ideal, as shown in Figure 7.3.

TABLE 7.1   Ideal Retrace Trade Set-Up Conditions

Definition	In a retrace trade set-up, a market participant waits for the first retrace after a breakout to make a purchase (bullish breakout/retrace sequence) or a short sell (bearish breakout/retrace sequence). A fast retrace occurs within six bars, whereas a delayed retrace occurs after more than six bars have occurred but within 60 bars.
Ideal General Market and Sector Alignment Conditions	For a stock that experiences a bullish breakout prior to the retest and regenerate sequence, the ideal case is a bullish or sideways sector and general market trend for the same and next higher time frame and sector and market are not extended (the probability for trend failure relative to time duration is reasonably small).
	For a stock that experiences a bearish breakout prior to the retest and regenerate sequence, the ideal case is a bearish or sideways sector and general market trend for the same and next higher time frame, not extended (the probability for trend failure relative to time duration is reasonably small).
	Note: In both of the preceding cases, this will appear to be the case even when a long term major market transition is in its infancy, transitioning from bullish to bearish or from bearish to bullish. In such a case, more and more stocks will begin to show as divergent with the general market trend on the intermediate- and long-term time frames, and in this case the probability of a trend failure is higher than it appears to be. Anticipating long term trend changes, though fraught with error, is possible, but that's a subject for another time. This is the proverbial case where the trend is only wrong in two instances: at the top and at the bottom. It is the reason that a market participant must always protect their capital through judicious use of stop loss orders.
	Note also that for slow delayed retraces, if a short-term trend is to be traded, note that the short-term sector and general market trends may actually weaken, which should not necessarily dissuade a trader from making the trade. Look to the intermediate-term trend for guidance.

TABLE 7.1 (*Continued*)

Ideal Stock Trade Triggers	The trade triggers leading to the highest probability trades naturally consist of a number of factors. They include the following: • If applicable, complementary retest and regenerate signals across multiple time frames. Complementary retest and regenerate signals need not be simultaneous. • Confluent trends on the next higher time frame. • Trends that are not too extended as identified in the trend failure probability tables (see the Appendix) across each of the time frames at the time of the retest and regenerate sequence. • Light volume retest on the retest and regenerate sequence for the current time frame and, if applicable, across multiple time frames. • Confirmed breakouts have preference over suspect breakouts. Clearly the most ideal situation is where all three time frames break out together, are all confirmed and retest and regenerate with lighter volume compared to both the breakout bar and the prior swing point bar, and are supported by the general market and sector trends. Given the plethora of ideal conditions, it is unlikely that this case will be encountered other than a few rare times. The more likely case is to see a combination of these ideal conditions. The more, the better.

The reason for a less than ideal assessment is, first, because the trend transition in the general market is suspect—volume did not expand—and second, when McDonald's performed its first retest and regenerate sequence on the daily chart, the retest on the general market came on heavier volume. This sort of behavior where one market or stock is stronger or weaker than another is commonly referred to as *positive* or *negative divergence*. In this case, the stock was stronger than the market. If you want to purchase McDonald's stock, you would prefer both the stock and the market to be strong, but if there is divergence, you want the instrument you are trading to be stronger—not the other way around.

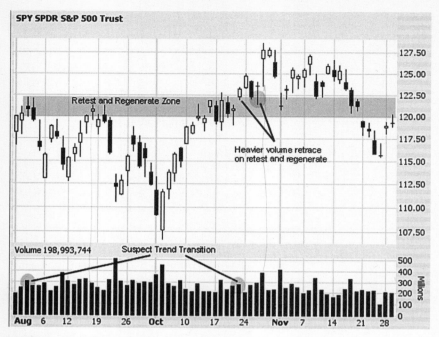

FIGURE 7.3   SPDR S&P 500 Trust—Short-Term Time Frame (SPY) (August 29, 2011 to November 29, 2011)

Finally, to wrap up this analysis, here is how the general market appeared at the time McDonald's did its first retrace on the retest and regenerate sequence for the weekly chart. Again, there is divergence and the stock is stronger than the general market.

Although the attributes surrounding the stock were ideal, clearly the general market is not the most ideal set-up on the broader market, as the trends are weaker. The trend transition was confirmed (good) for the broader market as seen in Figure 7.4, but the intermediate term is now a sideways trend, not bullish.

The reason for examining this first retest and regenerate trade set-up in such detail is to walk through all the questions that need to be asked and answered as presented in Table 7.1, for those criteria are the decision points that require sufficient affirmation in order to proceed with the trade. They are the ideal case. Few trades are ideal though, thus a trader needs to decide how much less than ideal is acceptable.

Markets are not precise. An overshoot and undershoot are to be expected. When trading, you have to build in a bit of error margin as was described in Chapter 6 with respect to stops. The same is true of entry into

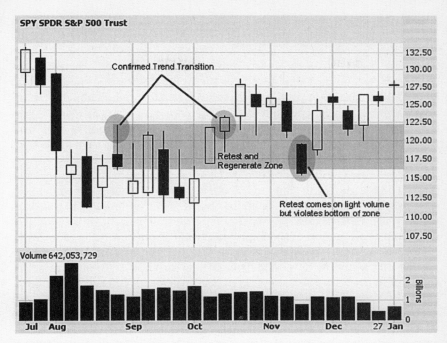

FIGURE 7.4 SPDR S&P 500 Trust—Intermediate-Term Time Frame (SPY) (July 18, 2011 to January 3, 2012)

a position. One cannot assume that a bit of an overshoot rules out the trade. It just has to be monitored carefully as a result. In the end, the probability of a trade succeeding or failing is based on all the data available, and rarely will all the data be perfectly aligned or available. If they were, most traders would be millionaires. The reality is always far from the ideal. The ideal is what you shoot for, but the reality is usually a bit less. View the trade in the context of all competing probabilities, and do not let one blemish dissuade you from the trade. What matters is, of all the trades possible of which a trader is aware, is this trade the best of the best and is that good enough to actually trade?

To continue with this analysis, another factor not yet incorporated is the failure rate probabilities presented in Chapters 1 through 3 for trend and trade failures. Essentially, when a bullish or bearish trend is in its infancy, it is a lot less likely to fail quickly as compared to when the trend is mature. All fast retest and regenerate sequences involving swing point breakouts are more likely to be in their infancy on the current time frame when the first retrace occurs. Table A1.1 from the Appendix shows that short-term confirmed trends ranging from one to five bars experience trend failure rates at less than 4 percent. Consulting the same table for short-term suspect trends (which is what the general market had transitioned to), the failure rate for one to five bars is just less than 5 percent. So, on a short-term time frame, the odds of the trend failing are reasonably small.

When examining Table A1.2 from the Appendix for intermediate-term trends, the failure rate probabilities for McDonald's remains highly favorable registering in at 4 percent again. This ends up being true for the general market as well since the trend transition on the intermediate-term time frame is from a bearish to a sideways trend. From Chapter 1 we know that, in general, 70 to 80 percent of all sideways trends fail within the first 15 bars (see "Sideways Trend Persistence" in Chapter 1). Now, it could be the case that the sideways trend "fails" and becomes bearish, but it is equally possible it "fails" and becomes a bullish trend. What is known, is that it is unlikely to remain sideways for very long and the benefit of the doubt is given to a continuation of the improving trend (from bearish to sideways).

So the bottom line question is, as it should be, should a trader have purchased the first retrace on McDonald's on the short-term time frame (as seen in Figure 7.1)? The answer is probably yes as it offered a high probability of trade success, and the reward-to-risk of the trade was favorable enough to make the trade. But "probably yes" is not good enough. When trying to decide if a trade is a high probability trade, it is best to list the key criteria and then see if, at the current time, a sufficient number of those criteria are met. If they are, then they get a check mark. If not, then they do not. If enough check marks are garnered, then the trade is worthwhile; otherwise it is not.

Using the McDonald's question of whether the first retrace should be bought, Table 7.2 sizes it up.

When working through the checklist and then adding up the number of criteria that are met, the McDonald's trade evaluates to seven out of nine possible check marks. Rather than trying to weight the values, a thumbs-up or -down is all that is needed. If six or more criteria are met, then enough positives are evident to indicate that the trade has a reasonably high probability of succeeding. Since only the highest probability trades should be considered, then only those that score high enough across the board should be considered. Realize that this will sometimes overlook trades that are worth taking, but on the flip side, it will keep a trader out of trades that should not be pursued.

With nine possible criteria to meet, after significant study it appears that the tipping point for a high probability is that six or more be met. Naturally, the more the better, but at least six are needed to qualify. Note that this checklist works for bullish and bearish trade set-ups.

Constructing a trade entry decision ledger is well worth the effort. It can be easily placed into a spreadsheet and removes a considerable amount

TABLE 7.2 Trade Entry Decision Ledger for McDonald's Corporation on First Retrace on Daily Time Frame

Item	True?	Description
General market aligned for the same time frame and is not extended	✓	Short-term trend suspect bullish
General market aligned for next higher time frame and is not extended	✓	Intermediate sideways
Sector aligned for the same time frame and is not extended	✓	Short-term trend suspect bullish
Sector aligned for next higher time frame and is not extended		Intermediate bearish
Trend for stock's current time frame is not extended	✓	Failure probability rate for short-term trend is <50%
Trend for stock's next higher time frame is not extended	✓	Failure probability rate for intermediate-term trend is <50%
Complementary retest and regenerate signals across multiple time frames *or* confluent trends on the next higher time frame	✓	Short and intermediate-term trends transitioned to bullish
Light volume retest on the retest and regenerate sequence		Heavier than breakout bar, lighter than prior swing point bar
Confirmed versus suspect breakout	✓	Confirmed
Total Criteria Met	7	If six or more items are true, then check potential reward versus risk to make a final trading decision

of the emotion from the entry decision. Does the trade add up or not? Which trades, among all the trades available, are the "best" trades? The decision table allows a trader to take a lot of the guesswork out of this decision process.

Carrying the example further, the same question of whether a trade is worth making is also applicable to the first retrace on the weekly time frame (Figure 7.2), which correlates to the second retrace on the daily time frame. Again, the answer is yes once the decision tree is constructed, as shown in Table 7.3

A couple more comments regarding values for the Decision Ledger rows are in order. For the failure rate probabilities, just use 50 percent as the dividing line. If less than 50 percent, then the criteria is deemed as

TABLE 7.3   Trade Entry Decision Ledger for McDonald's Corporation on First Retrace on Weekly Time Frame

Item	True?	Description
General market aligned for the same time frame and is not extended	✓	Intermediate sideways
General market aligned for next higher time frame and is not extended	✓	Long-term trend suspect bullish
Sector aligned for the same time frame and is not extended		Intermediate bearish
Sector aligned for next higher time frame and is not extended	✓	Long-term trend suspect bullish
Trend for stock's current time frame is not extended	✓	Failure probability rate for short-term trend is <50%
Trend for stock's next higher time frame is not extended		Failure probability rate for intermediate-term trend is >50% (64.24% per Table A1.2)
Complementary retest and regenerate signals across multiple time frames *or* confluent trends on the next higher time frame	✓	Intermediate-term trends transitioned to bullish and long-term trend remains bullish
Light volume retest on the retest and regenerate sequence	✓	Lighter than breakout bar, lighter than prior swing point bar
Confirmed versus suspect breakout	✓	Confirmed
Total Criteria Met	7	If six or more items are true, then check potential reward versus risk to make a final trading decision

met, otherwise it is not. When considering the next higher time frame, if the current time frame is the long-term time frame, then the "next higher time frame," would be the "longer" term time frame. In the examples used here, that would be the "quarterly" bar chart where each bar represents three months of data rather than one.

Another area of confusion might be what to do if the instrument being examined is the sector or the general market. In those cases, should that portion of the decision tree be skipped over? In such a case, the simplest way to handle the situation is to simply consider the decision criteria as having been fulfilled since, after all, what is being examined is the sector or the general market.

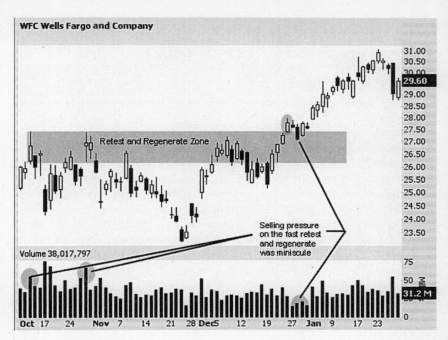

FIGURE 7.5 Wells Fargo and Company—Short-Term Time Frame (WFC) (October 10, 2011 to January 27, 2012)

The decision tree in Table 7.3 works out to the same reading as Table 7.2 but for different reasons on the breakout buy for McDonald's on the intermediate-term time frame. As has been said many times, the market does not provide the ideal case (nine check marks) in the majority of the set-ups it provides. When they do come along, the market participant needs to capitalize on their existence with confidence and size.

McDonald's is one example of a fast retrace that sets up a high probability trade off a confirmed bullish breakout. Figure 7.5 is an example of a high probability trade off a suspect bullish breakout to show that the trend need not be *confirmed*.

In this example, the breakout was suspect but the critical item is that the fast retrace to retest and regenerate showed absolutely no volume on the retest comparatively. There were no sellers. At the same time that this occurred, the sector was actually showing relative strength as compared to Wells Fargo (not shown) and the general market had successfully completed its retest and regenerate after its suspect breakout, as was seen previously in Figure 7.4. The weekly chart on Wells Fargo (not shown) had also just broken out on a suspect bullish trend transition, and it too was doing the immediate retest and regenerate on extremely light volume.

Suspect trends no longer need to be feared but can be embraced if the entire trade as measured through the Trade Entry Decision Ledger registers six or more of the nine criteria being met.

For what it is worth, the first retest and regenerate sequence on the McDonald's chart (Figure 7.1) as well as the Wells Fargo chart (Figure 7.5) both yielded trades that have higher than average possibilities as they both register six or more of the criteria as positive. As a market participant with limited time and resources, an individual will always experience trade-offs between varying possibilities. Naturally there are more factors beyond those listed here that determine whether a high probability trade should be taken. For example, a trader may already be overweight one sector and thus should not add more risk to trades within that particular sector. It may also be the case that three trades show up but the resources for just one more is available. The decision process previously described is to simply identify those trades with the highest probability for success. The next item is that they offer a reward-to-risk ratio that is worthwhile. Beyond that there are all the other issues that may come to be bear on whether a trade is made or not.

Fast Retrace into a Retest and Regenerate Sequence for Bearish Trends

Fast retraces into retest and regenerate zones for bearish trends are essentially the same as those witnessed for bullish trends. Figure 7.6 looks at a fast bearish first retrace into a retest and regenerate zone.

In 2007, a number of the financial concerns began to show signs of serious deterioration, and Citigroup was one of them. Figure 7.6 is a snapshot of Citigroup after it had turned quite bearish and exhibits one of many retest and regenerate sequences as it wound its way to near financial oblivion.

This example was chosen to contrast other aspects of a retest and regenerate sequence that a trader is likely to see. McDonald's was an easy trade. Citigroup is not.

To start with, it is a bearish trend rather than a bullish trend. Bearish trends are more apt to be confirmed when compared to bullish trends, although this one is actually suspect. Another difference is that this time frame is intermediate rather than daily. Continuing on with differences, this bearish trend has been in place for 35 bars already, while the trend had just transitioned in the McDonald's example.

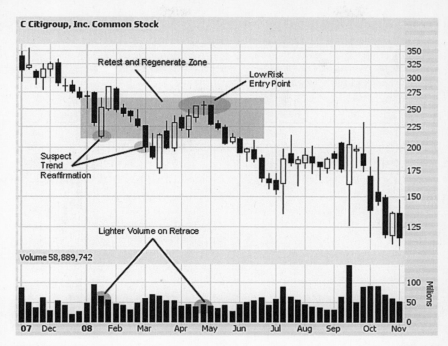

FIGURE 7.6 Citigroup—Intermediate-Term Time Frame (C) (November 5, 2007 to November 11, 2008)

Although an immediate retrace like the McDonald's example in Figure 7.1, in this case the retrace happened on the very next bar and continued to bounce for eight weeks before finally exhausting itself near the top of the retest and regenerate zone. Note the volume comparison at the peak of the retrace as compared to the top of swing point bar that was broken. Volume was much lighter. Also note that the immediate retrace showed volume was slightly higher on the first bar that retested, then about even on the second. After that it gradually became lighter and lighter as the retrace pushed higher and higher in price, which is typical of a retrace that has a higher probability of failure.

Looking at this list of dissimilarities when compared to the bullish example of McDonald's, it is almost as if this is not even the same type of trade set-up—but it is. In the market, there almost always seems to be something to worry about when putting on a trade—something that is not quite right.

Taking inventory and referring back to Table 7.1, the question is, is this a trade worth pursuing? In hindsight it clearly was, but was it at the time? In March of 2008, the stock had already lost 61 percent of its value from the

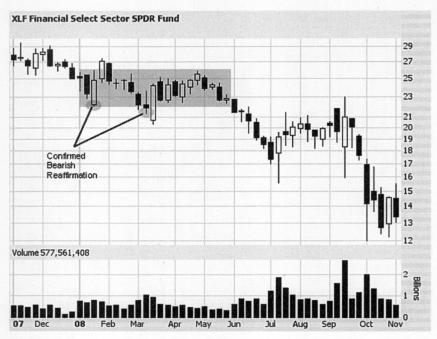

FIGURE 7.7 Financial Select Sector SPDR Fund—Intermediate-Term Time Frame (XLF) (November 5, 2007 to November 11, 2008)

peak 2007 price. Surely that would make one gasp to think that shorting a stock that had already been hit that hard would make sense. Rather than try to rationalize the trade, just consider the ideal conditions for a fast retrace and see if they dissuade or persuade a trader to take the trade.

First off, did the general market and sector trends complement the trade or were they against it? Figure 7.7 is the sector trend, and it also was bearish at the time and proceeded to reaffirm its bearish trend on the very next weekly bar when compared to the Citigroup chart.

Looking at the chart, the sector was supportive of a further move south from a trend perspective. But how extended was it in terms of time? At this point in time, the bearish trend had been in place for 32 weeks (not shown), which is becoming reasonably extended. A quick look at Table A1.5 in the Appendix shows the cumulative failure rate for a suspect trend that has persisted for this amount of time is at 70.61 percent; thus, from a time perspective, the sector is already extended into its downtrend.

So the sector is stretched on the intermediate-term view, but what about the long-term trend? Figure 7.8 shows it as having just transitioned to bearish.

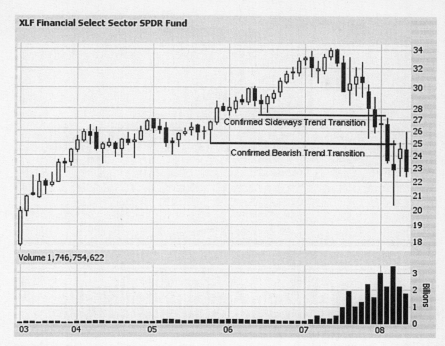

FIGURE 7.8 Financial Select Sector SPDR Fund—Long-Term Time Frame (XLF) (March 1, 2003 to May 1, 2008)

Appendix Table A1.6 tells us that long-term confirmed bearish trends that are two bars in length have a failure rate of 2.21 percent, so clearly this sector is not oversold on this time frame. The probabilities clearly suggest that a market participant should not expect this sector to run inordinately higher any time soon. That is the big take-away.

WHAT IS THE TRADING SIGNIFICANCE?

Long-term bearish trend transitions occur infrequently—on the order of once every two to four years. When they do change, however, their transition should be viewed as significant because they take an inordinate amount of time to transition once more.

Since all trend measures are lagging indicators, a good portion of the sell-off may have already transpired so they are by no means *a reason* to go short. The long term has to be anticipated by examining trend changes on the intermediate-term trend.

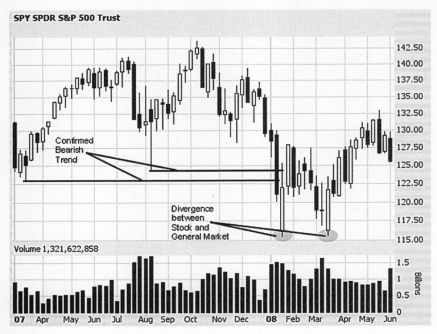

FIGURE 7.9 SPDR S&P 500 Trust—Intermediate-Term Time Frame (SPY) (February 2, 2007 to June 2, 2008)

What about the general market? Was it supportive of further selling or was it stretched too? Figure 7.9 considers that question.

By broadening the view to the long-term general market, the bearish trend was not stretched at all at this juncture but instead was just getting underway, having only recently turned bearish (10 bars). Again referring to Table A1.5, the probability for a trend failure in March of 2008 for the general market was only 16.8 percent. Do note, though, that once the next weekly bar prints, the trend failure rate almost doubles to 30.27 percent, which is higher but still well below 50 percent.

So far, from observing the respective failure rates for the intermediate and long sector trends and the same for the intermediate market, the conclusion is that, intermediate term, the sector selloff is pretty stretched and could use a reset, but long term indicators suggest that the selling is unlikely to end just yet, and the general market is just starting to catch the same selling fervor as what the individual stocks have already been experiencing. That is what happens at major turns—the sectors, and then the general markets, slowly begin to reflect what the individual stocks that comprise them have been saying for some time.

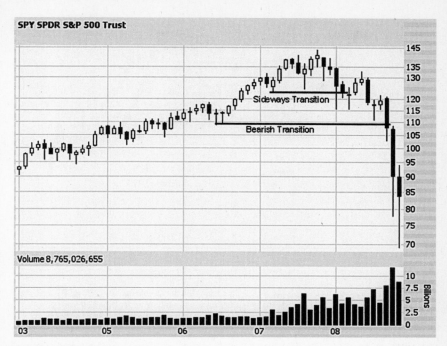

FIGURE 7.10 SPDR S&P 500 Trust—Long-Term Time Frame (SPY) (November 3, 2003 to November 3, 2008)

Finally, Figure 7.10 examines the monthly general market to see if it complements or contradicts what has been observed so far. In March of 2008, it had transitioned from bullish to sideways and did so in a confirmed mode.

From a time perspective and using the work from Chapter 1, Figure 1.14, roughly 45 percent of all long-term sideways trends fail when between one and five bars. In March of 2008, the sideways trend was one bar in duration and, given that, the transition to a sideways trend did not provide any actionable indication of the next move (lower or higher). To try to gain a better understanding, more legwork is needed to examine the trend transition paths for other sectors that also were beginning to transition from bullish to sideways and bearish on the long-term trends (not shown).

Given the preceding analysis, three of four criteria are met for the general market and sector alignment conditions. There is significant negative divergence in the stock and sector as compared to the general market, though the general market has transitioned out of a bullish state to sideways, which has to happen if it is going to bearish.

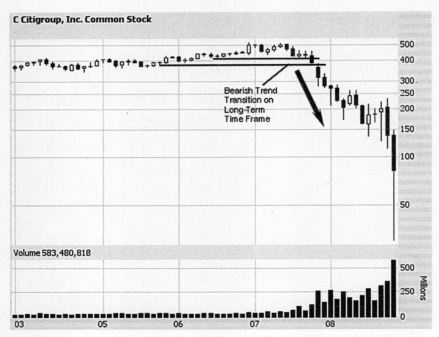

FIGURE 7.11 Citigroup—Long-Term Time Frame (C) (November 3, 2003 to November 3, 2008)

Turning to the stock trade triggers, does the long-term trend in Citigroup complement the intermediate-term trend where the trade is being considered? Figure 7.11 considers that question.

Like the sector, Citigroup's long-term trend was bearish and was five bars into that long-term confirmed bearish trend, which suggests a failure probability rate of 2.21 percent that is about to turn to 17.88 percent on the next monthly bar. Thus, it is complementary of the intermediate-term bearishness and, when viewed from this time frame, the potential for the selling is still in its early stages.

Referring back to Figure 7.6, the immediate retrace exhibits a reasonably significant volume surge at the bottom of the retest and regenerate zone. Combine that with the intermediate term being rather stretched, and anyone wanting to short Citigroup had indication that it had a reasonably high potential to bounce further than just the lower edge of the retest and regenerate zone.

Contrast this with McDonald's, which was a confirmed breakout that was not stretched at all on the short- or intermediate-term time frames when it broke its swing point. In Figure 7.1, McDonald's had just undergone six weeks of consolidation on the short-term time frame before breaking out in a confirmed manner. A minor retrace into the retest and regenerate had a higher probability of occurring than a deep retrace.

In Citigroup, the latest breakout on the intermediate-term time frame was suspect, and it came 35 bars into the trend, which yields a failure probability rate of 70.61 percent (Table A1.5), implying that a trader needs to be slower to pull the trigger as the probability for failure is much higher than desired. That need not kill the trade idea but should delay the decision a bit.

Given all the information to the trader at the time, six of the nine criteria are met (see Table 7.4) and thus the trade meets the criteria to be placed, but the reward-to-risk dynamics are not nearly as favorable for the

TABLE 7.4 Trade Entry Decision Ledger for Citigroup on Retrace Set-Up on the Weekly Time Frame

Item	True?	Description
General market aligned for the same time frame and is not extended	✓	Intermediate-term trend bearish and is not extended
General market aligned for next higher time frame and is not extended	✓	Long-term trend intermediate transitioning from bullish
Sector aligned for the same time frame and is not extended		Bearish but very extended already
Sector aligned for next higher time frame and is not extended	✓	Long-term trend recently turned bearish and thus is not extended
Trend for stock's current time frame is not extended		Failure probability rate for short-term trend is >50% (70.61%)
Trend for stock's next higher time frame is not extended	✓	Failure probability rate for intermediate-term trend is <50%
Complementary retest and regenerate signals across multiple time frames *or* confluent trends on the next higher time frame	✓	Intermediate-term trends transitioned to bullish and long-term trend remains bullish
Light volume retest on the retest and regenerate sequence on current time frame	✓	Lighter than breakout bar, lighter than prior swing point bar
Confirmed versus suspect breakout		Confirmed
Total Criteria Met	6	If six or more items are true, then check potential reward versus risk to make a final trading decision

immediate initiation. Given the stretched intermediate-term time frame, the fact that it is a suspect break to the downside, and the reward-to-risk criteria, more than likely a trader would pass until the reward-to-risk criteria are more favorable, which is what happened toward the end of April.

There are plenty of examples of fast retraces for bullish and bearish trade set-ups. Many examples are scattered throughout the charts on all time frames and for many differing stocks. With a standard template for evaluating potential trades, the best trades can be sought out and the mediocre ones avoided.

WHAT IS THE TRADING SIGNIFICANCE?

It is not enough to have a high probability of success in order to place a trade. The trade always has to additionally offer enough reward as compared to risk. Trades cannot be taken unless both criteria are met—higher than average success probability and higher than average reward-to-risk.

Slow Retrace into a Retest and Regenerate Sequence for Bullish Trends

A slow retrace into a retest and regenerate zone for bullish trends is one of the highest probability trades available. The second retrace on the daily time frame in the McDonald's example (Figure 7.1) that started this chapter is an example of such a set-up. It exemplifies all the characteristics that a trader would want and could profit by.

A look through the data shows that slow retraces into retest and regenerate zones tend to cluster around those periods when the general market tends to take another leg higher or lower after a consolidation period, providing the opportunity for many stocks to replicate that behavior. The breakouts tend to be stronger and rather than receiving a quick retest and regenerate sequence, price retraces have to wait until the first leg up completes before the next consolidation phase begins and prices slowly drip back toward their pre–take off levels. That slow retrace typically comes on lighter volume, and once price pulls back into the retest and regenerate zone, they have typically extended themselves, which is what makes this such a high probability trade.

At the opposite end of the spectrum, after an extended period without a retrace to the retest and regenerate zone, the stock suffers a fast retrace that happens in just a few bars and that covers a large price range. Naturally, this type of behavior tends to be much more difficult to purchase or short sell, although it can offer the same opportunity. This type of hard and fast retrace after an extended period since the original breakout works because most of the time it ends up creating a range trade at worst. The fast and hard retrace quickly reaches a state of exhaustion on the retrace as was described and characterized in Chapter 6 for the range trade set-up.

As an example of a fast retrace after an extended period of elevating above a breakout without a retest and regenerate sequence, in May of 2009 Wall Street suffered a rapid selloff that has since come to be known as the flash crash. In a very short period of time, most all bids disappeared and the market was left careening lower in a free fall vacuum. Rather than a slow retrace to a retest and regenerate zone, Figure 7.12 exhibits a rapid retrace to the aforementioned zone after a significant period of time had passed since the breakout. The stock highlighted here is Yum! Brands, a large restaurant chain, and the dizzying plunge actually ended up being nothing more than a retrace into a retest and regenerate zone that had seemingly been left behind for good.

As you can see from Figure 7.12, it took 24 bars on the short-term time frame for the retest and regenerate sequence to play out, and when it did,

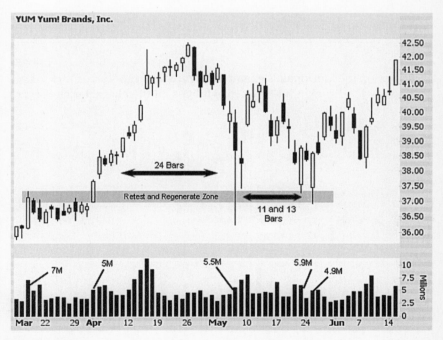

FIGURE 7.12   Yum! Brands—Short-Term Time Frame (YUM) (March 15, 2010 to June 15, 2010)

it all came at once. Note that the retest and regenerate zone in this figure is different than previous ones, and that has to do with how quickly the retest occurs. When it comes after more than six bars, it is more likely to test only the near end of the previously broken swing point bar rather the far side of that bar.

Given this, the plunge on the flash crash was probably not something to buy even if desired since it pushed so far down on the retest and regenerate after so many bars had transpired. As time progressed though, other opportunities arose with two more retraces into the retest and regenerate zone. Figures 7.13 through 7.16 exhibit the weekly charts for Yum! Brands, the sector, and the general market to provide the context needed for a decision.

Once more, using the Trade Entry Decision Ledger, a reasonably rational decision can be made regarding a purchase of Yum! Brands on the final retrace into retest and regenerate zone, purchased on May 23, 2010, as seen in Table 7.5. In this particular case, when looking back, the decision that this was not a high enough probability trade resulted in a missed opportunity. The decision fell short of what is needed, with a

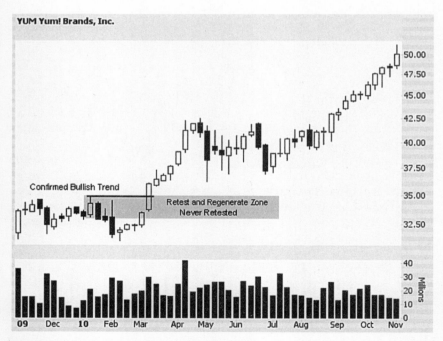

FIGURE 7.13 Yum! Brands—Intermediate-Term Time Frame (YUM) (November 1, 2009 to November 1, 2010)

FIGURE 7.14 Consumer Discretionary Select Sector SPDR—Intermediate-Term Time Frame (XLY) (July 6, 2009 to August 9, 2010)

valuation of only four criteria met. That will happen and in this case, a lot of risk did appear to be in the market. Missed opportunities are easy to make up when compared to failed trades that require far more effort to overcome.

There are many examples like Yum! Brands, such as Intel Corporation, which, in Figure 7.16, shows a slow retrace back to the retest and regenerate zone that offers up a great entry despite the obvious increased volume on the retrace as compared to the breakout bar and the prior swing point high bar. When the decision tree is computed (not shown) this does represent an excellent buying opportunity.

Slow retraces off of breakouts offer traders some of the highest probability for success trades available. They exist in bullish and, as will be shown, in bearish scenarios. The difficulty in taking advantage of these trades is to be patient enough to wait for them to set up. In many cases it will take 15 to 30 or 40 bars for the set-up to arrive. In a trader/investor's busy life, such a set-up can easily be forgotten and overlooked by the time it arrives. Given their high probability win ratio though, they are best not forgotten.

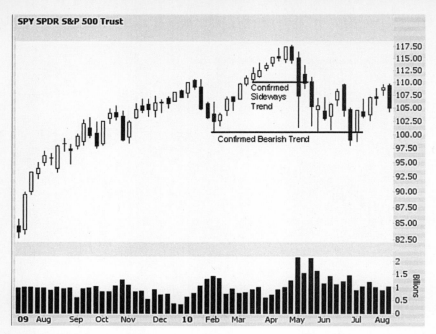

FIGURE 7.15 SPDR S&P 500 Trust ETF—Intermediate-Term Time Frame (SPY) (July 6, 2009 to August 9, 2010)

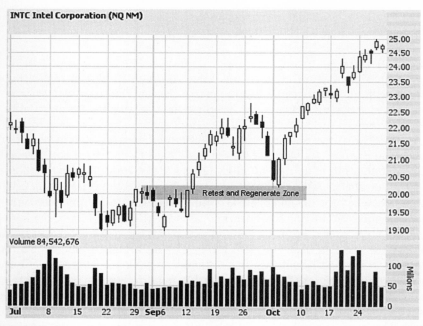

FIGURE 7.16 Intel Corporation—Short-Term Time Frame (INTC) (November 1, 2009 to November 1, 2010)

TABLE 7.5 Trade Entry Decision Ledger for Yum! Brands

Item	True?	Description
General market aligned for the same time frame and is not extended		Short-term trend bearish
General market aligned for next higher time frame and is not extended		Intermediate-term trend sideways
Sector aligned for the same time frame and is not extended		Short-term trend bearish
Sector aligned for next higher time frame and is not extended		Intermediate-term trend sideways
Trend for stock's current time frame is not extended	✓	Trend sideways. Not ideal but not a negative.
Trend for stock's next higher time frame is not extended	✓	Failure probability rate for intermediate-term trend is <50%
Complementary retest and regenerate signals across multiple time frames *or* confluent trends on the next higher time frame	✓	Intermediate-term trend for YUM never even retests
Light volume retest on the retest and regenerate sequence	✓	Lighter than breakout bar, lighter than prior swing point bar
Confirmed versus suspect breakout		Confirmed
Total Criteria Met	4	If six or more items are true, then check potential reward versus risk to make a final trading decision

Slow Retrace into a Retest and Regenerate Sequence for Bearish Trends

Slow retraces for bearish trends are not as common as bullish trends because bearish trends tend to exhaust to the downside reaching targets and thus, once they begin to rise to retest and regenerate, they end up trading through the test area and heading lower. The most workable slow retrace seen with bearish trends typically comes off some event that markedly drives prices lower on a swing point break and many times involves either a large wide price bar break lower or gap down. The plunge finally abates and prices crawl back to where they first broke down after more than six bars, and in these situations one can experience a secondary pounding in share price.

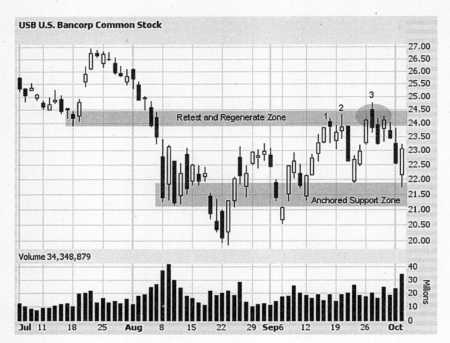

FIGURE 7.17 U.S. Bancorp—Short-Term Time Frame (USB) (July 5, 2011 to November 4, 2011)

An example of this is shown in Figure 7.17, where U.S. Bancorp was caught in a plunge along with the rest of the market in August of 2011, only to much later lift back to retest and attempt to regenerate and head lower once more.

In this example, the selling began in July and by the first week of August it turned into a rout. The swing point low from the middle of July was broken and volume expanded on the break. The push lower was intense and volume expanded greatly. A revisit to the retest and regenerate zone would not occur for another six weeks and is demarcated by a 1 on Figure 7.17. There were two other points—2 and 3—where the trade decision was available. Since they all occurred closely together and volumes did not deviate much, it ends up that all three occurrences yield the same result as shown in the Trade Entry Decision Ledger in Table 7.6.

In each of these three trade entry opportunities, the probability of a trade success was extremely high and the reward-to-risk favorable enough to make the trade. Assuming a trader took each of the three possible entry points, all three yielded high probability trades with good reward-to-risk ratios using a stop above the retest and regenerate zone and a target back to the anchored support zone on the short sell. In the case of entry 3, the stop

TABLE 7.6 Trade Entry Decision Ledger for U.S. Bancorp

Item	True?	Description
General market aligned for the same time frame and is not extended	✓	Short-term trend bearish
General market aligned for next higher time frame and is not extended	✓	Intermediate-term trend sideways
Sector aligned for the same time frame and is not extended	✓	Short-term trend bearish
Sector aligned for next higher time frame and is not extended	✓	Intermediate-term trend sideways. Not ideal but not a negative.
Trend for stock's current time frame is not extended	✓	Failure probability rate for short-term trend is trend is <50%
Trend for stock's next higher time frame is not extended	✓	Failure probability rate for intermediate-term trend is <50%
Complementary retest and regenerate signals across multiple time frames *or* confluent trends on the next higher time frame		Intermediate-term trend for USB retests but with increased volume
Light volume retest on the retest and regenerate sequence	✓	Lighter than breakout bar, lighter than prior swing point bar
Confirmed versus suspect breakout	✓	Confirmed
Total Criteria Met	8	If six or more items are true, then check potential reward versus risk to make a final trading decision

loss would have triggered since the average true range was $.81, and even the conservative 25 percent would have placed the stop at just $.20 above the high of the swing point low bar that defined the retest and regenerate zone. Even so, a reentry into the trade was possible that same day or the following couple of days had that happened.

This example brings the stop loss calculations presented in Chapter 5 back into fold. Stop loss orders are placed above and below resistance and support on the assumption that anchored resistance and support should stop the advance or fall in price. Is the same true of a retest and regenerate zone?

For the most part, yes it is, although as a trader you are free to choose more conservative stop loss exit points if you wish. In so doing though, you have to adjust your entry so that the reward-to-risk remains at least 2:1 but

FIGURE 7.18 Best Buy Company—Intermediate-Term Time Frame (BBY) (December 13, 2010 to December 19, 2011)

more preferably 3:1 or 4:1. That is the trade-off. A more conservative stop loss requires a more conservative entry point to make the reward-to-risk equation work in most cases. In this particular case, there was not really a better stop loss area anyway.

As with other examples previously, these set-ups occur over and over again on various time frames. Figure 7.18 shows a retest and regenerate sequence for Best Buy Company, which began to suffer tremendously from the pressure Amazon brought to bear on its retail electronics business model.

BREAKOUT TRADE SET-UPS

Breakout trades, in general, are typically not the ideal time to step into a trade, but as with most things, there are exceptions. In the case of breakout trades, these exceptions are extremely costly to ignore because they can lead to outsized percentage moves in the context of a high probability trade.

The data from Chapter 5's Figure 5.9 clearly demonstrates that most breakouts return to the scene of the crime. In fact, more than 80 percent of all breakouts, regardless of the qualified trend type or time frame, return to retest and regenerate. In the same chapter, Figure 5.10 further indicates that some 70 percent to 80 percent of all of these return within five bars of the breakout. So, the $10 million question is, are there any similarities in the miniscule number of breakouts that do not return to retest and regenerate within five bars? Is there is some common set of characteristics that would lead a trader to enter into a trade for those breakouts that have a high probability of success? If so, that would be a great edge to possess.

The downside of jumping on a breakout trade is quite obviously that the potential for a reversal is high, as just discussed. The risk of not entering the trade on the breakout is that if retrace to a retest and regenerate zone does not happen, then the opportunity to capture a significant percentage gain is lost and those breakouts that do not retrace are the trades that offer the potential for the unbelievable gains one seeks. The old saying on Wall Street is that "A bull market doesn't let you in and a bear market doesn't let you out."

From years of observation and now a methodical analysis of the data, it turns out that breakout trading opportunities that succeed tend to fall into two camps. In retrace trades, there are slow retraces and fast retraces. In breakout trading opportunities, there are breakouts that burst higher and those that crawl. Both can end up as successful trades but the crawling breakouts have a higher potential to turn into a retrace trade set-up with the varying probabilities that apply to those trade types. Burst breakouts are the gems a trader searches for.

The next couple of sections address these two breakout trade set-ups with the idea that a trader is always seeking the burst breakouts but may instead encounter a crawl breakout. The ideal breakout trade set-up conditions are outlined in Table 7.7.

Crawling Breakout Trade Set-Ups

There are breakout trades that surge higher and those that, for whatever reason, initially just mill around. Those breakouts that mill around are, for the purposes of this book, referred to as crawling breakouts. Although crawling breakout trades can work higher without a retrace, they do not surge higher, which is the more desirable trade set-up.

Crawling breakout trade set-ups appear to occur for several reasons, of which three are most common:

1. The stock breaking out is already stretched in terms of price and/or time.

TABLE 7.7	Ideal Breakout Trade Set-Up Conditions
Definition	In a breakout trade set-up, a market participant enters into a trade when it is clear that it is breaking out on the time frame being traded. For breakout trade set-ups, the trade entry is to trade in the direction of the breakout making the purchase (bullish breakout sequence) or a short sell (bearish breakout sequence) once the breakout looks to hold.
Ideal General Market and Sector Alignment Conditions	For a stock that experiences a bullish breakout, the ideal case is a bullish or sideways sector and general market trend for the same and next higher time frame and sector and market are not extended (the probability for trend failure relative to time duration is reasonably small).
	For a stock that experiences a bearish breakout, the ideal case is a bearish or sideways sector and general market trend for the same and next higher time frame, not extended (the probability for trend failure relative to time duration is reasonably small).
	Note: In both of the preceding cases, this will appear to be the case even when a long-term major market transition is in its infancy, transitioning from bullish to bearish or from bearish to bullish. In such a case, more and more stocks will begin to show as divergent with the general market trend on the intermediate- and long-term time frames, and in this case the probability of a trend failure is higher than realized. Anticipating long term trend changes, though fraught with error, is possible but that's a subject for another time. This is the proverbial case where the trend is only wrong in two instances: at the top and at the bottom. It is the reason that a market participant must always protect his or her capital through judicious use of stop loss orders.
Ideal Stock Trade Triggers	The trade triggers leading to the highest probability trades naturally consist of a number of factors. They include:
	• Multiple clustered swing points that are broken on the current time frame (two or more swing point breaks desired)
	• Complementary swing point breakouts on multiple time frames. A break of clustered swing points on multiple time frames offers the highest probability
	• Trends that are not too extended as identified in the trend failure probability tables (see the Appendix) across the current and next higher time frame at the time of the breakout
	• The breakout has no obvious anchored resistance just beyond the current breakout area
	• Confirmed breakouts have preference over suspect breakouts

TABLE 7.7 (Continued)
Clearly the most ideal situation is for all three time frames to breakout together with each time frame breaking over clustered swing points; for all breakouts to be confirmed; and for all breakouts to be supported by the general market and sector. Such a situation is the ultimate set-up. Given the plethora of ideal conditions, it is unlikely that this case will be encountered other than a few rare times. The more likely case is to see a combination of these ideal conditions. The more the better.

2. A breakout on one time frame encounters support or resistance on another.
3. The general sector and market alignment characteristics are not as favorable when compared to surging breakout trade set-ups.

Naturally, the focus of a trader should be to identify those breakout trade set-ups that possess the vast majority of the trade set-up conditions identified in Table 7.7, thus increasing the odds of capturing a surging breakout trade set-up rather than a crawling trade set-up.

Figures 7.19 and 7.20 provide an example of a breakout trade that initially crawls rather than surges. In this case, there was resistance on the next longer term time frame that held things up.

Figure 7.19 displays the short-term time frame for U.S. Bancorp and two clustered swing point highs that are part and parcel of breakout trades that have the potential to surge higher.

Looking back at Table 7.7, other potential downsides to this breakout trade from the stock-only perspective shows the breakout as being suspect rather than confirmed.

In fact, on closer analysis, the short-term (daily) chart price stalls right at the $27 to $27.50 area, which is represented as the higher swing point as witnessed on the intermediate-term time frame visible in Figure 7.20. Once the intermediate-term swing points break, then the trade turns into more of a surge breakout than a crawler until once more it hits resistance at the long term swing point (not shown).

Despite these deficiencies, the breakout trade does eventually get on track and begin to work higher, but it does not surge immediately. To evaluate breakout trade set-ups. It has been filled out for the U.S. Bancorp breakout trade set-up conditions as an example.

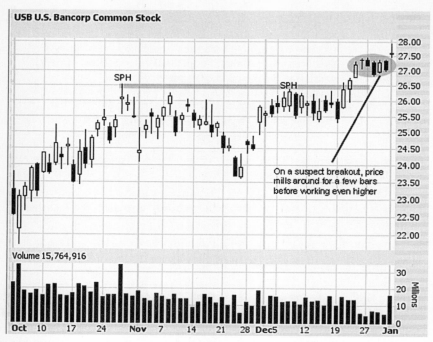

FIGURE 7.19 U.S. Bancorp—Short-Term Time Frame (USB) (October 3, 2011 to January 3, 2011)

Although the decision checklist provides a trader with a way to leave emotion out of the decision equation, it also will never be a replacement for common sense. The U.S. Bancorp trade ended up as a breakout trade that crawled higher prior to taking off. When examining the decision ledger, the first four items all garner true values but all exhibit sideways trends. Sideways trends are considered as having met the criteria because they are not a negative, but they are not a strong positive either. Rather than try to make up special rules, just remember that the decision ledger is focused on clear negatives in the case of trend. For a breakout trade set-up there are 10 criteria, versus 9 for retrace trades. If more than three criteria are negative then the trade is not considered viable from a success probability perspective and should most likely be passed over. Two trade set-ups may garner a value of eight, for example, but one may very well represent a much stronger trading candidate than the other. That would be true in this example if the first four items were all bullish rather than sideways. That would make this trade set-up much stronger, as would no obvious anchored resistance just beyond the current breakout area.

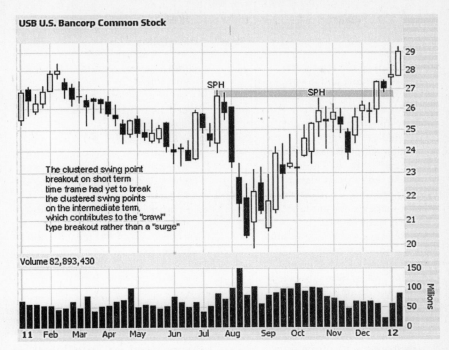

USB U.S. Bancorp Common Stock

The clustered swing point
breakout on short term
time frame had yet to break
the clustered swing points
on the intermediate term,
which contributes to the "crawl"
type breakout rather than a "surge"

Volume 82,893,430

FIGURE 7.20 U.S. Bancorp (USB)—Intermediate-Term Time Frame (January 1, 2011 to January 3, 2012)

Surging Breakout Trade Set-Ups

The powerful breakout trades have a common characteristic that, unless you are specifically searching for it, likely goes unnoticed. That characteristic is clustered swing point breakouts across multiple time frames with no obvious resistance beyond. With each of the following chart examples, you can pull up your own charts to see how, in almost all cases, the general market and sector support was present in the following figures as well. Also, refer to Table 7.7 and see how most if not all of the stock trade triggers are met.

The first figure is for the general equity market and for a breakout to the downside. Recall from Chapter 2, bearish breakouts have an extremely high probability of extending lower to profit targets quickly (Figures 2.7 and 2.8) and Figure 7.21 is an example of that in the general market. The set-up in this case that provides a large fast downdraft is the breaking of the two clustered swing point lows, which unleashes a torrent of selling. Note that if viewed on a daily chart (not shown), the exit was triggered on August 4, when the swing point low from March 16 was undercut as well

TABLE 7.8 Trade Entry Decision Ledger for U.S. Bancorp's Breakout Trade Set-Up

Item	True?	Description
General market aligned for the same time frame and is not extended	✓	Trend sideways. Not ideal but not a negative.
General market aligned for next higher time frame and is not extended	✓	Trend sideways. Not ideal but not a negative.
Sector aligned for the same time frame and is not extended	✓	Trend sideways. Not ideal but not a negative.
Sector aligned for next higher time frame and is not extended	✓	Trend sideways. Not ideal but not a negative.
Trend for stock's current time frame is not extended	✓	Just breaking out so not extended
Trend for stock's next higher time frame is not extended	✓	Trend sideways. Not ideal but not a negative.
Multiple clustered swing points that are broken on the breakout for this time frame	✓	
Complimentary swing point breakouts on multiple time frames	✓	
The breakout has no obvious anchored resistance just beyond the current breakout area		There is additional resistance via swing points on intermediate-term and long-term time frames just beyond the current breakout price point
Confirmed versus suspect breakout		Suspect
Total Criteria Met	8	If seven or more items are true, then check potential reward versus risk to make a final trading decision

as the previous day's low just above \$122 for the short-term time frame. In this case both the daily and the weekly charts exhibited breaks of multiple swing point lows in a reasonably simultaneous fashion.

For every trade there needs to be a targeted profit exit and that is very true for bearish bets, for they tend to extend fast and furiously. In *Trend Qualification and Trading*,[1] there was quite a bit of discussion on utilizing

---

[1]L.A. Little, *Trend Qualification and Trading* (Hoboken, NJ: John Wiley & Sons, 2011), Chapters 7 and 8, pages 127–187.

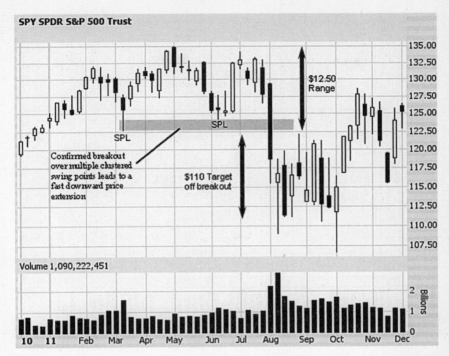

FIGURE 7.21 SPDR S&P 500 Trust—Intermediate-Term Time Frame (SPY) (December 6, 2010 to December 5, 2011)

anchored support and resistance zones as well projection mechanisms to find target price points. Chapter 6 of that book continued and extended the price projection thoughts to consider trading floors/ranges. These patterns play out over and over where the range of the trading floor is used to define the range of the upcoming floor once a breakout occurs. This is especially useful in bullish price projections but works equally well for downward price direction.

In Figure 7.21, a price projection of $110 is easily calculated by taking the width of the upper trading floor (measuring from the lower swing point to the highs) and subtracting that width from the lowest swing point low that was broken. It is a simple calculation and works reasonable well as a back-of-the-envelope calculation.

Moving to another example, Figure 7.22 is a weekly chart of International Business Machines (IBM). In this chart, the breakout clearly hurdles two clustered swing point highs, although it occurs as a suspect breakout.

As seen, price hurls higher, though without any repentance. There is no retest and regenerate sequence, and Figure 7.23 provides a clue as to

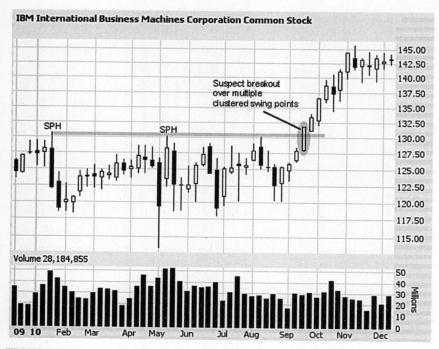

FIGURE 7.22   International Business Machines—Intermediate-Term Time Frame (IBM) (December 14, 2009 to December 13, 2010)

why, for the long-term time frame also witnessed a swing point breakout as well.

Although only one swing point was broken on the long-term time frame, it did hurl IBM forward, breaking to all-time highs, and it came after a 10 month consolidation period so the trends were not extended. The fact that IBM broke out on both the long- and intermediate-term time frames indicates (see the Appendix) that the cumulative probability for a failure is virtually zero, and if you pull up a daily chart, you will see that it, too, had just transitioned so its probability of a fast failure was also low.

Thus, even though the trend was suspect, it was the only negative of the entire trade set-up criteria. The general market and sector were supportive of the move (not shown); multiple clustered swing points were broken on the intermediate-term and the short-term time frames (not shown), while a single swing point was broken on the long-term time frame, taking prices to all-time highs. Not a single time frame suffered from an extended trend. No wonder the breakout succeeded and surged rather than crawled. Find a breakout that surges and you will almost always find these conditional set-ups being met.

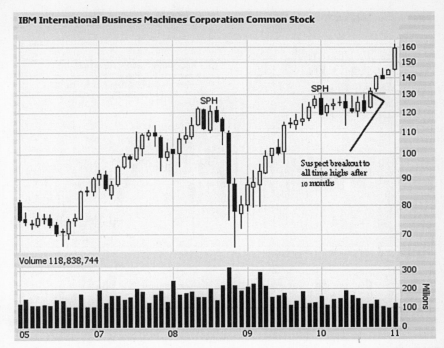

FIGURE 7.23 International Business Machines—Long-Term Time Frame (IBM) (December 1, 2005 to December 1, 2011)

Here's another one: Hasbro Incorporated. Figure 7.24 is an intermediate-term time frame (weekly bars), which shows how two clustered swing point lows are broken on the week of September 29, 2008, when prices decidedly broke lower.

This particular chart was chosen to show that even though most of the decision criteria needed to enter into a breakout trade set-up were met, it does not always prevent a retest and regenerate sequence from occurring. Naturally, the downside of entering into a breakout set-up is that price is somewhat extended already when a trader enters into the trade, and if the breakout ends up being false, the risk on the trade is greater than would otherwise be the case on a retrace trade set-up, for your stop needs to be placed on the far side of the retest and regenerate zone.

In the case of Hasbro, unless a trader was willing to risk back to the far side of the retest and regenerate zone as a stop loss target, then the trade would likely be a loss on the whipsaw back higher two bars later. This assumes the trader did not exit or take partial profits on the immediate follow through bar, and that is a reasonable assumption since the projected

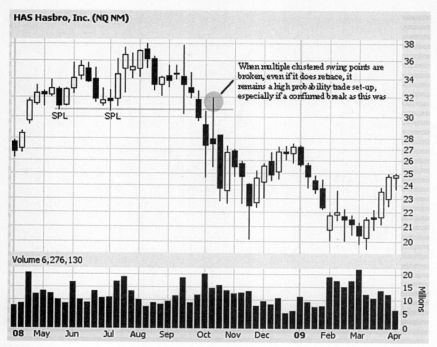

FIGURE 7.24   Hasbro Inc.—Intermediate-Term Time Frame (HAS) (April 7, 2008 to April 6, 2009)

extension lower comes at roughly at $23 and was yet unmet (using the trading floor price projection mechanism mentioned earlier).

Sometimes breakout trades come along when prices have been severely depressed for an extended period of time. In Figure 7.25, Affymax had previously suffered a tremendous bout of selling, having plunged from over $23 to a low of less than $6 in one fatal month. That was in June of 2010, and for more than 22 months prices had languished in large range, building a base to eventually surge back higher from. In this chart, the gap area is just above the leftmost bar.

Although this may not be the sort of chart one might envision when considering a breakout trade, breakouts come in all shapes and sizes. They just need the majority of the criteria to be met to give them a chance to surge higher or lower.

In this case, there were five clustered swing points that had accumulated on the weekly chart, which, when broken, served to slingshot prices higher. You can rest assured that there were many stops sitting above this clustered set of five swing points. In this particular breakout trade set-up,

FIGURE 7.25 Affymax Inc.—Intermediate-Term Time Frame (AFFY) (August 2, 2010 to December 1, 2010)

the monthly time frame also experienced two swing point breaks as part of this same breakout (not shown). Again, almost all the desired criteria were synchronized to support such a surge.

The preceding examples all have the same characteristics and clearly the idea of clustered swing points across multiple time frames is the key criterion. Sometimes the trade set-up is generous where the shorter term time frame will offer a low risk entry on a retrace set-up while the longer term time frame is a clean breakout trade set-up. That was the case in Autodesk. Figure 7.26 is the short-term time frame using daily bars and displaying the retest and regenerate sequence, while Figure 7.27 is a clean breakout trade set-up. In both cases, multiple swing points are aligned on multiple time frames leading to a fast surge lower in price once the ball gets rolling.

There are times when the breakout comes on a huge gap up, making the trade extremely hard to enter into. In such situations one has to improvise with scale in techniques to get a foot in the door if the majority of the breakout trade set-up conditions appear to be in place. Google in 2005 is such an example, as shown in Figures 7.28 and 7.29.

FIGURE 7.26   Autodesk, Inc.—Short-Term Time Frame (ADSK) (July 29, 2008 to October 6, 2008)

The Google case is particularly hard to buy into given the risk on the trade set-up. It is not as strong as other cases pointed out previously in terms of the trade set-up criteria and forces a purchase at a price point that is some $25 more than the prior day and $15 to $20 more than the prior swing point highs.

In these situations, the best thing a trader can do is to be patient. Keep the stock on the radar for the eventual retest and regenerate sequence and continue to work other trades that become available. That does not make this a bad trade set-up; it remains a good one, but the high probability trades require two things—high probability for success and a reward-to-risk set-up that favors that trade. In this case, the latter is a hard case to make.

Finally, Figures 7.30 and 7.31 are just one more example where, if a trader is able to create a system that forewarns of potential breakouts across clustered swing points on differing time frames, the reward potential is significant.

Breakout trades offer the unique opportunity to harvest huge gains in reasonably short periods of time without significant risk. They have a very particular set-up condition and are valuable to seek out.

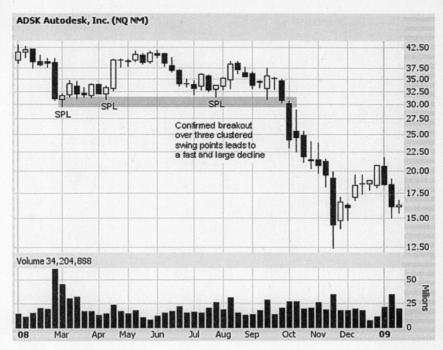

FIGURE 7.27 Autodesk, Inc.—Intermediate-Term Time Frame (ADSK) (January 22, 2008 to January 20, 2009)

CONSIDERING OTHER TRADE SET-UPS

As was first communicated in Chapter 5, there really are just two types of trade set-ups—retraces and breakouts. The data presented in Chapter 5 focused solely on breakouts and retraces centered on swing points. Breakouts and retraces can and do occur in at least one other case that does not necessarily have to involve a swing point. That case is anchored support and resistance zones where price can break out (up or down) and can retrace too.

When doing the analysis, what one finds is that a high percentage of all anchored support and resistance zones have swing points associated with them, and for this reason anchored zones without swing points were relegated to a minor role in the trade set-up considerations. When retrace to an anchored support or resistance zone occurs after a breakout through the zone, the trade set-up decision criteria are envisioned as essentially the same as for swing point breakouts followed by a retrace to a retest and regenerate zone. The only significant difference is that the retest and

FIGURE 7.28 Google Inc.—Short-Term Time Frame (GOOG) (July 21, 2005 to October 21, 2005)

regenerate zone is the anchor zone that was broken. The stop out becomes the far side of the anchored zone, and the idea is to enter the trade on a retrace into the zone if that retrace comes back with lighter volume as compared to the anchor bars that anchor the zone. Always use the worst case on the comparison. For example, if price breaks higher and there are two anchors with 1 million and 2 million shares, respectively, a retrace to the anchored zone should be compared to the 1 million shares and should be lighter on the retrace since that is the hardest comparison.

Breakout trades that do not involve swing points are problematic, because the key decision criterion on whether to enter such a trade is the break of multiple swing points across multiple time frames. If no swing points are involved in the breakout, then that removes the essential decision criterion. Some work has been done to consider breakouts over multiple anchor zones across multiple time frames but the evidence is inconclusive.

For these reasons, trade set-ups that do not involve swing points are not currently considered viable trade set-ups.

GOOG Google Inc. (NQ NM)

SPH

Simultaneous breakouts on
multiple time frames have an
excellent probability of producing
significant percentage moves

Volume 33,782,590

Millions

05 May   Jun   Jul   Aug   Sep   Oct   Nov   Dec   06   Feb   Mar   Apr

FIGURE 7.29   Google Inc.—Intermediate-Term Time Frame (GOOG) (April 11,
2005 to April 10, 2006)

TRADE SET-UP RATIONALE AND THOUGHTS

Trade set-ups happen for many reasons. They do not all succeed nor do
they all fail. In fact, all the work presented in this book seeks to understand what those probabilities look like so that increasingly informed decisions are possible. This chapter closes with a few additional trade set-up
thoughts. Considered are questions such as, "What causes these trade set-
ups?" and "Is there any value in a trade set-up coming up short and not
actualizing?"

Valuation-Altering Events

The repeating pattern of retraces off of breakouts occurs for many reasons, and it is sometimes good to consider why these set-ups occur. In
many cases individual stocks just get dragged higher and lower because
the general market is either lifting or falling. In those cases, once the

FIGURE 7.30 Jazz Pharmaceuticals—Short-Term Time Frame (JAZZ) (August 6, 2010 to November 5, 2010)

market takes a rest, the stock drifts back and performs a retest and re-generate zone.

In some cases there are special events that trigger price escalation either higher or lower, and these events may happen in concert with a general market move or be completely separate from it. The event can be the discovery of some new oil field for a large oil firm or expanded reserves for a mineral exploration company. On the negative side, a common occurrence for biotechnology companies is the denial of application by the Food and Drug Administration.

Another regular occurrence that happens every three months is earnings reports, which effectively operate the same way as some new one-time event. Since there are thousands of stocks, each earnings season inevitably witnesses a consequential number of stocks seeing large surges or drops in share price as a result of earnings disclosures.

The commonality between all these special situations is that in each case, something shifts the perceived value of the company, and it does so in a reasonably significant way. The result usually shows itself on the charts

FIGURE 7.31 Jazz Pharmaceuticals—Intermediate-Term Time Frame (JAZZ) (March 1, 2010 to March 3, 2011)

as a high volume and, in many cases, a wide price spread bar, and it usually involves a swing point.

Failure to Surpass a Swing Point

When a swing point is tested but does not break, there is still information to be gleaned. How the swing point is attacked reveals information about future possibilities. How often the swing point is attacked over time is another informational item.

Consider that a swing point typically demarcates the unknown. It usually sits at the edge of a price range beyond which is unchartered price territory. Sometimes the unchartered territory only applies to one time frame, other times to multiple ones. Most importantly, a swing point represents the price point that, heretofore, market participants have been unwilling to cross from a price paid perspective. In other literature this area is typically referred to as a supply line when speaking of resistance in an attempt for prices to march higher. The inverse is true as well; there can be and are bid supply lines as well (support).

When a bid or ask supply line is attacked, the force of the attack is the critical component to consider. Was the marauding party large or small? To tell this, you look to volume. Compare the force of the attack to the volume that is sitting at the swing point. If volume swells as compared to the swing point yet price is rejected, more than likely the attack is going to continue. The probability that it happens immediately or a few bars later is additional detective work that remains to be done, but trading experience shows that it will most likely reoccur.

The preceding description leaves out one other important factor to consider as part of swing points being tested. Many times a swing point demarcates a trading floor, and the swing point does not stand in isolation but as part of a larger anchored support or resistance zone. When this is the case, the volume test described earlier is a test against the volume associated not with just the swing point but with the anchor bars that form the zone.

The information release is attached to, what else, volume. If a swing point is hit and volume expands, then the probabilities increase that the breakout is not over—just delayed. Figure 7.32 is an example of this scenario. Notice that this is how breakout trade set-ups develop. When this happens long enough and over multiple time frames, all that is required is a spark to explode prices higher or, in bearish cases, lower.

Trades That Fail

No matter what you do in trading, there will always be trades that should work but just inexplicably fail. When that happens, you just have to stop out, take the loss, and move on. Unfortunately, what tends to happen is that wins and losses in trading occur in clusters, and a trader is almost always faced with a string of trades that fail rather than just one or two.

The reason for this is not that hard to understand since most traders trade one or two patterns, and they do it repeatedly independent of larger influences like the general market and sector strength or weakness. In many cases this is even true of classical trade set-ups like a triangle or a head and shoulders pattern, where volume trails are ignored and the pattern itself is traded independent of telltale signs that might suggest that the probability of trade success may be less than desirable.

When a string of failures comes along, initially traders are slow to react and, to some degree, deny the first sting of the losses that come their way, thinking it will turn in their favor. After the sting grows to a steady burn, the impulse is to exit and stand aside, which is not a bad response per se. The problem, however, is that the larger reason for why the trades are failing is not understood, and thus, the next few attempts to reenter trades using

FIGURE 7.32 Pfizer, Inc.—Short-Term Time Frame (PFE) (August 17, 2009 to November 17, 2009)

the same patterns once more fall flat on their face and then the questions of methods and process begin in earnest.

The simple fact is that something larger in scope is likely taking place that is either being ignored or not understood. It does not invalidate one's work. It really has not changed the longer run probabilities; it is just that short term, those probabilities are not reflective of the longer term probabilities. It is a time to stand aside, let the charts reset, and then put the same game plan back to work afterward. There is really nothing more that can be done. The long run probabilities will play out over time, but in the short run they can become skewed. It is part of life and part of trading.

SUMMARY

The best trade set-ups are those where the probability of the trade success is high and the reward-to-risk significant. Slow retraces to the retest and regenerate zone generally provide high probability winning trades.

Breakout trades, though difficult to find, when they do occur produce gains in relatively short periods of time, making them excellent trading opportunities, and if the trade triggers line up correctly, they offer high probability win rates as well.

To aid the trader in making the decision on whether to enter a trade, a trade entry decision ledger is offered. It is simple in construction and helps to reinforce unemotional trading decisions. It will sometimes pass on good trading opportunities, and that is incorporating a rational rather than emotional approach. What it will also do though is to keep a trader out of trades that he has no business making. That is the real value.

There are trades that are subpar, trades that are average, and trades that really shine with potential. Your job is to find the diamonds in the rough. With Chapters 5 to 7 under your belt, you now have the correct tools and knowledge to mine for those diamonds.

CONCLUSION

Unleashing Trade Potential

I remember my first read of Robert D. Edwards and John Magee's classic *Technical Analysis of Stock Trends* many years ago.[1] There were references like "in our experience" and an occasional reference to implied probabilities that this or that pattern should play out as described. In all cases no underlying data was offered. When that classic book was written there were no computers, and thus there was no easy way to systematically compile and present the data behind the assertions presented. It is unreasonable to fault Edwards and Magee with not having provided such underlying data, but in this day and age those limitations are no longer applicable.

As you have seen, a significant effort has been put forth in both identifying and enumerating the various failure probability rates that exist for both trends and trades across the three accepted time frames. A decade of data was systematically analyzed over a period of time that witnessed the end of the Dotcom crash followed by the arrival of another bull market followed by yet another crash and subsequent bull market run. This test bed of data was analyzed based on the concept of qualified trend identification, swing point tests, anchored support and resistance and, of course, trend trading set-ups. The results of this analysis are scattered throughout the book, and the trend and trade failure probability rates are presented in the Appendix for reference purposes.

---

[1] Robert D. Edwards and John Magee, *Technical Analysis of Stock Trends*, 7th ed. (Boca Raton, FL: St. Lucie Press, 1998).

Although there are no absolutes in trading, there are probabilities and putting the probabilities on your side has significant value. The fundamental influences on price are numerous and seemingly beyond analysis, but despite this, a systematic and consistent analysis of the charts with the neoclassical approach based on price, volume, and time as measured through tests can yield information on true supply and demand across all tradable instruments and all time frames. When a range, retrace, or breakout trade set-up presents itself, one need only ask oneself if the critical factors are properly aligned. Are the failure probability rates approaching nosebleed levels or are they fresh and young? Are the qualified trends for individual stocks congruent with sector and general market trends? If a retrace trade set-up, are the failure probabilities low based on the time spent performing the retrace? How has the retest and regenerate sequence played out? What about the characteristics of a breakout trade? Have multiple swing points broken on multiple time frames?

The market offers opportunity no matter what the direction. These trade possibilities are present in all markets. High probability range trades set up after extended runs once a final surge takes place. They can be bearish and bullish in their makeup. Both bullish and bearish retrace and breakout trades are almost always present as well. If a trader is able to recognize the pattern and utilizes the trade entry decision ledgers offered to evaluate the trade potential, all that is left is to wrap a viable trading plan around it. After that, it is just about trade execution and management.

These are the keys to exceptional trading success, and those keys have now been passed to you. What you do with them is up to you and you only. You can refuse to accept them. You can accidentally misplace them for a while. You may never even grasp the promise that they hold. For many of you though, you can do as I have. You can grab them and run with them— all the way to the bank!

Data Tables

Throughout this book numerous references are made to various failure probability matrixes. Due to the extensive amount of data, only a subset of the data compiled was presented, but for the serious reader, the raw data tables are presented here for completeness.

Two notes regarding this data first, though. First, although this data is constantly evolving, the pace of that evolution is rather slow, and thus the trend failure rate probabilities presented below should hold true for some period of time. Second, these data points are across all stocks in all sectors for each of the three major indexes (S&P 500, NASDAQ, and AMEX), and thus the sample and population sampled are roughly equal.

For current trend failure probability rates and eventually the inclusion of virtual sector trend probability failure rates, visit us at Technical Analysis Today (www.tatoday.com).

CHAPTER 1: IDENTIFYING AND QUALIFYING TREND PROBABILITIES

In Chapter 1, the first set of probabilities referenced data gathered from January of 2002 through July of 2011 and encompassed both bullish and bearish trends based on trend failures. The following tables were utilized to construct the charts that appeared in the first half of Chapter 1.

Trend Failure Probabilities for Bullish and Bearish Trends

TABLE A1.1 Bullish Short-Term Time Frame Trend Probability Failure Rates

Number Bars	Confirmed Trend Percentages		Suspect Trend Percentages		Difference Confirmed versus Suspect	
	Individual	Cumulative	Individual	Cumulative	Difference	Cumulative
0 to 1	0.20%	0.20%	0.17%	0.17%	0.03%	0.188%
1 to 5	3.36%	3.56%	4.24%	4.41%	−0.88%	0.188%
6 to 10	10.05%	13.61%	11.74%	16.15%	−1.69%	2.181%
11 to 15	12.43%	26.04%	12.84%	28.98%	−0.41%	6.069%
16 to 20	11.63%	37.67%	11.93%	40.92%	−0.30%	6.663%
21 to 25	10.31%	47.99%	9.88%	50.79%	0.44%	6.173%
26 to 30	9.01%	57.00%	8.52%	59.31%	0.49%	5.077%
31 to 35	7.74%	64.74%	7.15%	66.46%	0.59%	4.365%
36 to 40	6.39%	71.13%	5.89%	72.35%	0.50%	3.656%
41 to 45	5.75%	76.88%	5.29%	77.64%	0.46%	3.011%
46 to 50	4.48%	81.36%	4.24%	81.88%	0.24%	2.707%
51 to 55	3.54%	84.90%	3.49%	85.37%	0.05%	2.181%
56 to 60	2.91%	87.81%	2.74%	88.10%	0.17%	1.806%
61 to 65	2.65%	90.47%	2.43%	90.53%	0.22%	1.435%
66 to 70	2.21%	92.68%	1.98%	92.51%	0.23%	1.287%
71 to 75	1.79%	94.47%	1.82%	94.33%	−0.03%	1.064%
76 to 80	1.44%	95.91%	1.47%	95.80%	−0.03%	0.986%
81 to 85	1.27%	97.17%	1.29%	97.09%	−0.02%	0.817%
86 to 90	1.10%	98.28%	1.10%	98.19%	0.00%	0.728%
91 to 95	0.97%	99.25%	0.99%	99.19%	−0.02%	0.636%
96 to 100	0.75%	100.00%	0.81%	100.00%	−0.06%	0.585%

TABLE A1.2 Bullish Intermediate-Term Time Frame Trend Probability Rates

Number Bars	Confirmed Trend Percentages		Suspect Trend Percentages		Difference Confirmed versus Suspect	
	Individual	Cumulative	Individual	Cumulative	Difference	Cumulative
0 to 1	0.12%	0.12%	0.15%	0.15%	−0.03%	0.138%
1 to 5	3.70%	3.82%	4.70%	4.85%	−1.00%	0.138%
6 to 10	10.52%	14.35%	11.21%	16.06%	−0.69%	2.411%
11 to 15	12.54%	26.88%	12.65%	28.71%	−0.11%	5.856%
16 to 20	12.60%	39.48%	13.01%	41.72%	−0.41%	6.649%
21 to 25	10.43%	49.91%	10.51%	52.22%	−0.08%	6.848%
26 to 30	8.50%	58.41%	8.66%	60.88%	−0.16%	5.474%
31 to 35	7.22%	65.62%	7.04%	67.92%	0.18%	4.480%
36 to 40	6.09%	71.71%	6.08%	73.99%	0.01%	3.622%
41 to 45	5.36%	77.07%	4.89%	78.88%	0.47%	3.122%
46 to 50	4.81%	81.88%	4.17%	83.05%	0.64%	2.510%
51 to 55	3.76%	85.64%	3.21%	86.26%	0.56%	2.142%
56 to 60	3.22%	88.86%	2.67%	88.93%	0.55%	1.656%
61 to 65	2.46%	91.32%	2.22%	91.16%	0.23%	1.386%
66 to 70	2.01%	93.33%	2.05%	93.21%	−0.04%	1.162%
71 to 75	1.51%	94.84%	1.54%	94.75%	−0.02%	1.076%
76 to 80	1.32%	96.17%	1.33%	96.07%	0.00%	0.819%
81 to 85	1.19%	97.36%	1.13%	97.21%	0.06%	0.715%
86 to 90	0.95%	98.31%	1.07%	98.28%	−0.13%	0.619%
91 to 95	0.90%	99.20%	0.91%	99.19%	−0.02%	0.591%
96 to 100	0.80%	100.00%	0.81%	100.00%	−0.01%	0.511%

TABLE A1.3 Bullish Long-Term Time Frame Trend Probability Failure Rates (Note: For period from 2002 through 2006 only)

Number Bars	Confirmed Trend Percentages		Suspect Trend Percentages		Difference Confirmed versus Suspect	
	Individual	Cumulative	Individual	Cumulative	Difference	Cumulative
0 to 1	0.32%	0.32%	0.19%	0.19%	0.14%	−0.14%
1 to 5	4.86%	5.19%	5.66%	5.85%	−0.80%	0.66%
6 to 10	14.70%	19.89%	16.79%	22.64%	−2.09%	2.75%
11 to 15	21.19%	41.08%	22.83%	45.47%	−1.64%	4.39%
16 to 20	19.24%	60.32%	18.87%	64.34%	0.38%	4.02%
21 to 25	12.11%	72.43%	11.13%	75.47%	0.98%	3.04%
26 to 30	10.27%	82.70%	9.06%	84.53%	1.21%	1.83%
31 to 35	9.62%	92.32%	8.49%	93.02%	1.13%	0.69%
36 to 40	7.14%	99.46%	5.85%	98.87%	1.29%	−0.59%
41 to 45	0.43%	99.89%	1.13%	100.00%	−0.70%	0.11%
46 to 50	0.11%	100.00%	0.00%	100.00%	0.11%	0.00%

212

APPENDIX: DATA TABLES

TABLE A1.4 Bearish Short-Term Time Frame Trend Probability Failure Rates

Number Bars	Confirmed Trend Percentages		Suspect Trend Percentages		Difference Confirmed versus Suspect	
	Individual	Cumulative	Individual	Cumulative	Difference	Cumulative
0 to 1	0.18%	0.18%	0.21%	0.21%	−0.03%	0.193%
1 to 5	4.32%	4.50%	5.42%	5.63%	−1.10%	0.193%
6 to 10	11.61%	16.11%	13.81%	19.44%	−2.20%	2.759%
11 to 15	14.46%	30.57%	15.25%	34.69%	−0.79%	7.168%
16 to 20	13.95%	44.52%	13.66%	48.35%	0.29%	7.965%
21 to 25	10.63%	55.15%	10.36%	58.71%	0.27%	7.086%
26 to 30	9.31%	64.46%	8.42%	67.13%	0.89%	5.308%
31 to 35	7.38%	71.84%	7.15%	74.28%	0.22%	4.292%
36 to 40	5.86%	77.70%	5.41%	79.69%	0.46%	3.637%
41 to 45	4.92%	82.63%	4.29%	83.98%	0.63%	2.751%
46 to 50	4.04%	86.67%	3.57%	87.56%	0.47%	2.191%
51 to 55	2.93%	89.61%	2.73%	90.28%	0.21%	1.834%
56 to 60	2.65%	92.25%	2.32%	92.60%	0.33%	1.416%
61 to 65	2.12%	94.38%	1.78%	94.38%	0.34%	1.218%
66 to 70	1.38%	95.75%	1.38%	95.76%	0.00%	0.953%
71 to 75	1.13%	96.89%	1.10%	96.86%	0.04%	0.760%
76 to 80	0.98%	97.86%	0.87%	97.73%	0.11%	0.622%
81 to 85	0.73%	98.59%	0.77%	98.49%	−0.04%	0.511%
86 to 90	0.56%	99.15%	0.57%	99.07%	−0.02%	0.463%
91 to 95	0.48%	99.63%	0.55%	99.62%	−0.06%	0.370%
96 to 100	0.37%	100.00%	0.38%	100.00%	−0.02%	0.357%

TABLE A1.5 Bearish Intermediate-Term Time Frame Trend Probability Failure Rates (Note: For period from 2002 through 2007 only)

Number Bars	Confirmed Trend Percentages		Suspect Trend Percentages		Difference Confirmed versus Suspect	
	Individual	Cumulative	Individual	Cumulative	Difference	Cumulative
0 to 1	0.10%	0.10%	0.27%	0.27%	−0.17%	0.17%
1 to 5	4.52%	4.62%	6.44%	6.71%	−1.92%	2.09%
6 to 10	14.09%	18.71%	16.28%	22.99%	−2.20%	4.28%
11 to 15	18.19%	36.90%	19.45%	42.44%	−1.26%	5.54%
16 to 20	16.88%	53.78%	16.48%	58.91%	0.40%	5.14%
21 to 25	10.90%	64.68%	10.14%	69.05%	0.77%	4.37%
26 to 30	9.16%	73.84%	8.30%	77.35%	0.86%	3.51%
31 to 35	6.32%	80.16%	5.16%	82.51%	1.16%	2.35%
36 to 40	4.83%	84.99%	4.34%	86.85%	0.49%	1.86%
41 to 45	4.76%	89.75%	3.91%	90.76%	0.85%	1.01%
46 to 50	3.48%	93.23%	3.42%	94.18%	0.06%	0.95%
51 to 55	2.30%	95.53%	2.04%	96.22%	0.26%	0.69%
56 to 60	1.31%	96.84%	1.24%	97.46%	0.07%	0.61%
61 to 65	0.85%	97.70%	0.65%	98.10%	0.20%	0.41%
66 to 70	0.74%	98.44%	0.55%	98.65%	0.19%	0.21%
71 to 75	0.52%	98.95%	0.45%	99.10%	0.07%	0.15%
76 to 80	0.31%	99.26%	0.39%	99.49%	−0.09%	0.23%
81 to 85	0.39%	99.65%	0.28%	99.78%	0.11%	0.12%
86 to 90	0.21%	99.86%	0.11%	99.89%	0.10%	0.03%
91 to 95	0.06%	99.92%	0.08%	99.97%	−0.03%	0.06%
96 to 100	0.08%	100.00%	0.03%	100.00%	0.06%	0.00%

TABLE A1.6 Bearish Long-Term Time Frame Trend Probability Failure Rates (All data included. Note: Data after 2007 skews suspect versus confirmed failure rates and extends the time it takes for a bear market to end. This was deemed a "safer" reading.)

Number Bars	Confirmed Trend Percentages		Suspect Trend Percentages		Difference Confirmed versus Suspect	
	Individual	Cumulative	Individual	Cumulative	Difference	Cumulative
0 to 1	0.05%	0.05%	0.11%	0.11%	−0.02%	0.068%
1 to 5	2.16%	2.21%	5.28%	5.39%	−3.52%	0.068%
6 to 10	15.67%	17.88%	17.13%	22.52%	−2.47%	2.073%
11 to 15	17.86%	35.74%	18.37%	40.89%	−0.86%	6.179%
16 to 20	15.74%	51.49%	15.41%	56.30%	1.24%	6.440%
21 to 25	21.79%	73.28%	17.73%	74.03%	4.50%	4.994%
26 to 30	17.02%	90.30%	16.43%	90.46%	1.38%	5.325%
31 to 35	5.86%	96.16%	6.14%	96.61%	0.33%	4.754%
36 to 40	2.93%	99.09%	2.32%	98.92%	0.53%	1.846%
41 to 45	0.86%	99.95%	1.02%	99.95%	−0.20%	0.894%
46 to 50	0.05%	100.00%	0.00%	99.95%	−0.29%	0.645%
51 to 55	0.00%	100.00%	0.05%	100.00%	−0.33%	0.328%
96 to 100	0.02%	100.00%	0.00%	100.00%	0.02%	0.041%

Trade Failure Probabilities for Bullish and Bearish Trend

The latter half of Chapter 1 considered *trade* failure probability rates. Figures 1.17 through 1.22 utilized the following raw data to construct the charts presented in the latter half of Chapter 1. This data encompasses the same period from 2002 to 2011 for bullish and bearish trends based on *trade* rather than *trend* failures.

TABLE A1.7 Bullish Short-Term Time Frame Trade Failure Probability Rates

Number Bars	Confirmed Trend Percentages		Suspect Trend Percentages		Difference Confirmed versus Suspect	
	Individual	Cumulative	Individual	Cumulative	Difference	Cumulative
0 to 1	22.58%	22.58%	26.36%	26.36%	−3.78%	3.78%
2 to 3	22.09%	44.66%	24.20%	50.56%	−2.12%	5.90%
4 to 5	11.16%	55.82%	11.58%	62.14%	−0.42%	6.32%
6 to 10	14.56%	70.38%	13.81%	75.95%	0.75%	5.58%
11 to 15	7.06%	77.43%	6.32%	82.27%	0.74%	4.84%
16 to 20	4.38%	81.81%	3.96%	86.23%	0.42%	4.42%
21 to 25	3.28%	85.09%	2.61%	88.84%	0.66%	3.76%
26 to 30	2.34%	87.43%	1.88%	90.72%	0.46%	3.30%
31 to 35	1.97%	89.40%	1.53%	92.25%	0.45%	2.85%
36 to 40	1.59%	90.99%	1.21%	93.46%	0.38%	2.47%
41 to 45	1.51%	92.49%	1.02%	94.48%	0.48%	1.98%
46 to 50	1.20%	93.69%	0.84%	95.32%	0.36%	1.63%
51 to 55	1.04%	94.73%	0.82%	96.14%	0.22%	1.40%
56 to 60	0.90%	95.63%	0.66%	96.80%	0.24%	1.17%
61 to 65	0.78%	96.41%	0.52%	97.32%	0.26%	0.91%
66 to 70	0.63%	97.04%	0.50%	97.82%	0.14%	0.77%
71 to 75	0.58%	97.62%	0.40%	98.21%	0.18%	0.59%
76 to 80	0.56%	98.18%	0.42%	98.64%	0.13%	0.45%
81 to 85	0.52%	98.70%	0.41%	99.05%	0.11%	0.34%
86 to 90	0.44%	99.14%	0.35%	99.39%	0.09%	0.25%
91 to 95	0.43%	99.57%	0.34%	99.73%	0.08%	0.17%
96 to 100	0.43%	100.00%	0.27%	100.00%	0.17%	0.00%

TABLE A1.8 Bullish Intermediate-Term Time Frame Trade Failure
Probability Rates

Number Bars	Confirmed Trend Percentages		Suspect Trend Percentages		Difference Confirmed versus Suspect	
	Individual	Cumulative	Individual	Cumulative	Difference	Cumulative
0 to 1	17.74%	17.74%	22.09%	22.09%	−4.36%	3.78%
2 to 3	20.28%	38.02%	23.78%	45.87%	−3.49%	5.90%
4 to 5	10.58%	48.60%	10.89%	56.76%	−0.31%	6.32%
6 to 10	14.44%	63.04%	13.04%	69.80%	1.41%	5.58%
11 to 15	7.72%	70.76%	6.24%	76.04%	1.48%	4.84%
16 to 20	5.26%	76.02%	4.26%	80.30%	1.00%	4.42%
21 to 25	3.82%	79.84%	2.96%	83.26%	0.86%	3.76%
26 to 30	2.97%	82.81%	2.38%	85.64%	0.59%	3.30%
31 to 35	2.47%	85.28%	2.34%	87.98%	0.13%	2.85%
36 to 40	2.13%	87.40%	2.21%	90.19%	−0.08%	2.47%
41 to 45	2.28%	89.69%	2.32%	92.51%	−0.04%	1.98%
46 to 50	1.52%	91.20%	1.20%	93.71%	0.32%	1.63%
51 to 55	1.30%	92.50%	0.98%	94.69%	0.32%	1.40%
56 to 60	0.86%	93.36%	0.52%	95.20%	0.34%	1.17%
61 to 65	0.75%	94.11%	0.36%	95.56%	0.39%	0.91%
66 to 70	0.77%	94.88%	0.49%	96.05%	0.28%	0.77%
71 to 75	0.96%	95.84%	0.87%	96.92%	0.09%	0.59%
76 to 80	0.76%	96.60%	0.55%	97.46%	0.21%	0.45%
81 to 85	0.77%	97.37%	0.55%	98.01%	0.23%	0.34%
86 to 90	0.91%	98.29%	0.64%	98.65%	0.28%	0.25%
91 to 95	0.73%	99.02%	0.52%	99.17%	0.21%	0.17%
96 to 100	0.98%	100.00%	0.83%	100.00%	0.15%	0.00%

TABLE A1.9 Bullish Long-Term Time Frame Trade Failure Probability Rates

Number Bars	Confirmed Trend Percentages		Suspect Trend Percentages		Difference Confirmed versus Suspect	
	Individual	Cumulative	Individual	Cumulative	Difference	Cumulative
0 to 1	16.25%	16.25%	20.66%	20.66%	−4.40%	4.40%
2 to 3	19.23%	35.48%	21.51%	42.17%	−2.28%	6.68%
4 to 5	10.29%	45.77%	10.63%	52.80%	−0.35%	7.03%
6 to 10	15.52%	61.29%	14.79%	67.59%	0.73%	6.30%
11 to 15	6.61%	67.90%	6.08%	73.68%	0.53%	5.77%
16 to 20	5.41%	73.32%	4.20%	77.88%	1.21%	4.56%
21 to 25	4.14%	77.46%	3.92%	81.79%	0.22%	4.34%
26 to 30	2.10%	79.55%	1.60%	83.39%	0.50%	3.84%
31 to 35	1.90%	81.45%	1.58%	84.97%	0.32%	3.52%
36 to 40	1.52%	82.97%	1.31%	86.28%	0.21%	3.31%
41 to 45	1.22%	84.19%	0.90%	87.18%	0.32%	2.98%
46 to 50	1.59%	85.79%	1.95%	89.12%	−0.35%	3.34%
51 to 55	1.47%	87.26%	1.14%	90.26%	0.33%	3.00%
56 to 60	2.06%	89.32%	1.27%	91.53%	0.79%	2.21%
61 to 65	2.24%	91.56%	2.04%	93.57%	0.21%	2.01%
66 to 70	1.11%	92.67%	0.98%	94.55%	0.13%	1.88%
71 to 75	0.70%	93.37%	0.44%	94.99%	0.26%	1.62%
76 to 80	1.00%	94.37%	0.57%	95.56%	0.43%	1.19%
81 to 85	0.38%	94.75%	0.48%	96.04%	−0.11%	1.29%
86 to 90	0.91%	95.66%	0.85%	96.89%	0.06%	1.23%
91 to 95	2.20%	97.87%	1.82%	98.71%	0.39%	0.84%
96 to 100	2.13%	100.00%	1.29%	100.00%	0.84%	0.00%

TABLE A1.10 Bearish Short-Term Time Frame Trade Failure Probability Rates

Number Bars	Confirmed Trend Percentages		Suspect Trend Percentages		Difference Confirmed versus Suspect	
	Individual	Cumulative	Individual	Cumulative	Difference	Cumulative
0 to 1	25.33%	25.33%	26.65%	26.65%	−1.32%	1.32%
2 to 3	23.59%	48.92%	25.23%	51.88%	−1.64%	2.96%
4 to 5	11.53%	60.45%	11.78%	63.67%	−0.26%	3.22%
6 to 10	13.23%	73.68%	13.28%	76.95%	−0.05%	3.27%
11 to 15	6.68%	80.36%	6.17%	83.12%	0.51%	2.76%
16 to 20	4.29%	84.64%	4.01%	87.13%	0.28%	2.48%
21 to 25	2.76%	87.41%	2.50%	89.62%	0.27%	2.21%
26 to 30	2.13%	89.54%	1.86%	91.48%	0.27%	1.95%
31 to 35	1.78%	91.32%	1.50%	92.99%	0.28%	1.67%
36 to 40	1.43%	92.75%	1.24%	94.22%	0.19%	1.48%
41 to 45	1.18%	93.92%	0.97%	95.19%	0.21%	1.27%
46 to 50	1.00%	94.93%	0.88%	96.07%	0.12%	1.14%
51 to 55	0.79%	95.72%	0.72%	96.79%	0.07%	1.08%
56 to 60	0.79%	96.51%	0.61%	97.41%	0.18%	0.90%
61 to 65	0.64%	97.15%	0.45%	97.86%	0.19%	0.71%
66 to 70	0.57%	97.72%	0.38%	98.24%	0.18%	0.52%
71 to 75	0.49%	98.21%	0.37%	98.61%	0.12%	0.40%
76 to 80	0.43%	98.64%	0.32%	98.93%	0.11%	0.29%
81 to 85	0.36%	99.00%	0.31%	99.24%	0.05%	0.24%
86 to 90	0.35%	99.35%	0.25%	99.49%	0.10%	0.14%
91 to 95	0.38%	99.73%	0.26%	99.75%	0.12%	0.02%
96 to 100	0.27%	100.00%	0.25%	100.00%	0.02%	0.00%

TABLE A1.11 Bearish Intermediate-Term Time Frame Trade Failure
Probability Rates

Number Bars	Confirmed Trend Percentages		Suspect Trend Percentages		Difference Confirmed versus Suspect	
	Individual	Cumulative	Individual	Cumulative	Difference	Cumulative
0 to 1	22.44%	22.44%	23.54%	23.54%	−1.10%	1.10%
2 to 3	22.05%	44.49%	24.88%	48.41%	−2.82%	3.92%
4 to 5	10.75%	55.24%	11.53%	59.95%	−0.78%	4.70%
6 to 10	13.99%	69.24%	13.62%	73.57%	0.37%	4.33%
11 to 15	6.75%	75.99%	6.26%	79.83%	0.49%	3.84%
16 to 20	3.94%	79.92%	3.14%	82.97%	0.79%	3.05%
21 to 25	3.04%	82.96%	2.48%	85.45%	0.56%	2.49%
26 to 30	2.88%	85.84%	2.15%	87.60%	0.73%	1.76%
31 to 35	1.88%	87.72%	1.81%	89.40%	0.08%	1.68%
36 to 40	1.60%	89.32%	1.34%	90.74%	0.26%	1.42%
41 to 45	1.84%	91.16%	1.57%	92.31%	0.27%	1.15%
46 to 50	1.65%	92.82%	1.25%	93.56%	0.40%	0.75%
51 to 55	1.14%	93.96%	1.17%	94.73%	−0.03%	0.77%
56 to 60	0.96%	94.92%	0.93%	95.66%	0.04%	0.74%
61 to 65	1.05%	95.97%	0.90%	96.56%	0.15%	0.59%
66 to 70	0.78%	96.75%	0.58%	97.14%	0.20%	0.39%
71 to 75	0.79%	97.54%	0.53%	97.67%	0.27%	0.12%
76 to 80	0.85%	98.39%	0.72%	98.39%	0.13%	−0.01%
81 to 85	0.53%	98.93%	0.51%	98.89%	0.02%	−0.03%
86 to 90	0.41%	99.34%	0.40%	99.29%	0.01%	−0.04%
91 to 95	0.38%	99.72%	0.43%	99.73%	−0.05%	0.01%
96 to 100	0.28%	100.00%	0.27%	100.00%	0.01%	0.00%

TABLE A1.12 Bearish Long-Term Time Frame Trade Failure Probability Rates

Number Bars	Confirmed Trend Percentages		Suspect Trend Percentages		Difference Confirmed versus Suspect	
	Individual	Cumulative	Individual	Cumulative	Difference	Cumulative
0 to 1	14.99%	14.99%	18.93%	18.93%	−3.94%	3.94%
2 to 3	19.51%	34.50%	22.25%	41.18%	−2.74%	6.68%
4 to 5	9.66%	44.16%	10.23%	51.41%	−0.57%	7.25%
6 to 10	17.95%	62.11%	15.85%	67.26%	2.10%	5.15%
11 to 15	8.40%	70.51%	6.94%	74.20%	1.46%	3.69%
16 to 20	4.84%	75.35%	4.69%	78.89%	0.15%	3.54%
21 to 25	2.68%	78.03%	2.68%	81.57%	0.00%	3.54%
26 to 30	3.72%	81.75%	3.54%	85.12%	0.17%	3.37%
31 to 35	6.50%	88.25%	5.76%	90.88%	0.74%	2.62%
36 to 40	3.89%	92.15%	3.36%	94.24%	0.53%	2.09%
41 to 45	3.84%	95.99%	2.68%	96.92%	1.16%	0.94%
46 to 50	2.02%	98.00%	1.25%	98.18%	0.76%	0.17%
51 to 55	0.35%	98.35%	0.39%	98.57%	−0.04%	0.22%
56 to 60	0.35%	98.70%	0.36%	98.93%	−0.01%	0.22%
61 to 65	0.30%	99.00%	0.21%	99.14%	0.08%	0.14%
66 to 70	0.30%	99.30%	0.32%	99.46%	−0.02%	0.16%
71 to 75	0.26%	99.56%	0.25%	99.71%	0.01%	0.15%
76 to 80	0.11%	99.67%	0.07%	99.79%	0.03%	0.12%
81 to 85	0.26%	99.93%	0.14%	99.93%	0.12%	0.00%
86 to 90	0.04%	99.96%	0.04%	99.96%	0.00%	0.00%
91 to 95	0.02%	99.98%	0.00%	99.96%	0.02%	−0.02%
96 to 100	0.02%	100.00%	0.04%	100.00%	−0.02%	0.00%

CHAPTER 2: ANCHOR ZONES: THE KEY TO TIMING TRADES

In Chapter 2 anchor zones were introduced and used to consider stop outs both for losses and profits for the same data set first analyzed in Chapter 1. The following tables contain the raw data from 2002 to 2011 for bullish and bearish trends based on trade terminations for bullish and bearish cases.

Bullish Profit and Loss Cases

TABLE A2.1 Bullish Short-Term Time Frame Trade Termination Observations in Profit Case

Number Bars	Confirmed Trend Percentages		Suspect Trend Percentages		Difference Confirmed versus Suspect	
	Individual	Cumulative	Individual	Cumulative	Difference	Cumulative
0 to 1	6.34%	6.34%	4.35%	4.35%	4.80%	−1.99%
2 to 3	7.44%	13.77%	7.61%	11.96%	14.50%	−1.81%
4 to 5	5.44%	19.21%	5.94%	17.90%	22.41%	−1.31%
6 to 10	9.20%	28.41%	10.69%	28.59%	36.43%	0.18%
11 to 15	6.30%	34.71%	7.43%	36.01%	45.60%	1.30%
16 to 20	5.50%	40.21%	5.36%	41.38%	52.80%	1.16%
21 to 25	4.20%	44.41%	4.78%	46.16%	58.21%	1.74%
26 to 30	3.87%	48.28%	3.70%	49.86%	62.42%	1.57%
31 to 35	3.07%	51.35%	3.22%	53.08%	66.00%	1.73%
36 to 40	2.80%	54.15%	2.61%	55.69%	68.93%	1.54%
41 to 45	2.77%	56.92%	2.43%	58.12%	71.67%	1.20%
46 to 50	2.07%	58.99%	2.07%	60.18%	73.87%	1.19%
51 to 60	4.03%	63.02%	4.53%	64.71%	77.52%	1.69%
61 to 70	4.17%	67.19%	4.24%	68.95%	80.66%	1.76%
71 to 80	4.13%	71.32%	3.59%	72.54%	83.32%	1.21%
81 to 90	3.70%	75.03%	2.90%	75.43%	85.40%	0.41%
91 to 100	2.90%	77.93%	2.72%	78.15%	87.21%	0.23%
101 to 110	2.63%	80.56%	2.97%	81.12%	88.94%	0.56%
111 to 120	2.57%	83.13%	2.72%	83.84%	90.61%	0.71%
121 to 130	2.93%	86.06%	2.43%	86.27%	92.15%	0.21%
131 to 140	2.53%	88.60%	2.46%	88.73%	93.67%	0.14%
141 to 150	2.37%	90.96%	2.43%	91.16%	95.02%	0.20%
151 to 160	2.27%	93.23%	1.99%	93.15%	96.20%	−0.08%
161 to 170	2.17%	95.40%	1.88%	95.04%	97.27%	−0.36%
171 to 180	2.00%	97.40%	1.67%	96.70%	98.30%	−0.70%
181 to 190	1.43%	98.83%	2.07%	98.77%	99.22%	−0.06%
191 to 200	1.17%	100.00%	1.23%	100.00%	100.00%	0.00%

TABLE A2.2 Bullish Short-Term Time Frame Trade Termination Observations in Loss Case

Number Bars	Confirmed Trend Percentages		Suspect Trend Percentages		Difference Confirmed versus Suspect	
	Individual	Cumulative	Individual	Cumulative	Difference	Cumulative
0 to 1	4.65%	4.65%	4.60%	4.60%	0.05%	−0.05%
2 to 3	9.70%	14.35%	11.11%	15.71%	−1.41%	1.36%
4 to 5	8.32%	22.67%	8.87%	24.58%	−0.55%	1.91%
6 to 10	15.08%	37.75%	15.47%	40.05%	−0.39%	2.30%
11 to 15	9.83%	47.58%	9.90%	49.95%	−0.08%	2.37%
16 to 20	8.04%	55.62%	7.39%	57.35%	0.64%	1.73%
21 to 25	5.73%	61.35%	5.64%	62.99%	0.09%	1.64%
26 to 30	4.26%	65.61%	4.42%	67.41%	−0.16%	1.80%
31 to 35	3.74%	69.35%	3.68%	71.09%	0.06%	1.74%
36 to 40	3.17%	72.52%	2.79%	73.88%	0.38%	1.36%
41 to 45	2.89%	75.41%	2.64%	76.52%	0.25%	1.11%
46 to 50	2.35%	77.77%	2.13%	78.65%	0.23%	0.89%
51 to 60	3.77%	81.53%	3.09%	81.75%	0.67%	0.21%
61 to 70	2.94%	84.47%	2.69%	84.44%	0.25%	−0.03%
71 to 80	2.24%	86.71%	2.35%	86.79%	−0.11%	0.08%
81 to 90	1.81%	88.52%	1.60%	88.39%	0.21%	−0.13%
91 to 100	1.76%	90.28%	1.23%	89.61%	0.53%	−0.67%
101 to 110	1.52%	91.80%	1.27%	90.88%	0.25%	−0.91%
111 to 120	1.30%	93.10%	1.46%	92.35%	−0.16%	−0.75%
121 to 130	1.26%	94.37%	1.11%	93.46%	0.15%	−0.90%
131 to 140	1.09%	95.46%	1.40%	94.86%	−0.31%	−0.60%
141 to 150	0.99%	96.45%	1.07%	95.93%	−0.08%	−0.52%
151 to 160	0.83%	97.28%	0.99%	96.92%	−0.16%	−0.36%
161 to 170	0.76%	98.03%	0.79%	97.70%	−0.03%	−0.33%
171 to 180	0.79%	98.82%	0.79%	98.49%	0.00%	−0.33%
181 to 190	0.60%	99.43%	0.75%	99.25%	−0.15%	−0.18%
191 to 200	0.57%	100.00%	0.75%	100.00%	−0.18%	0.00%

TABLE A2.3 Bullish Intermediate-Term Time Frame Trade Termination
Observations in Profit Case

Number Bars	Confirmed Trend Percentages Individual	Cumulative	Suspect Trend Percentages Individual	Cumulative	Difference Confirmed versus Suspect Difference	Cumulative
0 to 1	6.54%	6.54%	7.28%	7.28%	−0.74%	0.74%
2 to 3	9.20%	15.75%	7.70%	14.99%	1.50%	−0.76%
4 to 5	7.57%	23.31%	8.12%	23.11%	−0.56%	−0.20%
6 to 10	13.09%	36.40%	12.04%	35.15%	1.04%	−1.25%
11 to 15	10.84%	47.24%	10.15%	45.31%	0.68%	−1.93%
16 to 20	8.73%	55.96%	8.19%	53.50%	0.53%	−2.46%
21 to 25	7.50%	63.46%	7.28%	60.78%	0.22%	−2.68%
26 to 30	4.43%	67.89%	5.18%	65.97%	−0.75%	−1.93%
31 to 35	4.29%	72.19%	4.90%	70.87%	−0.61%	−1.32%
36 to 40	3.68%	75.87%	4.41%	75.28%	−0.73%	−0.59%
41 to 45	2.18%	78.05%	3.01%	78.29%	−0.83%	0.24%
46 to 50	1.70%	79.75%	1.68%	79.97%	0.02%	0.22%
51 to 60	3.75%	83.50%	3.57%	83.54%	0.18%	0.04%
61 to 70	3.20%	86.71%	2.87%	86.41%	0.33%	−0.29%
71 to 80	3.00%	89.71%	2.94%	89.36%	0.06%	−0.35%
81 to 90	2.18%	91.89%	2.17%	91.53%	0.01%	−0.36%
91 to 100	1.98%	93.87%	1.82%	93.35%	0.16%	−0.52%
101 to 110	1.57%	95.43%	1.47%	94.82%	0.10%	−0.61%
111 to 120	0.14%	95.57%	1.47%	96.29%	−1.33%	0.72%
121 to 130	0.95%	96.52%	0.84%	97.13%	0.11%	0.61%
131 to 140	0.61%	97.14%	0.42%	97.55%	0.19%	0.41%
141 to 150	0.75%	97.89%	0.98%	98.53%	−0.23%	0.64%
151 to 160	0.41%	98.30%	0.70%	99.23%	−0.29%	0.93%
161 to 170	0.20%	98.50%	0.21%	99.44%	−0.01%	0.94%
171 to 180	0.61%	99.11%	0.07%	99.51%	0.54%	0.40%
181 to 190	0.55%	99.66%	0.07%	99.58%	0.48%	−0.08%
191 to 200	0.34%	100.00%	0.42%	100.00%	−0.08%	0.00%

TABLE A2.4 Bullish Intermediate-Term Time Frame Trade Termination Observations in Loss Case

Number Bars	Confirmed Trend Percentages		Suspect Trend Percentages		Difference Confirmed versus Suspect	
	Individual	Cumulative	Individual	Cumulative	Difference	Cumulative
0 to 1	4.01%	4.01%	3.00%	3.00%	1.01%	−1.01%
2 to 3	7.98%	11.98%	10.60%	13.59%	−2.62%	1.61%
4 to 5	6.78%	18.76%	8.54%	22.14%	−1.76%	3.37%
6 to 10	13.70%	32.47%	13.96%	36.10%	−0.26%	3.63%
11 to 15	9.66%	42.13%	8.62%	44.72%	1.04%	2.59%
16 to 20	8.12%	50.25%	6.65%	51.38%	1.46%	1.13%
21 to 25	6.25%	56.50%	6.37%	57.74%	−0.11%	1.24%
26 to 30	5.09%	61.60%	5.01%	62.75%	0.08%	1.16%
31 to 35	4.22%	65.81%	5.54%	68.30%	−1.33%	2.48%
36 to 40	3.06%	68.87%	4.15%	72.44%	−1.09%	3.57%
41 to 45	2.85%	71.71%	3.29%	75.73%	−0.44%	4.01%
46 to 50	2.18%	73.89%	2.01%	77.74%	0.17%	3.85%
51 to 60	3.87%	77.76%	2.71%	80.45%	1.15%	2.69%
61 to 70	3.51%	81.27%	3.20%	83.66%	0.31%	2.38%
71 to 80	2.57%	83.84%	2.83%	86.49%	−0.27%	2.65%
81 to 90	3.16%	87.00%	2.09%	88.58%	1.07%	1.58%
91 to 100	2.85%	89.85%	2.51%	91.09%	0.34%	1.24%
101 to 110	3.65%	93.50%	3.24%	94.33%	0.41%	0.83%
111 to 120	3.16%	96.66%	2.83%	97.17%	0.33%	0.50%
121 to 130	0.98%	97.65%	0.66%	97.82%	0.33%	0.18%
131 to 140	0.32%	97.96%	0.53%	98.36%	−0.22%	0.40%
141 to 150	0.25%	98.21%	0.12%	98.48%	0.12%	0.27%
151 to 160	0.70%	98.91%	0.41%	98.89%	0.29%	−0.02%
161 to 170	0.46%	99.37%	0.53%	99.43%	−0.08%	0.06%
171 to 180	0.28%	99.65%	0.21%	99.63%	0.08%	−0.02%
181 to 190	0.18%	99.82%	0.16%	99.79%	0.01%	−0.03%
191 to 200	0.18%	100.00%	0.21%	100.00%	−0.03%	0.00%

TABLE A2.5 Bullish Long-Term Time Frame Trade Termination Observations in Profit Case

Number Bars	Confirmed Trend Percentages		Suspect Trend Percentages		Difference Confirmed versus Suspect	
	Individual	Cumulative	Individual	Cumulative	Difference	Cumulative
0 to 1	12.19%	12.19%	19.30%	19.30%	−7.12%	7.12%
2 to 3	26.52%	38.71%	21.20%	40.51%	5.32%	1.80%
4 to 5	16.13%	54.84%	16.77%	57.28%	−0.64%	2.44%
6 to 10	18.64%	73.48%	20.89%	78.16%	−2.25%	4.69%
11 to 15	10.39%	83.87%	9.49%	87.66%	0.90%	3.79%
16 to 20	6.09%	89.96%	4.11%	91.77%	1.98%	1.81%
21 to 25	4.66%	94.62%	1.90%	93.67%	2.76%	−0.95%
26 to 30	0.36%	94.98%	0.95%	94.62%	−0.59%	−0.36%
31 to 35	0.36%	95.34%	0.63%	95.25%	−0.27%	−0.09%
36 to 40	0.72%	96.06%	0.63%	95.89%	0.08%	−0.17%
41 to 45	1.08%	97.13%	0.63%	96.52%	0.44%	−0.61%
46 to 50	1.08%	98.21%	0.95%	97.47%	0.13%	−0.74%
51 to 60	1.43%	99.64%	0.00%	97.47%	1.43%	−2.17%
61 to 70	0.36%	100.00%	0.63%	98.10%	−0.27%	−1.90%
71 to 80	0.00%	100.00%	0.95%	99.05%	−0.95%	−0.95%
81 to 90	0.00%	100.00%	0.63%	99.68%	−0.63%	−0.32%
91 to 100	0.00%	100.00%	0.32%	100.00%	−0.32%	0.00%

TABLE A2.6 Bullish Long-Term Time Frame Trade Termination Observations in Loss Case

Number Bars	Confirmed Trend Percentages		Suspect Trend Percentages		Difference Confirmed versus Suspect	
	Individual	Cumulative	Individual	Cumulative	Difference	Cumulative
0 to 1	7.35%	7.35%	6.58%	6.58%	0.77%	−0.77%
2 to 3	17.54%	24.88%	17.11%	23.68%	0.43%	−1.20%
4 to 5	20.14%	45.02%	19.08%	42.76%	1.06%	−2.26%
6 to 10	20.62%	65.64%	22.70%	65.46%	−2.08%	−0.18%
11 to 15	13.98%	79.62%	14.80%	80.26%	−0.82%	0.64%
16 to 20	7.11%	86.73%	4.93%	85.20%	2.17%	−1.53%
21 to 25	5.45%	92.18%	3.62%	88.82%	1.83%	−3.36%
26 to 30	0.00%	92.18%	2.63%	91.45%	−2.63%	−0.73%
31 to 35	1.42%	93.60%	1.64%	93.09%	−0.22%	−0.51%
36 to 40	1.42%	95.02%	1.64%	94.74%	−0.22%	−0.29%
41 to 45	0.71%	95.73%	0.99%	95.72%	−0.28%	−0.01%
46 to 50	1.42%	97.16%	1.64%	97.37%	−0.22%	0.21%
51 to 60	2.13%	99.29%	1.64%	99.01%	0.49%	−0.28%
61 to 70	0.71%	100.00%	0.66%	99.67%	0.05%	−0.33%
71 to 80	0.00%	100.00%	0.00%	99.67%	0.00%	−0.33%
81 to 90	0.00%	100.00%	0.33%	100.00%	−0.33%	0.00%
91 to 100	0.00%	100.00%	0.00%	100.00%	0.00%	0.00%

Bearish Profit and Loss Cases

| TABLE A2.7 | Bearish Short-Term Time Frame Trade Termination Observations in Profit Case |

Number Bars	Confirmed Trend Percentages		Suspect Trend Percentages		Difference Confirmed versus Suspect	
	Individual	Cumulative	Individual	Cumulative	Difference	Cumulative
0 to 1	54.23%	54.23%	50.61%	50.61%	3.62%	−3.62%
2 to 3	17.49%	71.73%	18.91%	69.53%	−1.42%	−2.20%
4 to 5	7.20%	78.92%	7.87%	77.40%	−0.68%	−1.52%
6 to 10	8.05%	86.97%	8.69%	86.09%	−0.64%	−0.88%
11 to 15	3.82%	90.79%	3.81%	89.90%	0.02%	−0.90%
16 to 20	2.04%	92.83%	2.20%	92.10%	−0.16%	−0.74%
21 to 25	1.38%	94.21%	1.66%	93.76%	−0.28%	−0.45%
26 to 30	1.01%	95.23%	1.28%	95.04%	−0.27%	−0.19%
31 to 35	0.72%	95.95%	0.76%	95.80%	−0.04%	−0.15%
36 to 40	0.68%	96.63%	0.71%	96.51%	−0.03%	−0.12%
41 to 45	0.47%	97.10%	0.44%	96.95%	0.03%	−0.14%
46 to 50	0.33%	97.43%	0.36%	97.31%	−0.03%	−0.12%
51 to 60	0.55%	97.98%	0.58%	97.90%	−0.03%	−0.09%
61 to 70	0.45%	98.43%	0.46%	98.36%	−0.02%	−0.07%
71 to 80	0.30%	98.73%	0.39%	98.75%	−0.09%	0.02%
81 to 90	0.27%	99.00%	0.25%	99.00%	0.02%	0.00%
91 to 100	0.17%	99.17%	0.24%	99.24%	−0.07%	0.07%
101 to 110	0.16%	99.33%	0.06%	99.30%	0.10%	−0.03%
111 to 120	0.13%	99.46%	0.12%	99.42%	0.01%	−0.05%
121 to 130	0.14%	99.60%	0.14%	99.56%	0.00%	−0.04%
131 to 140	0.06%	99.66%	0.14%	99.70%	−0.09%	0.04%
141 to 150	0.08%	99.75%	0.09%	99.79%	0.00%	0.05%
151 to 160	0.07%	99.82%	0.05%	99.84%	0.02%	0.02%
161 to 170	0.06%	99.88%	0.04%	99.88%	0.02%	0.00%
171 to 180	0.04%	99.92%	0.03%	99.91%	0.00%	0.00%
181 to 190	0.05%	99.96%	0.06%	99.98%	−0.01%	0.01%
191 to 200	0.04%	100.00%	0.02%	100.00%	0.01%	0.00%

TABLE A2.8 Bearish Short-Term Time Frame Trade Termination Observations in Loss Case

Number Bars	Confirmed Trend Percentages		Suspect Trend Percentages		Difference Confirmed versus Suspect	
	Individual	Cumulative	Individual	Cumulative	Difference	Cumulative
0 to 1	25.04%	25.04%	20.06%	20.06%	4.98%	−4.98%
2 to 3	21.49%	46.53%	19.29%	39.35%	2.20%	−7.18%
4 to 5	10.58%	57.10%	11.11%	50.46%	−0.53%	−6.65%
6 to 10	12.65%	69.76%	13.87%	64.33%	−1.22%	−5.42%
11 to 15	7.41%	77.17%	8.14%	72.47%	−0.73%	−4.70%
16 to 20	4.74%	81.91%	5.86%	78.34%	−1.13%	−3.57%
21 to 25	3.35%	85.26%	3.59%	81.92%	−0.24%	−3.33%
26 to 30	2.29%	87.55%	2.67%	84.59%	−0.38%	−2.95%
31 to 35	1.82%	89.37%	2.60%	87.19%	−0.77%	−2.18%
36 to 40	1.67%	91.05%	1.70%	88.89%	−0.03%	−2.16%
41 to 45	1.36%	92.40%	1.46%	90.35%	−0.10%	−2.06%
46 to 50	0.77%	93.17%	1.16%	91.50%	−0.39%	−1.67%
51 to 60	1.51%	94.68%	1.83%	93.33%	−0.32%	−1.34%
61 to 70	1.12%	95.80%	1.16%	94.49%	−0.04%	−1.31%
71 to 80	0.89%	96.69%	0.84%	95.33%	0.05%	−1.35%
81 to 90	0.55%	97.24%	0.67%	96.00%	−0.12%	−1.23%
91 to 100	0.50%	97.74%	0.93%	96.94%	−0.43%	−0.80%
101 to 110	0.50%	98.24%	0.63%	97.57%	−0.13%	−0.67%
111 to 120	0.33%	98.58%	0.43%	98.00%	−0.09%	−0.58%
121 to 130	0.27%	98.85%	0.37%	98.38%	−0.11%	−0.47%
131 to 140	0.27%	99.11%	0.22%	98.60%	0.04%	−0.51%
141 to 150	0.20%	99.31%	0.28%	98.88%	−0.08%	−0.43%
151 to 160	0.18%	99.50%	0.32%	99.20%	−0.13%	−0.30%
161 to 170	0.13%	99.63%	0.24%	99.44%	−0.11%	−0.19%
171 to 180	0.12%	99.75%	0.26%	99.70%	−0.14%	−0.05%
181 to 190	0.15%	99.90%	0.17%	99.87%	−0.02%	−0.03%
191 to 200	0.10%	100.00%	0.13%	100.00%	−0.03%	0.00%

TABLE A2.9 Bearish Intermediate-Term Time Frame Trade Termination Observations in Profit Case

Number Bars	Confirmed Trend Percentages		Suspect Trend Percentages		Difference Confirmed versus Suspect	
	Individual	Cumulative	Individual	Cumulative	Difference	Cumulative
0 to 1	45.19%	45.19%	46.49%	46.49%	−1.30%	1.30%
2 to 3	14.39%	59.58%	15.88%	62.37%	−1.49%	2.79%
4 to 5	6.69%	66.28%	7.18%	69.55%	−0.48%	3.27%
6 to 10	9.58%	75.86%	8.56%	78.11%	1.02%	2.25%
11 to 15	5.73%	81.58%	5.03%	83.14%	0.69%	1.56%
16 to 20	2.96%	84.54%	2.53%	85.67%	0.43%	1.13%
21 to 25	2.16%	86.70%	1.96%	87.63%	0.19%	0.93%
26 to 30	1.77%	88.46%	1.60%	89.23%	0.16%	0.77%
31 to 35	1.43%	89.89%	1.36%	90.60%	0.06%	0.71%
36 to 40	1.38%	91.27%	1.28%	91.88%	0.09%	0.61%
41 to 45	0.71%	91.98%	0.70%	92.58%	0.01%	0.60%
46 to 50	1.05%	93.03%	1.02%	93.60%	0.03%	0.57%
51 to 60	1.50%	94.53%	1.34%	94.95%	0.15%	0.42%
61 to 70	1.14%	95.67%	0.90%	95.85%	0.24%	0.18%
71 to 80	0.80%	96.47%	0.58%	96.43%	0.22%	−0.03%
81 to 90	0.37%	96.84%	0.40%	96.83%	−0.03%	−0.01%
91 to 100	0.54%	97.38%	0.52%	97.35%	0.02%	−0.03%
101 to 110	0.39%	97.77%	0.40%	97.75%	−0.01%	−0.02%
111 to 120	0.29%	98.06%	0.46%	98.22%	−0.17%	0.15%
121 to 130	0.46%	98.52%	0.32%	98.54%	0.14%	0.01%
131 to 140	0.27%	98.79%	0.38%	98.92%	−0.11%	0.12%
141 to 150	0.49%	99.29%	0.36%	99.28%	0.13%	−0.01%
151 to 160	0.22%	99.51%	0.22%	99.50%	0.00%	−0.01%
161 to 170	0.12%	99.63%	0.10%	99.60%	0.02%	−0.03%
171 to 180	0.22%	99.85%	0.14%	99.74%	0.08%	−0.11%
181 to 190	0.10%	99.95%	0.16%	99.90%	−0.06%	−0.05%
191 to 200	0.05%	100.00%	0.10%	100.00%	−0.05%	0.00%

TABLE A2.10 Bearish Intermediate-Term Time Frame Trade Termination Observations in Loss Case

Number Bars	Confirmed Trend Percentages		Suspect Trend Percentages		Difference Confirmed versus Suspect	
	Individual	Cumulative	Individual	Cumulative	Difference	Cumulative
0 to 1	22.28%	22.28%	18.39%	18.39%	3.89%	−3.89%
2 to 3	15.67%	37.94%	14.91%	33.30%	0.76%	−4.64%
4 to 5	8.01%	45.96%	8.78%	42.08%	−0.77%	−3.88%
6 to 10	14.23%	60.19%	15.98%	58.06%	−1.75%	−2.13%
11 to 15	9.02%	69.21%	9.01%	67.07%	0.01%	−2.14%
16 to 20	5.43%	74.63%	5.90%	72.97%	−0.47%	−1.66%
21 to 25	4.49%	79.12%	4.41%	77.38%	0.08%	−1.74%
26 to 30	3.70%	82.82%	3.62%	81.00%	0.08%	−1.82%
31 to 35	2.84%	85.66%	2.23%	83.23%	0.61%	−2.43%
36 to 40	2.23%	87.89%	2.00%	85.23%	0.23%	−2.66%
41 to 45	1.58%	89.47%	1.76%	86.99%	−0.18%	−2.48%
46 to 50	2.66%	92.13%	1.53%	88.53%	1.13%	−3.60%
51 to 60	1.72%	93.86%	2.51%	91.04%	−0.78%	−2.82%
61 to 70	1.15%	95.01%	1.76%	92.80%	−0.62%	−2.20%
71 to 80	0.75%	95.76%	1.49%	94.29%	−0.73%	−1.47%
81 to 90	0.72%	96.48%	1.30%	95.59%	−0.58%	−0.89%
91 to 100	0.57%	97.05%	0.93%	96.52%	−0.35%	−0.54%
101 to 110	0.61%	97.66%	0.74%	97.26%	−0.13%	−0.40%
111 to 120	0.50%	98.17%	0.65%	97.91%	−0.15%	−0.26%
121 to 130	0.25%	98.42%	0.51%	98.42%	−0.26%	0.00%
131 to 140	0.54%	98.96%	0.37%	98.79%	0.17%	−0.17%
141 to 150	0.36%	99.32%	0.65%	99.44%	−0.29%	0.13%
151 to 160	0.22%	99.53%	0.09%	99.54%	0.12%	0.00%
161 to 170	0.22%	99.75%	0.19%	99.72%	0.03%	−0.03%
171 to 180	0.04%	99.78%	0.14%	99.86%	−0.10%	0.08%
181 to 190	0.22%	100.00%	0.09%	99.95%	0.12%	−0.05%
191 to 200	0.00%	100.00%	0.05%	100.00%	−0.05%	0.00%

TABLE A2.11   Bearish Long-Term Time Frame Trade Termination Observations in Profit Case

Number Bars	Confirmed Trend Percentages		Suspect Trend Percentages		Difference Confirmed versus Suspect	
	Individual	Cumulative	Individual	Cumulative	Difference	Cumulative
0 to 1	59.45%	59.45%	57.08%	57.08%	2.37%	−2.37%
2 to 3	14.04%	73.49%	14.76%	71.84%	−0.72%	−1.65%
4 to 5	7.43%	80.92%	5.90%	77.74%	1.53%	−3.18%
6 to 10	8.95%	89.87%	9.53%	87.27%	−0.58%	−2.61%
11 to 15	3.48%	93.35%	4.22%	91.48%	−0.74%	−1.87%
16 to 20	1.30%	94.65%	1.52%	93.00%	−0.21%	−1.65%
21 to 25	0.65%	95.31%	0.76%	93.76%	−0.11%	−1.55%
26 to 30	1.61%	96.91%	1.94%	95.70%	−0.33%	−1.21%
31 to 35	1.91%	98.83%	1.69%	97.39%	0.23%	−1.44%
36 to 40	0.48%	99.30%	1.18%	98.57%	−0.70%	−0.74%
41 to 45	0.39%	99.70%	0.76%	99.33%	−0.37%	−0.37%
46 to 50	0.09%	99.78%	0.34%	99.66%	−0.25%	−0.12%
51 to 60	0.04%	99.83%	0.00%	99.66%	0.04%	−0.16%
61 to 70	0.13%	99.96%	0.17%	99.83%	−0.04%	−0.13%
71 to 80	0.00%	99.96%	0.00%	99.83%	0.00%	−0.13%
81 to 90	0.04%	100.00%	0.17%	100.00%	−0.13%	0.00%
91 to 100	0.00%	100.00%	0.00%	100.00%	0.00%	0.00%

TABLE A2.12   Bearish Long-Term Time Frame Trade Termination Observations in Loss Case

Number Bars	Confirmed Trend Percentages		Suspect Trend Percentages		Difference Confirmed versus Suspect	
	Individual	Cumulative	Individual	Cumulative	Difference	Cumulative
0 to 1	22.84%	22.84%	24.33%	24.33%	−1.49%	1.49%
2 to 3	18.43%	41.27%	18.98%	43.31%	−0.55%	2.04%
4 to 5	9.70%	50.97%	12.17%	55.47%	−2.47%	4.50%
6 to 10	22.09%	73.06%	20.92%	76.40%	1.17%	3.34%
11 to 15	11.75%	84.81%	9.00%	85.40%	2.74%	0.60%
16 to 20	4.63%	89.44%	2.68%	88.08%	1.96%	−1.36%
21 to 25	3.56%	93.00%	3.89%	91.97%	−0.34%	−1.02%
26 to 30	4.09%	97.09%	4.38%	96.35%	−0.28%	−0.74%
31 to 35	2.05%	99.14%	2.19%	98.54%	−0.14%	−0.60%
36 to 40	0.43%	99.57%	0.97%	99.51%	−0.54%	−0.06%
41 to 45	0.32%	99.89%	0.00%	99.51%	0.32%	−0.38%
46 to 50	0.00%	99.89%	0.00%	99.51%	0.00%	−0.38%
51 to 60	0.00%	99.89%	0.00%	99.51%	0.00%	−0.38%
61 to 70	0.00%	99.89%	0.00%	99.51%	0.00%	−0.38%
71 to 80	0.11%	100.00%	0.00%	99.51%	0.11%	−0.49%
81 to 90	0.00%	100.00%	0.00%	99.51%	0.00%	−0.49%
91 to 100	0.00%	100.00%	0.49%	100.00%	−0.49%	0.00%

CHAPTER 3: BROADER INFLUENCES AFFECTING STOCKS

Chapter 3 considered the broader influences on a stock, which included the stock sector and the broader market. The data for each of these is included here for bullish and bearish sectors, both suspect and confirmed.

Bullish Sector Congruency

TABLE A3.1 Bullish Short-Term Time Frame Trend Failure Probability Rates Where Sector Data Congruency Was Present

Number Bars	Confirmed Trend Percentages		Suspect Trend Percentages		Difference Confirmed versus Suspect	
	Individual	Cumulative	Individual	Cumulative	Difference	Cumulative
0 to 1	0.21%	0.21%	0.16%	0.16%	0.05%	−0.05%
1 to 5	3.27%	3.48%	4.22%	4.38%	−0.95%	0.90%
6 to 10	9.18%	12.66%	10.89%	15.27%	−1.71%	2.61%
11 to 15	11.87%	24.53%	12.31%	27.58%	−0.43%	3.05%
16 to 20	12.11%	36.65%	11.78%	39.36%	0.33%	2.72%
21 to 25	10.38%	47.03%	9.82%	49.19%	0.56%	2.16%
26 to 30	9.13%	56.16%	8.39%	57.57%	0.75%	1.41%
31 to 35	7.44%	63.59%	6.78%	64.35%	0.65%	0.76%
36 to 40	6.26%	69.85%	5.93%	70.28%	0.33%	0.43%
41 to 45	5.62%	75.48%	5.19%	75.47%	0.43%	0.00%
46 to 50	4.56%	80.04%	4.31%	79.78%	0.26%	−0.26%
51 to 55	3.58%	83.62%	3.61%	83.39%	−0.03%	−0.23%
56 to 60	3.03%	86.65%	3.16%	86.55%	−0.13%	−0.10%
61 to 65	2.86%	89.51%	2.63%	89.18%	0.23%	−0.33%
66 to 70	2.37%	91.88%	2.09%	91.27%	0.29%	−0.62%
71 to 75	2.03%	93.92%	1.95%	93.22%	0.08%	−0.69%
76 to 80	1.58%	95.50%	1.81%	95.03%	−0.23%	−0.47%
81 to 85	1.42%	96.92%	1.48%	96.52%	−0.06%	−0.41%
86 to 90	1.17%	98.09%	1.33%	97.85%	−0.16%	−0.24%
91 to 95	1.11%	99.21%	1.26%	99.11%	−0.14%	−0.10%
96 to 100	0.79%	100.00%	0.89%	100.00%	−0.10%	0.00%

TABLE A3.2 Bullish Intermediate-Term Time Frame Trend Failure Probability Rates Where Sector Data Congruency Was Present

Number Bars	Confirmed Trend Percentages		Suspect Trend Percentages		Difference Confirmed versus Suspect	
	Individual	Cumulative	Individual	Cumulative	Difference	Cumulative
0 to 1	0.10%	0.10%	0.16%	0.16%	−0.06%	0.06%
1 to 5	2.83%	2.93%	3.74%	3.90%	−0.91%	0.97%
6 to 10	8.67%	11.60%	9.13%	13.03%	−0.46%	1.43%
11 to 15	11.81%	23.41%	11.91%	24.95%	−0.10%	1.54%
16 to 20	11.70%	35.11%	13.08%	38.03%	−1.39%	2.92%
21 to 25	10.60%	45.71%	10.35%	48.38%	0.25%	2.68%
26 to 30	8.80%	54.50%	8.62%	57.01%	0.17%	2.51%
31 to 35	7.82%	62.32%	6.85%	63.85%	0.97%	1.53%
36 to 40	6.32%	68.65%	6.60%	70.45%	−0.28%	1.81%
41 to 45	6.18%	74.83%	5.39%	75.85%	0.79%	1.02%
46 to 50	5.57%	80.40%	4.52%	80.37%	1.05%	−0.03%
51 to 55	3.66%	84.05%	3.19%	83.56%	0.47%	−0.50%
56 to 60	3.50%	87.55%	3.00%	86.55%	0.50%	−1.00%
61 to 65	2.38%	89.94%	2.21%	88.76%	0.17%	−1.18%
66 to 70	2.20%	92.14%	2.36%	91.12%	−0.16%	−1.02%
71 to 75	1.68%	93.82%	2.04%	93.16%	−0.36%	−0.65%
76 to 80	1.72%	95.53%	1.61%	94.77%	0.10%	−0.76%
81 to 85	1.48%	97.01%	1.58%	96.36%	−0.10%	−0.65%
86 to 90	1.11%	98.12%	1.38%	97.73%	−0.27%	−0.39%
91 to 95	0.95%	99.07%	1.27%	99.00%	−0.32%	−0.07%
96 to 100	0.93%	100.00%	1.00%	100.00%	−0.07%	0.00%

TABLE A3.3 Bullish Long-Term Time Frame Trend Failure Probability Rates Where Sector Data Congruency Was Present

Number Bars	Confirmed Trend Percentages		Suspect Trend Percentages		Difference Confirmed versus Suspect	
	Individual	Cumulative	Individual	Cumulative	Difference	Cumulative
0 to 1	0.12%	0.12%	0.00%	0.00%	0.12%	−0.12%
1 to 5	4.03%	4.15%	2.89%	2.89%	1.14%	−1.26%
6 to 10	9.98%	14.13%	9.65%	12.54%	0.33%	−1.59%
11 to 15	15.09%	29.22%	12.00%	24.54%	3.10%	−4.69%
16 to 20	14.40%	43.63%	14.45%	38.99%	−0.05%	−4.64%
21 to 25	11.29%	54.92%	10.96%	49.95%	0.33%	−4.97%
26 to 30	6.87%	61.79%	7.63%	57.58%	−0.76%	−4.21%
31 to 35	6.87%	68.66%	7.14%	64.72%	−0.27%	−3.94%
36 to 40	4.92%	73.58%	5.13%	69.85%	−0.21%	−3.73%
41 to 45	4.80%	78.38%	6.92%	76.77%	−2.12%	−1.61%
46 to 50	7.03%	85.41%	8.62%	85.39%	−1.59%	−0.02%
51 to 55	5.72%	91.13%	6.16%	91.55%	−0.44%	0.42%
56 to 60	5.11%	96.24%	5.29%	96.84%	−0.18%	0.60%
61 to 65	3.07%	99.31%	2.84%	99.67%	0.24%	0.36%
66 to 70	0.54%	99.85%	0.22%	99.89%	0.32%	0.04%
71 to 75	0.04%	99.88%	0.00%	99.89%	0.04%	0.01%
76 to 80	0.04%	99.92%	0.05%	99.95%	−0.02%	0.02%
81 to 85	0.08%	100.00%	0.05%	100.00%	0.02%	0.00%

Bearish Sector Congruency

| TABLE A3.4 | Bearish Short-Term Time Frame Trend Failure Probability Rates Where Sector Data Congruency Was Present |

Number Bars	Confirmed Trend Percentages		Suspect Trend Percentages		Difference Confirmed versus Suspect	
	Individual	Cumulative	Individual	Cumulative	Difference	Cumulative
0 to 1	0.13%	0.13%	0.11%	0.11%	0.02%	−0.02%
1 to 5	4.08%	4.21%	4.43%	4.54%	−0.35%	0.33%
6 to 10	10.80%	15.01%	12.00%	16.54%	−1.20%	1.53%
11 to 15	12.96%	27.97%	14.56%	31.10%	−1.60%	3.13%
16 to 20	16.51%	44.48%	15.52%	46.62%	0.99%	2.14%
21 to 25	9.91%	54.39%	10.12%	56.74%	−0.21%	2.35%
26 to 30	8.06%	62.45%	7.79%	64.53%	0.27%	2.07%
31 to 35	7.60%	70.06%	7.09%	71.61%	0.52%	1.56%
36 to 40	7.08%	77.14%	6.67%	78.29%	0.41%	1.15%
41 to 45	5.91%	83.05%	5.34%	83.62%	0.57%	0.57%
46 to 50	4.96%	88.01%	4.61%	88.23%	0.35%	0.23%
51 to 55	2.43%	90.43%	2.78%	91.01%	−0.35%	0.58%
56 to 60	3.46%	93.89%	2.51%	93.52%	0.95%	−0.37%
61 to 65	2.08%	95.98%	2.36%	95.88%	−0.28%	−0.09%
66 to 70	0.90%	96.87%	0.75%	96.63%	0.15%	−0.24%
71 to 75	0.80%	97.68%	0.83%	97.47%	−0.03%	−0.21%
76 to 80	0.79%	98.47%	0.76%	98.23%	0.03%	−0.24%
81 to 85	0.47%	98.94%	0.70%	98.93%	−0.23%	−0.01%
86 to 90	0.25%	99.20%	0.39%	99.32%	−0.13%	0.12%
91 to 95	0.44%	99.63%	0.43%	99.75%	0.00%	0.12%
96 to 100	0.37%	100.00%	0.25%	100.00%	0.12%	0.00%

TABLE A3.5 Bearish Intermediate-Term Time Frame Trend Failure Probability Rates Where Sector Data Congruency Was Present

Number Bars	Confirmed Trend Percentages		Suspect Trend Percentages		Difference Confirmed versus Suspect	
	Individual	Cumulative	Individual	Cumulative	Difference	Cumulative
0 to 1	0.03%	0.03%	0.04%	0.04%	−0.01%	0.01%
1 to 5	2.49%	2.53%	3.90%	3.94%	−1.40%	1.41%
6 to 10	12.09%	14.62%	14.20%	18.14%	−2.11%	3.52%
11 to 15	11.85%	26.47%	14.32%	32.46%	−2.47%	5.99%
16 to 20	9.98%	36.45%	9.74%	42.20%	0.24%	5.75%
21 to 25	18.56%	55.01%	15.83%	58.03%	2.73%	3.02%
26 to 30	18.36%	73.37%	14.97%	73.01%	3.38%	−0.36%
31 to 35	7.10%	80.47%	7.50%	80.50%	−0.39%	0.03%
36 to 40	5.32%	85.79%	4.75%	85.26%	0.57%	−0.54%
41 to 45	6.14%	91.93%	5.88%	91.14%	0.26%	−0.79%
46 to 50	2.78%	94.71%	2.68%	93.82%	0.10%	−0.89%
51 to 55	1.29%	96.01%	1.68%	95.50%	−0.38%	−0.51%
56 to 60	1.58%	97.58%	1.38%	96.88%	0.20%	−0.71%
61 to 65	0.92%	98.50%	1.11%	97.99%	−0.19%	−0.51%
66 to 70	0.41%	98.91%	0.48%	98.47%	−0.07%	−0.44%
71 to 75	0.25%	99.16%	0.54%	99.02%	−0.29%	−0.15%
76 to 80	0.28%	99.45%	0.34%	99.35%	−0.05%	−0.10%
81 to 85	0.14%	99.59%	0.25%	99.60%	−0.11%	0.01%
86 to 90	0.14%	99.73%	0.08%	99.69%	0.06%	−0.05%
91 to 95	0.13%	99.86%	0.21%	99.90%	−0.08%	0.04%
96 to 100	0.14%	100.00%	0.10%	100.00%	0.04%	0.00%

TABLE A3.6 Bearish Long-Term Time Frame Trend Failure Probability Rates Where Sector Data Congruency Was Present

Number Bars	Confirmed Trend Percentages		Suspect Trend Percentages		Difference Confirmed versus Suspect	
	Individual	Cumulative	Individual	Cumulative	Difference	Cumulative
0 to 1	0.05%	0.05%	0.00%	0.00%	0.05%	−0.05%
1 to 5	1.94%	1.99%	4.40%	4.40%	−2.46%	2.42%
6 to 10	17.70%	19.69%	21.09%	25.49%	−3.39%	5.80%
11 to 15	21.82%	41.50%	22.48%	47.97%	−0.66%	6.47%
16 to 20	15.76%	57.26%	16.57%	64.54%	−0.81%	7.28%
21 to 25	24.66%	81.92%	18.66%	83.20%	6.00%	1.28%
26 to 30	15.62%	97.54%	14.37%	97.57%	1.25%	0.03%
31 to 35	2.13%	99.67%	2.20%	99.77%	−0.07%	0.10%
36 to 40	0.33%	100.00%	0.23%	100.00%	0.10%	0.00%

Bullish General Market Congruency

TABLE A3.7 Bullish Short-Term Time Frame Trend Failure Probability Rates Where General Market Data Congruency Was Present

Number Bars	Confirmed Trend Percentages		Suspect Trend Percentages		Difference Confirmed versus Suspect	
	Individual	Cumulative	Individual	Cumulative	Difference	Cumulative
0 to 1	0.14%	0.14%	0.14%	0.14%	0.00%	0.00%
1 to 5	3.23%	3.37%	6.19%	6.34%	−2.97%	2.97%
6 to 10	9.03%	12.39%	10.32%	16.65%	−1.29%	4.26%
11 to 15	11.94%	24.34%	11.66%	28.32%	0.28%	3.98%
16 to 20	12.42%	36.76%	11.90%	40.21%	0.52%	3.46%
21 to 25	10.61%	47.37%	9.64%	49.85%	0.97%	2.49%
26 to 30	8.95%	56.32%	8.30%	58.16%	0.65%	1.84%
31 to 35	7.59%	63.91%	6.94%	65.09%	0.66%	1.18%
36 to 40	6.47%	70.38%	6.04%	71.13%	0.44%	0.75%
41 to 45	5.78%	76.16%	5.26%	76.39%	0.52%	0.23%
46 to 50	4.20%	80.37%	4.00%	80.39%	0.21%	0.02%
51 to 55	3.35%	83.72%	3.30%	83.69%	0.05%	−0.03%
56 to 60	2.99%	86.71%	3.09%	86.78%	−0.10%	0.07%
61 to 65	2.58%	89.29%	2.32%	89.09%	0.26%	−0.19%
66 to 70	2.23%	91.52%	2.01%	91.11%	0.22%	−0.41%
71 to 75	2.03%	93.55%	1.98%	93.09%	0.05%	−0.46%
76 to 80	1.67%	95.22%	1.85%	94.94%	−0.18%	−0.28%
81 to 85	1.42%	96.63%	1.53%	96.47%	−0.11%	−0.16%
86 to 90	1.32%	97.96%	1.34%	97.81%	−0.02%	−0.15%
91 to 95	1.25%	99.20%	1.16%	98.97%	0.09%	−0.24%
96 to 100	0.80%	100.00%	1.03%	100.00%	−0.24%	0.00%

TABLE A3.8 Bullish Intermediate-Term Time Frame Trend Failure Probability Rates Where General Market Data Congruency Was Present

Number Bars	Confirmed Trend Percentages		Suspect Trend Percentages		Difference Confirmed versus Suspect	
	Individual	Cumulative	Individual	Cumulative	Difference	Cumulative
0 to 1	0.06%	0.06%	0.11%	0.11%	−0.05%	0.05%
1 to 5	2.01%	2.07%	3.09%	3.21%	−1.09%	1.14%
6 to 10	8.47%	10.54%	9.28%	12.49%	−0.81%	1.95%
11 to 15	10.71%	21.24%	10.80%	23.28%	−0.09%	2.04%
16 to 20	10.89%	32.13%	12.80%	36.08%	−1.91%	3.95%
21 to 25	9.70%	41.83%	10.25%	46.33%	−0.55%	4.50%
26 to 30	8.19%	50.02%	8.13%	54.47%	0.06%	4.44%
31 to 35	7.67%	57.70%	6.78%	61.24%	0.90%	3.55%
36 to 40	6.66%	64.35%	6.24%	67.49%	0.41%	3.13%
41 to 45	6.85%	71.21%	4.96%	72.44%	1.89%	1.24%
46 to 50	6.27%	77.48%	4.65%	77.09%	1.62%	−0.38%
51 to 55	3.46%	80.93%	2.81%	79.91%	0.64%	−1.03%
56 to 60	3.54%	84.47%	2.90%	82.81%	0.64%	−1.67%
61 to 65	2.53%	87.00%	2.34%	85.14%	0.19%	−1.85%
66 to 70	2.42%	89.42%	2.94%	88.08%	−0.52%	−1.33%
71 to 75	2.27%	91.69%	2.77%	90.86%	−0.50%	−0.83%
76 to 80	2.37%	94.06%	2.35%	93.21%	0.02%	−0.85%
81 to 85	2.09%	96.15%	2.04%	95.25%	0.05%	−0.89%
86 to 90	1.41%	97.56%	1.71%	96.96%	−0.29%	−0.60%
91 to 95	1.20%	98.76%	1.58%	98.54%	−0.39%	−0.21%
96 to 100	1.24%	100.00%	1.46%	100.00%	−0.21%	0.00%

TABLE A3.9 Bullish Long-Term Time Frame Trend Failure Probability Rates Where General Market Data Congruency Was Present

Number Bars	Confirmed Trend Percentages		Suspect Trend Percentages		Difference Confirmed versus Suspect	
	Individual	Cumulative	Individual	Cumulative	Difference	Cumulative
0 to 1	0.05%	0.05%	0.00%	0.00%	0.05%	−0.05%
1 to 5	1.60%	1.65%	1.80%	1.80%	−0.20%	0.15%
6 to 10	5.48%	7.13%	4.68%	6.48%	0.80%	−0.65%
11 to 15	8.88%	16.01%	8.07%	14.55%	0.81%	−1.46%
16 to 20	10.92%	26.93%	9.94%	24.50%	0.97%	−2.43%
21 to 25	10.43%	37.36%	8.21%	32.71%	2.22%	−4.65%
26 to 30	10.53%	47.89%	10.23%	42.94%	0.30%	−4.95%
31 to 35	11.26%	59.15%	10.73%	53.67%	0.52%	−5.47%
36 to 40	6.36%	65.50%	7.28%	60.95%	−0.92%	−4.55%
41 to 45	6.55%	72.05%	8.36%	69.31%	−1.81%	−2.74%
46 to 50	7.47%	79.52%	8.79%	78.10%	−1.32%	−1.43%
51 to 55	7.42%	86.95%	8.65%	86.74%	−1.22%	−0.20%
56 to 60	8.01%	94.95%	8.36%	95.10%	−0.35%	0.15%
61 to 65	4.32%	99.27%	4.39%	99.50%	−0.08%	0.22%
66 to 70	0.53%	99.81%	0.29%	99.78%	0.25%	−0.02%
71 to 75	0.05%	99.85%	0.00%	99.78%	0.05%	−0.07%
76 to 80	0.05%	99.90%	0.07%	99.86%	−0.02%	−0.05%
81 to 85	0.10%	100.00%	0.14%	100.00%	−0.05%	0.00%

Bearish General Market Congruency

TABLE A3.10 Bearish Short-Term Time Frame Trend Failure Probability Rates Where General Market Data Congruency Was Present

Number Bars	Confirmed Trend Percentages		Suspect Trend Percentages		Difference Confirmed versus Suspect	
	Individual	Cumulative	Individual	Cumulative	Difference	Cumulative
0 to 1	0.19%	0.19%	0.13%	0.13%	0.06%	−0.06%
1 to 5	3.70%	3.89%	4.18%	4.31%	−0.48%	0.42%
6 to 10	9.43%	13.33%	10.31%	14.63%	−0.88%	1.30%
11 to 15	11.46%	24.78%	12.61%	27.23%	−1.15%	2.45%
16 to 20	13.92%	38.71%	13.72%	40.95%	0.21%	2.24%
21 to 25	8.85%	47.56%	9.58%	50.53%	−0.72%	2.97%
26 to 30	7.27%	54.83%	7.92%	58.45%	−0.65%	3.61%
31 to 35	7.56%	62.39%	7.08%	65.53%	0.48%	3.14%
36 to 40	7.56%	69.95%	6.88%	72.40%	0.68%	2.45%
41 to 45	6.98%	76.93%	6.22%	78.63%	0.75%	1.70%
46 to 50	5.59%	82.52%	5.14%	83.76%	0.46%	1.24%
51 to 55	3.09%	85.60%	3.41%	87.17%	−0.32%	1.56%
56 to 60	4.98%	90.59%	3.53%	90.70%	1.45%	0.12%
61 to 65	3.34%	93.93%	3.25%	93.95%	0.10%	0.02%
66 to 70	1.73%	95.66%	1.91%	95.86%	−0.18%	0.20%
71 to 75	1.38%	97.03%	1.29%	97.15%	0.08%	0.12%
76 to 80	1.44%	98.48%	1.00%	98.15%	0.44%	−0.32%
81 to 85	0.79%	99.26%	1.08%	99.23%	−0.29%	−0.03%
86 to 90	0.21%	99.47%	0.35%	99.58%	−0.15%	0.11%
91 to 95	0.27%	99.73%	0.20%	99.79%	0.06%	0.05%
96 to 100	0.27%	100.00%	0.21%	100.00%	0.05%	0.00%

TABLE A3.11 Bearish Intermediate-Term Time Frame Trend Failure Probability Rates Where General Market Data Congruency Was Present

Number Bars	Confirmed Trend Percentages		Suspect Trend Percentages		Difference Confirmed versus Suspect	
	Individual	Cumulative	Individual	Cumulative	Difference	Cumulative
0 to 1	0.04%	0.04%	0.02%	0.02%	0.02%	−0.02%
1 to 5	1.80%	1.84%	2.50%	2.51%	−0.69%	0.67%
6 to 10	9.53%	11.37%	11.76%	14.28%	−2.24%	2.91%
11 to 15	9.77%	21.14%	12.41%	26.69%	−2.64%	5.55%
16 to 20	9.50%	30.64%	8.73%	35.42%	0.77%	4.78%
21 to 25	18.22%	48.85%	15.74%	51.16%	2.47%	2.31%
26 to 30	23.37%	72.22%	19.58%	70.75%	3.78%	−1.47%
31 to 35	12.13%	84.35%	13.02%	83.77%	−0.89%	−0.58%
36 to 40	5.23%	89.57%	4.85%	88.62%	0.37%	−0.95%
41 to 45	5.21%	94.79%	5.06%	93.68%	0.15%	−1.11%
46 to 50	2.20%	96.99%	2.39%	96.07%	−0.19%	−0.92%
51 to 55	1.04%	98.03%	1.29%	97.36%	−0.25%	−0.67%
56 to 60	0.73%	98.76%	0.84%	98.20%	−0.10%	−0.56%
61 to 65	0.44%	99.20%	0.56%	98.76%	−0.12%	−0.44%
66 to 70	0.19%	99.39%	0.38%	99.14%	−0.19%	−0.25%
71 to 75	0.12%	99.51%	0.26%	99.41%	−0.15%	−0.10%
76 to 80	0.18%	99.69%	0.17%	99.58%	0.01%	−0.11%
81 to 85	0.06%	99.76%	0.17%	99.76%	−0.11%	0.00%
86 to 90	0.09%	99.85%	0.03%	99.79%	0.06%	−0.05%
91 to 95	0.04%	99.88%	0.10%	99.90%	−0.07%	0.01%
96 to 100	0.12%	100.00%	0.10%	100.00%	0.01%	0.00%

TABLE A3.12 Bearish Long-Term Time Frame Trend Failure Probability Rates Where General Market Data Congruency Was Present

Number Bars	Confirmed Trend Percentages		Suspect Trend Percentages		Difference Confirmed versus Suspect	
	Individual	Cumulative	Individual	Cumulative	Difference	Cumulative
0 to 1	0.00%	0.00%	0.00%	0.00%	0.00%	0.00%
1 to 5	1.55%	1.55%	2.91%	2.91%	−1.36%	1.36%
6 to 10	19.17%	20.73%	20.85%	23.76%	−1.68%	3.04%
11 to 15	21.37%	42.10%	23.47%	47.24%	−2.10%	5.14%
16 to 20	14.97%	57.07%	15.32%	62.56%	−0.36%	5.49%
21 to 25	24.48%	81.55%	19.30%	81.86%	5.18%	0.32%
26 to 30	17.77%	99.32%	17.36%	99.22%	0.41%	−0.09%
31 to 35	0.68%	100.00%	0.78%	100.00%	−0.09%	0.00%

About the Author

L.A. Little brings a unique perspective to technical analysis, incorporating more than three decades of trading and engineering experience when analyzing the markets. As an author of multiple trading titles and with degrees in Telecommunications (MS), Computer Information Systems (BS), Philosophy (BA), and Computer Science (AAS), L.A.'s holistic approach to trading has been to redefine some of the most basic concepts in technical analysis and to devise methodologies that systematically examine them. His philosophical background first requires crisp definitions beginning with the most basic concept of technical analysis: trend. As part of the definition, L.A. introduces his neoclassical approach to technical analysis, virtually turning it upside down. With his approach, trends are qualified, trend lines are replaced with anchored zones, and the technician is provided with a methodology that allows for the measurement of supply and demand at critical junctures on the charts.

L.A. has written extensively for many popular publications such as *Stocks and Commodities*, *Active Trader*, TheStreet.com, RealMoneyPro .com, and Minyanville.com; has appeared on numerous radio shows; and has presented his concepts at regional and international conferences. He is a professional money manager who trades his own accounts and manages investment funds for qualified investors from his Colorado-based home office at the foot of the Rocky Mountains.

L.A. writes and produces live Internet-based video programs daily on his own website, Technical Analysis Today (www.tatoday.com), sharing valuable and interesting market observations while calling the market's twists and turns daily. The concepts presented in both this book and his prior work, *Trend Qualification and Trading*, are embodied in a set of services that are available at Technical Analysis Today for the serious student, investor and/or trader. He can be reached at tat@tatoday.com.

Index

Stay in touch!

Subscribe to our free Finance and Accounting eNewsletters at
www.wiley.com/enewsletters

Visit our blog: **www.capitalexchangeblog.com**

 Follow us on Twitter
@wiley_finance

 "Like" us on Facebook
www.facebook.com/wileyglobalfinance

 Find us on LinkedIn
Wiley Global Finance Group

⊛WILEY Global Finance
WHERE DATA FINDS DIRECTION